Canoeing
Michigan Rivers

A Comprehensive Guide To 45 Rivers

Canoeing Michigan Rivers

A Comprehensive Guide To 45 Rivers

Third Edition
Revised 2013

text
Jerry Dennis

original maps and photographs
Craig Date

Thunder Bay Press

Holt, Michigan

Canoeing Michigan Rivers, Third Edition
© Copyright 2013 by Jerry Dennis and Craig Date

Published by Thunder Bay Press
2325 Jarco Drive, Holt MI 48842

First printing June 1986
Second printing August 1986
Third printing June 1987
Fourth printing September 1988
Fifth printing February 1990
Sixth printing February 1991
Seventh printing May 1992
Eighth printing July 1993
Ninth printing April 1995
Tenth printing February 1997

First printing, Revised Edition, February 2001
Second printing, Revised Edition, March 2005
Third printing, Revised Edition, May 2007
Fourth printing, Revised Edition, December 2009

First printing, Third Edition, May 2013

ISBN: 978-1-933272-33-7
Library of Congress Control Number: 2013936913

Text: Jerry Dennis
Original Edition maps: Craig Date
Revised Edition maps: Gary W. Barfknecht
Third Edition maps: Julie Taylor
Cover design: Chelsea Bay Design
Front cover photo: Presque Isle River by Craig Date
Back cover photo: Sturgeon River, Cheboygan County by Craig Date
All black-and-white photos are by Craig Date unless otherwise noted.
Third edition book design by Julie Taylor and Amelia Turkette

Printed in the United States of America
by McNaughton & Gunn, Inc. | Saline, Michigan

To Gail

CONTENTS

The authors wish to express their gratitude to the Sawyer Canoe Company and Mad River Canoes for generously assisting in our equipment needs during the research of this book.

We would also like to thank the many people who helped and supported us, especially Mike and Marcy McCumby, Mark and Denise Wilkes, Gerald and Eva Dennis, Paul Maurer, Dick and Tricia Armstrong, Elaine Dennis, Wayne Overberg, Bob and Daisy Kostus, Barry and Terry Barto, Jerry Weese and Andy Willey.

Other Books By Jerry Dennis

THE WINDWARD SHORE: A WINTER ON THE GREAT LAKES
(University of Michigan Press, 2011)

THE LIVING GREAT LAKES: SEARCHING FOR THE HEART OF THE INLAND SEAS
(St. Martin's Press, 2003)

LEELANAU: A PORTRAIT OF PLACE IN PHOTOGRAPHS AND TEXT
(with photographs by Ken Scott)(Petunia Press, 2000)

FROM A WOODEN CANOE: REFLECTIONS ON CANOEING, CAMPING, AND CLASSIC EQUIPMENT
(St. Martin's Press, 1999)

THE RIVER HOME: AN ANGLER'S EXPLORATIONS
(St. Martin's Press, 1998)

THE BIRD IN THE WATERFALL: A NATURAL HISTORY OF OCEANS, RIVERS, AND LAKES
(HarperCollins, 1996)

A PLACE ON THE WATER: AN ANGLER'S REFLECTIONS ON HOME
(St. Martin's Press, 1993)

IT'S RAINING FROGS AND FISHES: FOUR SEASONS OF NATURAL PHENOMENA AND ODDITIES OF THE SKY
(HarperCollins, 1992)

Introduction
To The Third Edition

Nearly thirty years ago Craig and I set out to paddle the lengths of our favorite rivers and write a book about them. We were very young then and very ambitious and had no idea what we were getting into. We figured we could do two rivers every weekend and have the book wrapped up in six months.

Two years later we floated around a bend on the Shiawassee River, saw Craig's red pick-up parked beside the Fergus Road Bridge, and realized that our work was done. By then we had paddled 1,500 miles on nearly 50 rivers and were a little older and maybe a little wiser for the experience. Our relief that the journey was over was exceeded only by our regret that it was over. Even then we knew we would always look back on those two years as a magical time in our lives.

As it turned out, all the years since have been pretty magical, in part because we've never stopped going to the rivers. Our appreciation for them just gets stronger. Though we've spent a fair amount of time exploring rivers on several continents, we always return to Michigan convinced that ours are the loveliest and most interesting rivers in the world. Each has an aroma, color, composition of bed, banks, and surrounding valley that adds up to a character as unique as a fingerprint. We're convinced that we could be blindfolded and led to any river in Michigan and know exactly where we are.

For this, our most fully revised edition to date, Craig and I revisited every river, drove all the roads, checked all the access sites, campgrounds, dams, and bridges, and made note of everything that has changed. Many roads that were once gravel are now paved. A few bridges are gone. Campgrounds have closed. A major dam on the Boardman River has been dismantled (with more scheduled for removal in the near future). And we found a few errors in the book that had slipped past us during earlier revisions.

We were heartened to note that the rivers themselves have changed very little. This isn't entirely true, of course. The Kalamazoo endured a devastating oil spill that is still not completely cleaned up. The Pigeon suffered a blow when a private dam on the upper river released a surge of silt that decimated the trout population. This was the second time in twenty-some years that the same dam failed because of the abysmally poor judgment of the owners.

Other changes have been more positive. Thanks to the efforts of many people many of the rivers in southern Michigan are cleaner than they were in the 1980s – so much so that Craig and I plan to include several of them in a future edition of this book. Northern rivers have benefited as well, especially from erosion controls that reduce the amounts of sand and silt entering them and reforestation that is keeping their waters shaded and cooler. More gravel and cooler water means more aquatic life and that of course means healthier rivers.

After a lifetime on the water, Craig and I are still thrilled every time we push off into a river and feel the current grab our boat and pull us toward the first bend and what we might discover beyond it. We hope that this book, the labor of our youth and middle-age, is in some small way an aid to your own enjoyment.

(For more information about Michigan rivers, including news and updates of interest to paddlers, anglers, and anyone else who cares about rivers, go to www.canoeingmichiganrivers. net.)

Introduction
To The Second Edition

A lot of water has flowed under the bridge since the day in February 1984 when my college friend Craig Date and I decided to try writing a book together. We had no idea how much time and work it would take, or even if it would ever be published, but we knew it would be a great excuse to spend a lot of time on rivers. If we broke even, we figured, we'd be ahead. We never dreamed that seventeen years later Canoeing Michigan Rivers would be considered the bible of paddling in Michigan.

This new edition is probably a bit overdue. Over the years we've received many letters from readers, most sharing their experiences but a few pointing out errors in our text and maps. We corrected the most serious of the errors in each of the reprints (there have been ten), and felt we were keeping the book reasonably updated. Lately, though, we realized that a major overhaul was necessary. Campgrounds, bridges, dams, roads, and access sites have altered over the years, making some of our information obsolete. The final nudge came from a critic on a web site who declared that our book was "outdated but still useful" (a phrase we fear applies to the authors as well). Clearly, it was time to update.

Most of the updating took place during several weeks in the summer and fall of 2000, when I poked around in all the Upper Peninsula rivers and most of the northern Lower Peninsula rivers described in the book. For the remainder of them I turned to the telephone and internet, and to friends around the state who generously shared their knowledge of the waters they know best.

Of course a lot has changed since the first edition. Among the most significant changes was legislation that required "run-of-the-river" management of hydro-electric dams on the Au Sable, Manistee, and Muskegon. Before, water was released in a system called "peak-flow," to meet power demand whenever it was needed. Fluctuations in flow made the rivers terribly low one day and dangerously high the next, causing erosion and making it difficult for many aquatic organisms to survive. Stabilizing the flow has increased fish populations and cleaned the rivers. Paddling below the dams is a lot more fun now.

Another change is an increase in U.S. Forest Service regulations. Paddlers, anglers, and campers on rivers flowing through national forests in the Lower Peninsula are subject to many more rules than they were in 1986. In some cases— the Pine comes to mind—permits and quotas have limited the number of river users and have probably done some good. Others I'm not so sure about. Upper Peninsula rivers, many of which flow through national forests, have so far remained largely unregulated.

Readers familiar with the first edition of Canoeing Michigan Rivers will notice some modifications. Gary Barfknecht has produced new maps that are easier to read and more accurate than the old ones (sorry, Craig). Photos are placed where they belong. Appendices are updated and a comprehensive list of canoe liveries has been added.

Other alterations aren't so obvious. At the urging of many readers, I've "softened" the estimated paddling times for most of the rivers. During our research, Craig and I always paddled steadily, trying to be as consistent as possible from river to river, and ended up maintaining a pace that was faster than most people like to go. We've received a few complaints about that. We also heard about a group of paddlers who tried to complete a section of the Fox River in five hours, as we had, and ended up abandoning their canoes and bushwhacking through the swamp in the middle of the night. I hope they've forgiven us. If they can give the Fox (and our book) another chance, I'm sure they'll find the new paddling times more realistic—and the Fox a fine river.

In fact, they're all fine. I don't know where this book or its authors will be 17 years from now, but I'm pretty confident that the rivers will remain in good shape. The single consistent note in all the letters we've received is that the rivers are lovely and enchanting and of immeasurable value. May they flow bright and clean forever.

Introduction
To The First Edition

This book was conceived on a February weekend on the Pine River. That trip—our antidote to cabin fever—began and ended so inauspiciously that it has earned an honored listing in our personal archives under "Chalk It Up to Experience." It began early Saturday morning in a search for Edgetts Bridge—lost on roads with names like 50 and 48½, guided by a vague hand-drawn map and even vaguer local advice. It ended Sunday evening when we found our way back to that remote bridge and discovered that our vehicles had been broken into and ransacked.

During the drive home that night we decided something had to be done. There had been too many trips marred by insufficient and inaccurate information. There had been too many hours spent driving in circles on unfamiliar roads, too much confusion over access sites and bridge names, and too many days spent hauling canoes over logjams and fallen trees on rivers we would never have attempted had we been warned ahead of time. Obviously it was time to invest in a good guide to Michigan rivers.

But there was no such guide. So, to make a long story short, we decided we would create one, and—two years and about 1,500 miles of canoeing later— you are holding the result in your hands.

For us, though, the story goes far beyond the pages of this book. It, itself, is enough reward for those two years work, but there have been so many bonuses along the way that several more volumes would be necessary to give them their due. Our friends and families and the many people we met on the rivers have been a continuous source of pleasure and surprise. What we learned about canoes and canoeing—especially whitewater canoeing—has added immeasurably to our enthusiasm for a sport we had already enjoyed for many years. And all of those out-of-the-way corners of Michigan we stumbled into have given us a new appreciation for a state we thought we knew pretty well.

But the greatest bonus—and the one we will carry with us the longest—has to do with the rivers themselves. We would never have begun this book if we did not care for rivers, and in candid moments we have been willing to admit that the entire project was designed to give us an excuse to be near them more.

Even after the hundreds of hours afloat, the miles of driving, the long days and too-short nights, the bad jokes and worse food, the rain, the snow, the mosquitoes and deer flies, and the mornings when all we wanted to do was stay curled up in our sleeping bags—but dragged ourselves to the canoe anyway—our appreciation for the rivers has not abated. It has, in fact, grown.

If there is one thing we hope for Canoeing Michigan Rivers it is this: That everyone who reads it and uses it will find his or her appreciation for Michigan rivers growing too.

PREFACE

We have made every effort to compose this guidebook in a manner that will make it a useful—and enjoyable —tool. Following are some explanations of the logic behind our terms and methods:

RIVERS

It is already apparent to us that there are going to be some readers who will be disappointed or even angered to learn that a favorite river or section of river has been omitted from this book. All blame or credit has to be placed squarely on the authors' shoulders.

From the beginning we were determined to include only those rivers we found to be particularly appealing to us. Our standards are simple. We prefer not to paddle on polluted water, or through long stretches of crowded, dirty, noisy surroundings, or in the company of too many powerboats and water skiers. We looked for rivers that offer beauty, variety and challenge, and that, if not remotely situated, had qualities that were interesting and appealing in their own right.

That is not to say that every river we omitted is dull or tainted with industrial waste. We have left out some fine rivers—perhaps enough for a second volume of this book—and simply missed some others. In the end, our decisions were based on our own prejudices but resulted, we hope, in a good representation of the best moving water in Michigan's two peninsulas.

COUNTIES

County names are listed at the beginning of each river description and appear in the order of the river's passage. The first county listed, then, contains the upstream or beginning reaches of the described river; the last county contains the end of the river or the final section we describe.

START / END

This refers only to the initial put-in and final take-out of the portion of the river described.

MILES

All river miles given are the result of our own measurements using a map measurer to trace each winding mile of every river on U.S. Geological Survey topographical maps. This is the most careful measurement system we could devise and is, we believe, quite accurate. Discrepancies with other sources are somewhat baffling. For instance, the length of the Au Sable from Grayling to Oscoda is variously reported as 180 to 240 miles. Repeated measurements of 1:24,000 scale topographical maps convinced us that the actual length is 114 miles. Perhaps what is most relevant is that all miles listed in this book resulted from the same method and will, therefore, be consistent from one river to the next.

HOURS

Because paddling time varies greatly according to ability, river character, water conditions and weather, we have included a range of times for each section of river only as a general guide. In a section listed as, say, a 3 to 5 hour trip, 3 hours is the time it took us at a steady, moderately fast pace while 5 hours is the time we estimate casual paddling and floating will take. We have tried to remain consistent from river to river, but again, the times should be regarded as general references only.

GRADIENT

Gradient is the measure of a river's descent and is expressed in feet per mile. A 10 ft/mile gradient means that the river drops 10 feet for each mile of lateral distance. We arrived at the gradient of each river by counting contour lines on topographical maps. On rivers where gradient varies greatly from section to section, we have listed the section gradients separately; otherwise, the figure listed is a good average for the entire river.

The gradient of a river is a fairly good gauge of its speed and difficulty, although other factors such as water volume, bottom type and number of obstructions also have to be considered. Generally, a descent of 10 feet/mile will create rapids. Anything over 15 feet/mile is certain to have some exciting water. A gradient over 20 feet/mile demands careful planning and preparation.

CAMPGROUNDS

All streamside campgrounds that we know of—both public and private—are marked on the maps or are listed in the descriptions. In some cases, campgrounds in the general vicinity are noted, but usually only when there are few on the rivers themselves.

SKILL REQUIRED

This, again, is intended as a general guide. The numerals I, II, III and IV refer to the river rating system devised by the American Whitewater Affiliation. Level I, for example, is used to recommend the ability of paddlers to negotiate rapids designated as Class I in the

Presque Isle River above South Boundary Road (photo by Gail Dennis)

International Scale of River Difficulty (see Appendix A). Level I, therefore, could be considered beginner or novice, level II intermediate, and level III and higher advanced or expert.

TOPOGRAPHICAL MAPS

We have listed the quadrant names of maps that cover rivers we consider remote enough, fast enough, or otherwise challenging enough to warrant special attention. Those who want maps of other rivers can get an index from the U.S. Geological Survey and other agencies where topos are available. The maps are also available at many canoe and outfitting shops.

MISCELLANEOUS

This is a book for paddlers and is written from a paddler's perspective. Therefore, all directions—such as right and left, up and down, and above and below—unless otherwise noted, are based on usual downstream progress.

Although we have made every effort to ensure that the information contained in this book is accurate, it is entirely possible that we have made an occasional mistake. We would be grateful to receive corrections, suggestions or comments of any kind. Please email Jerry Dennis at jcdennis@charter.net (or visit his website at www.jerrydennis.net). Snail mail should be addressed to Jerry Dennis and Craig Date, care of Thunder Bay Press, 2325 Jarco Drive, Holt, MI 48842.

MAP LEGEND

Symbols used on maps included with individual river descriptions.

—————— PAVED

- - - - - GRAVEL

▨ WATERFALLS

\\\ RAPIDS

❶ POINTS OF INTEREST
(see text)

⚑ CAMPGROUNDS

MICHIGAN NATURAL RIVERS PROGRAM

Michigan's Natural Rivers Act (Act 231) was initiated in 1970 for the purpose of protecting certain rivers from unwise development and use. The objectives of the program are

1. General: To preserve and protect the ecologic, aesthetic and historic values and enhance the many recreational values of the river and adjacent lands.

2. Water Quality: To maintain or improve water quality consistent with the designated classification of the river and adhere to the concept of non-degradation of water quality.

3. Free-Flowing Condition: To maintain existing free-flowing conditions where they presently exist for the purpose of preserving this part of the natural environment of the river.

4. Fish and Wildlife Resource: To maintain, protect and enhance desirable fish and wildlife populations and plant communities.

5. River Environment: To protect riverbanks, the flood plain and other adjacent river areas essential to the perpetuation of the total environment of the river system.

There are three categories of Natural Rivers in Michigan's program. They are

Wilderness: A free-flowing river, with essentially primitive, undeveloped adjacent lands.

Wild-Scenic: A river with wild, forested borders that is near developed lands and is moderately accessible.

Country-Scenic: A river in an agricultural setting—with pastoral borders and some homes—that is readily accessible.

Rapids on the Upper Peninsula's Black River (photo by Gail Dennis)

Designated Michigan Natural Rivers

Wilderness River: Two Hearted
Wild-Scenic Rivers: Au Sable, Betsie, Boardman, Fox, Jordan, Kalamazoo, Manistee (upper), Pere Marquette, Pigeon, Pine, Rifle
Country-Scenic: Boardman*, Flat, Huron, Rogue**, White*

* Some sections of the Boardman and White rivers are designated Wild-Scenic and others are designated Country-Scenic.
** The Rogue River is not included in this guide.

National Wild And Scenic Rivers Program

The National Wild and Scenic Act, like the Michigan Natural Rivers Act, is intended to preserve and protect rivers with outstanding aesthetic, scenic, historic and other features. Rivers are designated as Wild, Scenic or Recreational. As of early 2001, more than 150 rivers (or portions of rivers), were included in the national program.

Rivers are designated according to accessibility and are divided into the following categories:
*   **Wild** — Is accessible only by trail, is undeveloped and generally unpolluted.
*   **Scenic** — Is accessed by some roads but is mainly a trail-access river.
*   **Recreational** — Is developed along the shoreline and is easily accessible by roads.

In Michigan, the following rivers are included in the National Wild and Scenic Rivers Program:
Wild: Ontonagon**
Scenic: Au Sable, Black (Gogebic), Indian*, Ontonagon**, Pere Marquette, Pine, Presque Isle*, Sturgeon (Delta County)*
Recreational: Indian*, Ontonagon**, Paint, Presque Isle*, Sturgeon (Delta County)*

Further information about the national program can be obtained on the Web at www.nps.gov/rivers

* Has portions designated both as Scenic and Recreational
** Several sections of the East, Middle, Cisco, and West branches of the Ontonagon have been designated as Wild, Scenic, and Recreational.

Au Sable backwaters

LOWER PENINSULA RIVERS

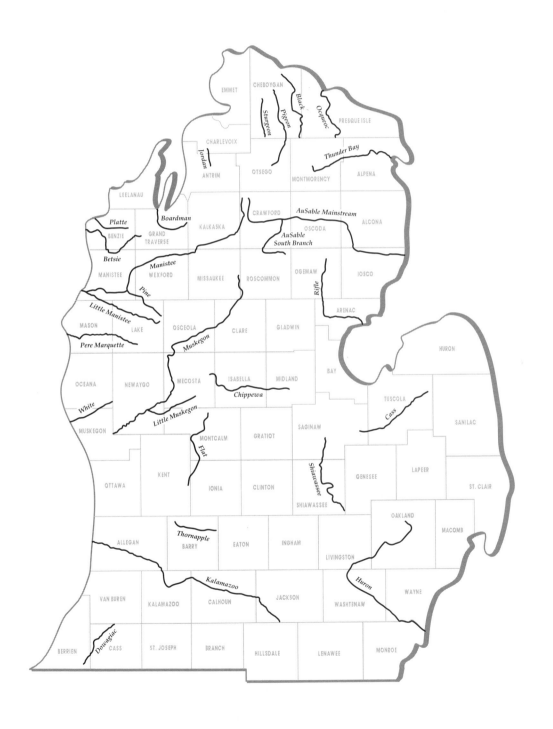

Au Sable River Mainstream

COUNTIES: Crawford, Oscoda, Alcona, Iosco
START/END: Grayling to Oscoda
MILES: 114
GRADIENT: Grayling to Parmalee Bridge—5.2 ft/mile
Parmalee Bridge to Oscoda—less than 3 ft/mile
PORTAGES: Six dams, fairly easy
RAPIDS / FALLS: None
CAMPGROUNDS: Numerous
CANOE LIVERIES: Numerous (see Appendix D)
SKILL REQUIRED: I

Long famous as one of the finest trout streams in the Midwest, the Au Sable is undoubtedly the best-known Michigan river and is deserving of its double designation as both a National Wild and Scenic River and a Wild-Scenic Michigan Natural River. It first gained the attention of sportsmen in the mid-19th century when its abundant grayling population became known. By the early 20th century, overfishing and years of bottom-scouring log drives had contributed to the extinction of the grayling, but brook, brown and rainbow trout—introduced in the 1890s—flourished and have continued to attract anglers.

Today the Au Sable's popularity among fishermen is nearly matched by its popularity among canoeists. Clear water, consistent flow, easy access and attractive surroundings make it a nearly ideal river for beginners and families, at least in the upper reaches, before the impoundments. Crossing those man-made ponds can be hard work, even dangerous when the wind is up.

The Au Sable isn't perfect. It suffers for its popularity, especially on summer weekends, when canoes and tubes appear in unending procession, and anglers wade at every bend or float down in riverboats. Much of the year, you can expect the sounds of the river to be punctuated with the boom and rattle of artillery and machine-gun fire from the nearby National Guard Artillery Range. It's a bizarre intrusion.

Nonetheless, the Au Sable is a premier river and one of the finest canoeing (and fishing) destinations in the Midwest. It also makes one of the best canoe-camp expeditions in the Lower Peninsula. Plan on at least 6 days (6 hours of paddling per day) to paddle from Grayling to Oscoda (keeping in mind that the winners of the annual Au Sable Marathon do it in less than 24 hours). Although the series of dams beginning at Mio hinder progress—and the reservoirs are distressingly long—portages are clear and well-marked, and numerous campgrounds and long stretches of state and national forests make the Au Sable a good choice for extended camping/canoeing trips.

Anglers should note that special regulations apply to certain sections of the river, including flies-only, no-kill in the "Holy Water" from Burton's Landing to Wakeley Bridge.

GRAYLING to WAKELEY BRIDGE
14 MILES / 5 ½ – 6½ HOURS

Although the Au Sable's beginnings are 20 miles north of Grayling, the river above the town is usually considered too small and brushy for enjoyable canoeing. It is interesting that, near the town of Frederick, the upper Au Sable comes within a few miles of the upper Manistee River, and for centuries that area was the site of portages by native Americans using the two rivers as a cross-state canoe route.

Access in Grayling ❶ is not as simple as you might imagine. There is a city park on the upstream side of the M-72 Bridge, but jumbled rocks at the site of the old dam under the bridge makes it necessary to portage the busy highway. Canoe liveries just downstream will usually grant permission to launch non-rental canoes from their property; the one we asked charged a modest fee for overnight parking. An alternative is to put in at any of the numerous access sites and campgrounds a short distance downstream from Grayling.

The river in town is small, shallow and narrow—with sand and gravel bottom— and is shaded by maples and willows. Current is steady and moderate—typical

of most of the river all the way to Lake Huron. After the little East Branch of the Au Sable joins the mainstream, just outside of the Grayling city limits, the river widens. From here to Wakeley Bridge the river is 25 – 40 feet wide and 1 – 3 feet deep, with sand or gravel bottom and beds of aquatic vegetation lining the shore areas. The water is remarkably clear and cold. Terrain is low hills of hardwoods with cedars and occasional tag alders near the river. Homes and cottages are frequent but scattered.

Access and parking are good at Au Sable River Canoe Campground, Burton's Landing State Forest Campground, and Keystone Landing State Forest Campground—all 1½ to 2½ hours below Grayling. ❷ Camping facilities are primitive (water, toilets and picnic tables). All three campgrounds are often crowded on summer weekends. Canoe Campground is especially popular and is used as a put-in and take-out site by canoe liveries.

Access and parking are good at the public site 200 yards downstream and on the right, below Stephan Bridge. ❸ The access site at Wakeley Bridge ❹ is a few hundred yards downstream on the right and has good access. Parking is a hundred yards up the road.

WAKELEY BRIDGE to PARMALEE BRIDGE
16.5 MILES / 5 – 7 ½ HOURS

Below Wakeley Bridge the river deepens and slows somewhat and enters a series of turns and switchbacks with deep pools at the bends. There are likely to be fewer canoes than in the section above. Cottages are frequent, but they tend to be widely spaced. The bottom is predominantly sand and silt, and large numbers of drowned logs and stumps line the banks.

A short distance downstream is Whitepine Canoe Forest Campground, ❺ a good choice for an overnight trip from Grayling (6 to 7 hours paddling time). It is considered a "group" campground because of the large size of its sites, and offers only primitive facilities—toilets and potable water. Access is limited to canoeists only, with the two-track road leading to the campground privately owned and posted.

The junction with the South Branch of the Au Sable is approximately 2 miles below Whitepine Campground. From here to Rainbow Bend State Forest Campground is a long stretch of wide, slow, relatively deep (3 to 6 feet) water known as Conners Flats or

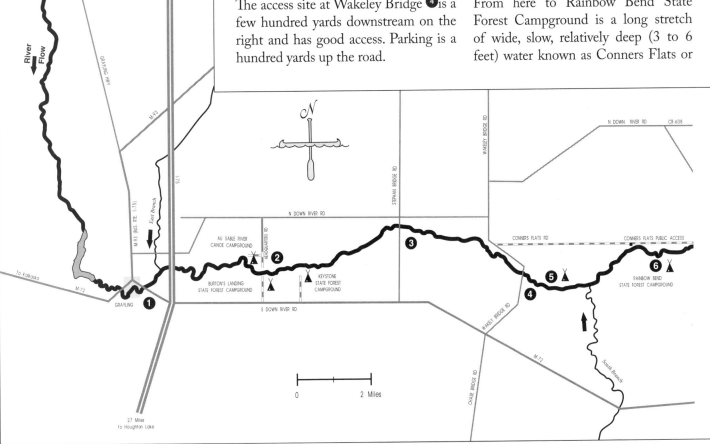

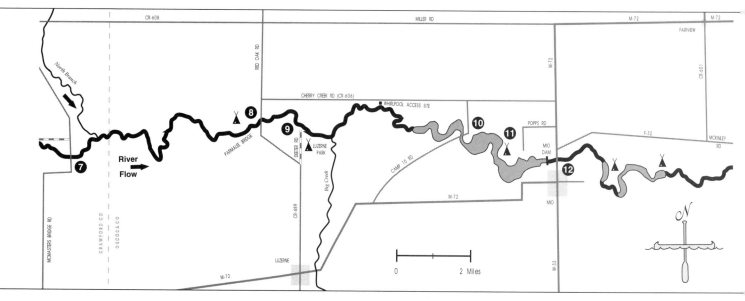

the Stillwater. Conners Flats Public Access, with good parking and access and vault toilets, is reached off Conners Flats Road and is 1½ to 2 hours below Wakeley Bridge.

Rainbow Bend State Forest Campground ❻ is shortly after Conners Flats Public Access. This small, primitive campground, reached via Conners Flats Road, is difficult to spot from the river. Look for a sandy landing and trail on the left bank.

McMasters Bridge, ❼ with good access and parking, is a short distance downstream. From here to the junction with the North Branch of the Au Sable, expect faster current—though still far from difficult paddling conditions—gravel bottom, and some wide riffles with medium-size stones to avoid. Below the North Branch is another stretch of wide, slow flats followed by fairly fast, wide, interesting water, with gravel bottom and occasional large rocks the rest of the way to Parmalee Bridge.

The access and parking site at Parmalee ❽ is on the right, before the bridge. Parmalee State Forest Campground, with rustic sites for canoeists, is directly across the river from the public access site.

PARMALEE BRIDGE (RED OAK RD) to MIO DAM
12.5 MILES / 3 – 6 HOURS

We made this trip in a little more than

2 hours of steady paddling, with a tail wind that helped greatly in crossing Mio Pond. In fact, prevailing west winds are an aid on all of the Au Sable's impoundments, in contrast to the Manistee, Muskegon and other west-flowing rivers, where winds seem always to be a hindrance.

Below Parmalee Bridge are several miles of fine water, with wide, fairly shallow riffles—some fast enough to create broken water—alternating with narrow, deep, slow pools. Bottom is generally pea- to grapefruit-size stones with occasional large rocks to avoid.

Camping, access and picnic grounds are available at Luzerne Township Park, ❾ a short distance below Parmalee Bridge, at the end of Deeter Road.

Whirlpool Access Site, beside Cherry Creek Road, has good access and parking.

The river slows and widens at the beginning of Mio Pond, a mile before Camp 10 Bridge, ❿ where access and parking are good. From here to Mio Dam are several miles of slow water, bordered by marshy, undeveloped shore with the isolated feel of wilderness. The pond can be a piece of cake—or it can be a back-breaker. Wind is the key. Headwinds or strong winds from any direction can make crossing this and the larger ponds downstream tricky at best and exhausting or dangerous at worst. Keep an eye on the weather; if strong winds are predicted, wait them out.

Mio Pond State Forest Campground ⓫, with good access and parking and a canoe group camp and boat-ramp, is located on the left (north) shore halfway to the dam.

Portage Mio Dam on the right side of the powerhouse.

MIO DAM to MCKINLEY BRIDGE
14.5 MILES / 4 ½ – 7 HOURS

Put in below Mio Dam or just downstream on the right at the DNR access site below the M-72/M-33 Bridge, ⓬ where access and parking are good. Expect lots of company on this section during summer weekends. The river is wide (75 to 125 feet) and often fairly fast as it repeats the riffle/pool pattern of the water above Mio.

The river passes much of the way from Mio to Oscoda through the Huron National Forest, and camping is permitted only at the 102 individually designated sites scattered from 4001 bridge to Oscoda. Camping permits and reservations are required between May 15 and September 30 ($10 per night, as of 2013). Reservations must be made at least four days in advance and can be made online using the clumsy system at wwww.recreation. gov (search for "camping" in "Huron-Manistee National Forest".) A toll-free reservation number is offered: 1-877-444-6777. Reservations and permits

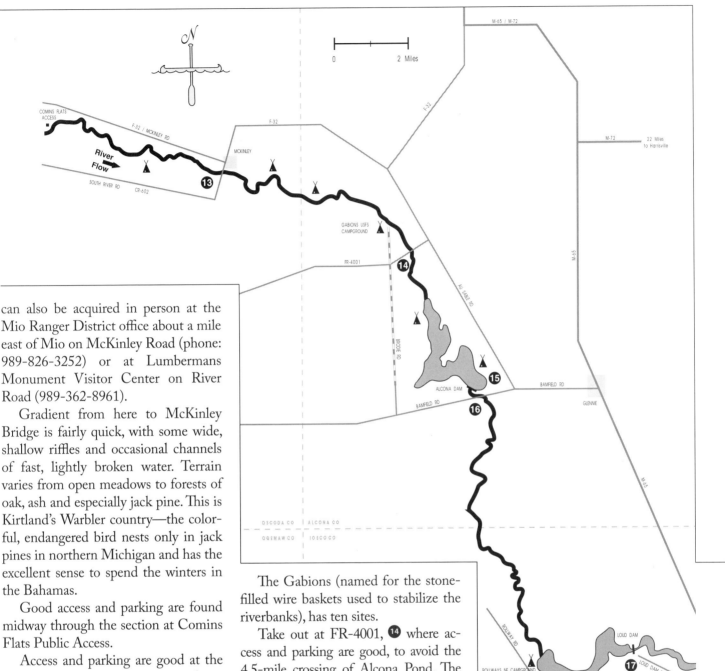

can also be acquired in person at the Mio Ranger District office about a mile east of Mio on McKinley Road (phone: 989-826-3252) or at Lumbermans Monument Visitor Center on River Road (989-362-8961).

Gradient from here to McKinley Bridge is fairly quick, with some wide, shallow riffles and occasional channels of fast, lightly broken water. Terrain varies from open meadows to forests of oak, ash and especially jack pine. This is Kirtland's Warbler country—the colorful, endangered bird nests only in jack pines in northern Michigan and has the excellent sense to spend the winters in the Bahamas.

Good access and parking are found midway through the section at Comins Flats Public Access.

Access and parking are good at the DNR public site upstream on right at McKinley Bridge, where there are vault toilets. ❸

MCKINLEY BRIDGE to ALCONA DAM
11.75 MILES / 4 – 6 HOURS

The river below McKinley Bridge continues much the same as the section above but is less accessible.

Several USFS campgrounds are located on the banks and do not require reservations. The first, Buttercup, is a small campground with rustic facilities used primarily by canoeists.

The Gabions (named for the stone-filled wire baskets used to stabilize the riverbanks), has ten sites.

Take out at FR-4001, ❹ where access and parking are good, to avoid the 4.5-mile crossing of Alcona Pond. The landing at 4001 is a fee site ($5/day), administered by the Huron National Forest.

Alcona Pond is a popular vacation spot used by large numbers of power boaters and water skiers. The shoreline is crowded with campers and vacation homes. Private and county campgrounds are located at the upper end, on the right shore, and at the lower end on the left. The lower one, Alcona Park, ❺ offers access and parking (for a fee) and many campsites with modern facilities.

Alcona Dam is a short distance from the park and can be portaged on the right.

ALCONA DAM to FIVE CHANNELS DAM
17.75 MILES / 6 – 9 HOURS

Put in below Alcona Dam ❻, at the public access on the left. From here to Loud Dam is a lovely, 15-mile stretch of wide (80 to 100 feet), deep water with moderate current and some stretches of faster riffles. This stretch is likely to be far less crowded than the more popular water upstream. There are few houses or other streamside development, and few intermediate access sites. Terrain is mostly high hills of hardwoods and pines, with high sand and clay banks common near the river. Much of the land is within the Huron National Forest.

Camping from here to Oscoda is allowed only on the designated campsites scattered along the river. These are single sites only, unlike the multiple-site campgrounds below Mio, and most can be reached only by river. Again, permits are required between May 15 and September 30 and can be purchased at Lumberman's Monument Visitor Center on River Road (near Cooke Pond), at the District Office east of Mio, or at the USFS website (see above).

Loud Pond **17** is smaller than Alcona Pond and much less populated. Portage the dam on the right. The portage is a 250-yard carry down a gravel road.

From here to Five Channels Dam **18** is a 3-mile stretch of backwaters. Portage the dam on the right at the ledge platform. There is good access and parking at Tailwater Access Site, below the dam on the right, where there is a vault toilet. Overnight parking is allowed here only with a USFS permit.

FIVE CHANNELS DAM to FOOTE DAM
15.5 MILES / 5 ½ – 8 ½ HOURS

Almost immediately below Five Channels Dam are the backwaters of Cooke Dam. This is another large impoundment, and high waves can be a problem. The shores are largely undeveloped, with many potentially good campsites—some at the feet of tremendous wooded hills that come down to the shore. There is a campground midway on the right shore at Lumberman's Monument; access, however, is very poor up 100-foot banks. Other campsites along the shore are much easier to reach.

Portage Cooke Dam **19** on the left. The river below remains crystal clear, and current is strong and steady as it opens into channels and bays with beds of weeds that offer cover for bass and pike. Good campsites are scattered along this undeveloped stretch.

Foote Pond, the largest of the Au Sable reservoirs, is a short distance downstream. Wind and waves can create problems on the huge pond, and crossing in a headwind can be discouraging. There is camping at Old Orchard Park, midway on the pond on the right shore. Portage Foote Dam **20** on the left. Access

and parking are good at the DNR public access a short distance below the dam, upstream and left of Rea Road Bridge.

FOOTE DAM to OSCODA
11.5 MILES / 4 ½ – 6 HOURS

The river below Foote Dam is wide (80 to 150 feet) and deep. Current is slow to moderate except immediately below the dam, where it is fairly swift. There are a few very wide, very shallow stretches of wadeable water and some beaches and sandbars where good picnicking is possible. But most of the way the river meanders through lowlands and hardwood forests, where there are only occasional suitable camp and picnic sites. Bottom is generally sand, and water tends to be discolored. This is popular steelhead- and salmon-fishing water and is likely to be crowded with anglers in the spring and fall.

Whirlpool Access Site is a USFS fee area with good parking, access and vault toilets.

In Oscoda there is good access and parking and vault toilets at the public site at River Road Bridge, as well as at the public boat-launching site **21** at the mouth of the river.

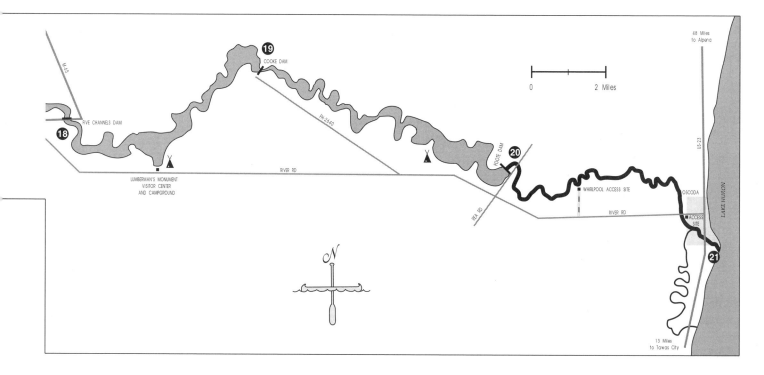

SOUTH BRANCH

COUNTIES: Roscommon, Crawford **START/END**: Roscommon to junction with Mainstream **MILES**: 21.5 **GRADIENT**: 2.5 ft/mile **PORTAGES**: None **RAPIDS/FALLS**: None **CAMPGROUNDS**: One **CANOE LIVERIES**: Numerous (see Appendix D) **SKILL REQUIRED**: I	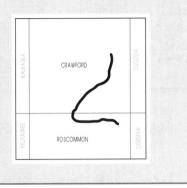

Like the mainstream of the Au Sable, the South Branch is rich in historic associations and has long been famous for classic fly-fishing for trout. Also like the mainstream, it is popular with canoeists seeking gentle family-suited water and near-wilderness settings.

The heart of the river flows through the Mason Tract, a several-thousand-acre sanctuary bequeathed to the state in 1954 by automobile-manufacturing-magnate George Mason. According to the dictates of the bequeathal, the land in the Mason property has been left to revert, as closely as possible, to the natural state of a Michigan forest. The few buildings that once existed have been removed, camping and picnicking are forbidden, and the numbers of roads and trails are kept at a minimum. The remains of Durant's Castle, Mason Chapel, and the foundations of one or two homes and cottages are nearly the only signs of human interference in the Mason Tract, which extends from Chase Bridge nearly to Smith Bridge.

Unlike the mainstream, water levels on the South Branch are quite variable. It is unusual for levels to vary more than 12 inches from spring to summer on the mainstream, but the South Branch will vary by as much as several feet and will often flow high and discolored during the spring or after heavy rains. Camping is limited to a state-forest campground at the end of the Mason Tract. Special fishing regulations include flies-only from Chase Bridge to the mouth.

MEAD'S LANDING to SMITH BRIDGE
13.5 MILES / 4 ½ – 6 ½ HOURS

Many paddlers, especially canoe-livery customers, put in at Roscommon, 3.5 miles above Steckert Bridge. However, access is difficult in Roscommon unless you get permission to launch from the liveries at the M-18 Bridge. Access is good at Wallace Park, a small community park immediately below the bridge, but parking is very limited.

We recommend starting a trip at Mead's Landing DNR Public Access ❶ where there is good access and parking (and vault toilets). It is located off Steckert Bridge Road, approximately 1 mile above Steckert Bridge.

Steckert Bridge has good parking, access and vault toilets at a DNR public site below a canoe livery and private campground.

The river here is 30 – 75 feet wide and 1 – 4 feet deep, with gentle current, mostly sand bottom and no serious obstructions. From Roscommon to Chase Bridge (6 miles, 2 to 3 hours) are a fair number of homes and cottages. But the banks are wooded and there is a feeling of serenity and isolation that peaks in the Mason property downstream.

Good parking and access are available at the DNR access site at Chase Bridge, ❷ at the beginning of the Mason Tract. On summer weekends we have found it advisable to put in here early in the morning to get ahead of canoe-livery customers.

Immediately below the bridge the river enters wooded hills of hardwoods, pines and cedars. Some tag alders line the banks. Bottom is gravel and occasional larger stones at midstream, with sand and silt along the edges. Century-old drowned logs remain from the lumbering era, when log drives were heavy on the entire Au Sable system. A few survivors of those days still linger: red pines and white pines 3 feet or more in diameter that tower over the river valley.

About 1¼ hours below Chase Bridge is a landing and sign announcing Durant's Castle. The 42-room mansion was built for William Durant (who founded General Motors in 1908) and included gables, turrets and separate servant's quarters. It burned in 1931 and was never rebuilt. Nothing remains today except the foundation and basement. Downstream one-half mile, the Mason Chapel commemorates George Mason and makes a good rest stop and picnic area.

Canoe Harbor State Forest Campground ❸ is a short distance upstream from Smith Bridge at the lower end of the Mason property. It is a primitive campground with 45 sites; canoe pick-up is prohibited.

Access and parking are good at Smith Bridge ❹ (M-72, or South Downriver Road) at the public site just downstream on the right. (Note that road access is about a mile west of the bridge on Old M-72.)

SMITH BRIDGE to
CONNORS FLATS PUBLIC ACCESS (MAINSTREAM)
7.5 MILES / 2 ½ – 4 HOURS

From Smith Bridge to the confluence with the mainstream is 5.5 miles of slow, winding, quite-deep water. Cottages and homes are scattered most of the way, and virtually all of the bordering land is private. The river is 60 – 85 feet wide and 2 – 5 feet deep, with very deep holes. Still water begins before the junction with the mainstream and extends downstream through Conners Flats.

Access and parking are good at Conners Flats Public Access or Rainbow Bend State Forest Campground, ❺ both on the mainstream about two miles below the junction of the two rivers.

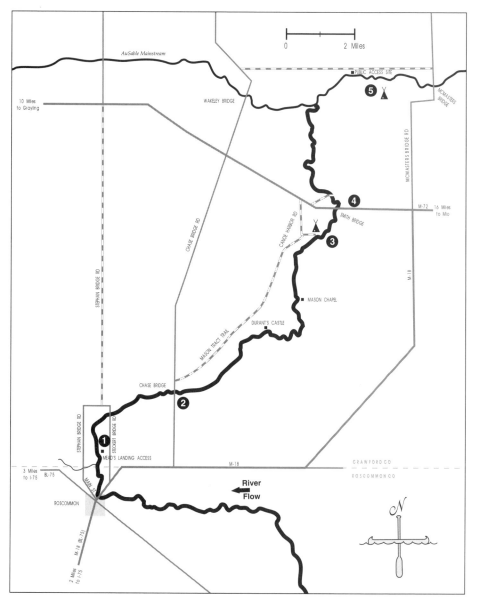

BETSIE RIVER

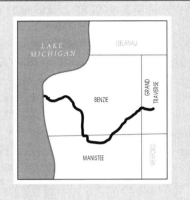

COUNTIES: Grand Traverse, Benzie, Manistee

START/END: Grass Lake to Elberta

MILES: 45

GRADIENT: Wallin Bridge to former Thompsonville Dam—5.6 ft/mile
All other sections—less than 4 ft/mile

PORTAGES: 2 small dams, occasional fallen trees

RAPIDS/FALLS: None

CAMPGROUNDS: Few

CANOE LIVERIES: Several (see Appendix D)

SKILL REQUIRED: Above Wallin—I; below Wallin—I-II

From its source in Green Lake, near Interlochen, to its mouth, at Elberta, the Betsie River offers an interesting variety of water. The usual order is reversed—expect the easiest canoeing in the upper reaches. There, current is slow to nearly nonexistent, and the river winds casually through marshlands and low wooded hills. Farther downstream, tight bends and moderate to moderately fast current create some fairly challenging water. Especially during high water, beginners may have difficulty negotiating quick turns and occasional fallen trees and other minor obstacles that occur much of the way from Wallin to Betsie Lake, above Elberta.

Campgrounds are limited, but state land along much of this Michigan Wild-Scenic River opens up possibilities for streamside camping. Fishing is for warm-water species above Wallin and for brown and rainbow trout below it. Salmon and steelhead runs in the spring and fall produce much fishing pressure, especially below Homestead Dam.

GRASS LAKE STATE FOREST CAMPGROUND to THOMPSONVILLE
10.5 MILES / 3 – 5 HOURS

The Betsie can be paddled from its origin in Green Lake, but access is poor at Betsie River Road, the first bridge below the lake. A better choice is the DNR public access site on Green Lake, two-fifths of a mile north of the mouth, where there is excellent access and parking and a restroom. From Green Lake, the Betsie flows slowly for four miles to the former Grass Lake Flooding, where the river winds slowly and shallow through the wetlands. Look for the access site and campground on the southwest shore, just before the dam. Portage the lowhead dam on the right.

Access and parking are good at the boat launch at Grass Lake State Forest Campground. ❶ The campground has primitive facilities and is usually uncrowded. Reynolds Road is narrow, winding, and bumpy; watch for the small "State Forest Campground" sign on the east side, about three miles south of Cinder Road.

The river below Grass Lake is shallow and warm enough in summer for swimming (though it tends to be rich with aquatic weed growth), and there is little current. In fact, strong winds can halt downstream progress. Like much of the Betsie, this upper section passes through uninhabited countryside of hardwood forests, meadows and occasional marshlands.

Downstream from the dam is a mile or two more of shallow, slow water. The river gradually quickens, however, until, upstream from Wallin, it becomes a gravel-bottomed, fairly fast trout stream. Access and parking are poor at Reynolds Road Bridge.

There is better access and roadside parking at Wallin Road Bridge. ❷ From here to Thompsonville is a fine 7-mile float. The river remains small—25 to 35 feet wide in most places—and is quick but not difficult for paddlers with basic skills. During summer's low water stay near the outside of bends to utilize the

most depth. Expect to scrape bottom or run aground occasionally in this section, especially where the river widens over gravel riffles. The countryside remains largely undeveloped, with only occasional streamside houses. Meadows and upland forests of hardwoods alternate, and there are frequent moss-covered clay-banks feeding the river with cold spring water.

There is fair access and roadside parking at Carmean Road Bridge and poor access at Thompsonville Road Bridge. The Little Betsie joins the mainstream here, contributing additional flow and colder water.

After King Road Bridge, also with fair access and roadside parking, there is about a mile of quick water winding through the marshland in what was previously the backwaters of the Thompsonville Dam, which washed out since the first edition of this book was published. A sharp bend and a quick, short rapids beneath the old railroad trestle mark the site of the washed-out dam. Good access and parking are available at the park, nature trail, and restroom at Gallagher Street Bridge ❸.

THOMPSONVILLE to COUNTY LINE ROAD BRIDGE
11.5 MILES / 3 ½ – 5 HOURS

Below Thompsonville, the river begins to change in character. There are several miles of moderately quick water similar to the stretch below Wallin but with more volume. The riverbed is gravel and sand with occasional large rocks. By Kurick Road Bridge, however, the current slows and the river widens and deepens. There remain stretches of quick, fairly shallow riffles, but they become less frequent. The more usual characteristic—and the one that predominates throughout the remainder of the river—is sand bottom dropping away into deep holes at every bend. Current is moderate and water tends toward cloudiness. Watch for logs and snags just below the surface and for fallen trees that can sometimes be a nuisance. During periods of high water, beginners might have difficulty with some of the frequent, very sharp bends. Much of this section is lined with thickets of tag alders and cedars, and there are fewer suitable resting places than in the upper reaches.

Access and parking are poor at Lindy Road. No access or parking are permitted at M-115 bridge.

Fair access and parking are available at Kurick Road Bridge. Psutka Road has fair access and poor parking.

Access is good and parking fair at North County Line Road Bridge. ❹

COUNTY LINE ROAD BRIDGE to HOMESTEAD DAM
11.5 MILES / 4 – 6 HOURS

From County Line Road, expect much of the same kind of water and terrain as in the section above. Hardwood forests rise in intersecting ridges above the river valley, and cedars and tag-alder thickets line the banks.

Access is poor at M-115 Bridge.

From here to Homestead Dam, the river winds tightly through lowlands and low wooded hills. Deadfalls, sweepers and small logjams are fairly frequent in the first several miles; some might require liftovers. Current is moderate to fairly quick. A few houses near M-115 give way to mostly undeveloped woods downstream. River depth is 1 to 6 feet; bottom is sand with sections of gravel and stone and very occasional larger rocks. Good campsites can be found, but they are scarce.

The backwaters of Homestead Dam were once a reservoir which still appears on some maps, but the demolition of the dam years ago (and replacement with a lowhead dam) drained the area. Now the river winds between sandbars and low banks overgrown with willows, cattails and marsh grasses.

Access and parking are good at Homestead Dam, where there are vault toilets. ❺ Portage the dam on the right at the developed landing.

HOMESTEAD DAM to ELBERTA
11.5 MILES / 4 – 6 HOURS

From Homestead to Elberta is a popular summer float, but keep in mind that in spring and fall the Betsie River is heavily fished for steelhead and salmon. Most fishing pressure is in the section below Homestead Dam, where anglers sometimes stand elbow to elbow, making it risky business to pass in a canoe.

The river is slow to moderate, is 35 to 50 feet wide, and passes mostly through lowland forests with cedars near the banks. Water is often discolored.

Just above the US-31 Bridge is a DNR access site, with restrooms and parking, and a 100-yard carry to the river.

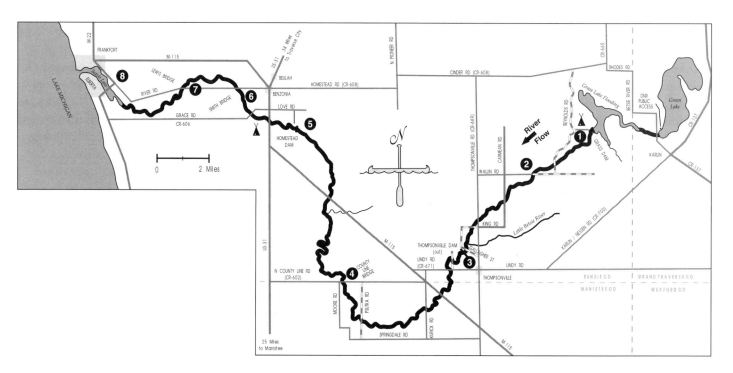

Huron River

There is a private landing and campground with supplies, at US-31, but no public access to the river.

Good access and parking are found at the DNR canoe access site a couple of bends below Grace Road Bridge. Note that the access road is 100 yards east of the bridge, on the right.

There is good access and parking at the public site just above Smith Bridge, ❻ the first of two bridges on River Road. The second, sometimes called Lewis Bridge, ❼ has good access and parking at a public access site above the bridge on the right.

From Lewis Bridge to Betsie Lake are several miles of slow, winding river through marshes before the river ends at Betsie Lake. Strong winds can make this stretch tedious, but abundant bird life is a strong draw.

No access or parking are allowed at the M-22 bridge at the mouth of the river, although there is fair access and very limited parking at the old railroad trestle ❽ just upstream of it, as well as below the bridge and to the left at the old, semi-abandoned marina at the southwest end of Betsie Lake.

Another alternative is to paddle the east shore of Betsie Lake to the municipal launch site in Frankfort.

BLACK RIVER

COUNTIES: Cheboygan, Presque Isle **START/END:** Clark Bridge to Black Lake MILES: 32.25 **GRADIENT:** 4 ft/mile **PORTAGES:** Two dams, moderately difficult **RAPIDS/FALLS:** Crocket Rapids, just above South Black River Road—Class I **CAMPGROUNDS:** None **CANOE LIVERIES:** None **SKILL REQUIRED:** I **TOPO. MAPS:** Hetherton, Tower, Atlanta (15 min.)	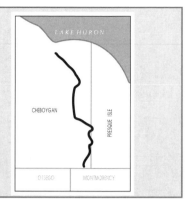

B etter known for outstanding brook-trout fishing than fine canoeing, the Black River is the most remote and least often paddled of Cheboygan County's major rivers. A generally slow-paced river, it meanders through long stretches of undeveloped woods and lowlands. Paddlers with basic skills should have no trouble during normal water levels. During high water the stretch of fast current above Crocket Bridge (South Black River Road) requires some caution.

There are sufficient access sites, especially above Tower Pond, but no on-bank campgrounds. State-forest camp-grounds are found near the river, above the sections described here, at Round Lake and Town Corner Lake. Public land in the Black Lake State Forest has the potential for streamside camping, although low ground and thickets of tag alders reduce the number of good sites.

Fishing is excellent for brook trout, with 18-inchers not uncommon, and to a lesser degree for brown trout. Northern pike and other warm-water species are found in the impoundments and in the lower section below Kleber Dam.

CLARK BRIDGE to CROCKET BRIDGE (SOUTH BLACK RIVER ROAD)
6 MILES / 2 – 3 HOURS

Although there is some canoeable water above Clark Bridge, a large area of private property at Black River Ranch limits access, and locally infamous "spreads" below Main River Bridge (not shown on map) make for discouraging prospects.

Access is excellent at Clark Bridge, ❶ with plenty of parking space available near the river. The river is 25 – 40 feet wide and 2 – 4 feet deep with much deeper holes. Water is clean but stained dark brown. Current is slow in the vicinity of the bridge but speeds up gradually as you move downstream. As the current increases, sand and silt bottom changes to gravel and stone. This section flows almost entirely through state-forest land, and most of the bordering land is low, with tag alders and marshes backing up to lowland forests. Higher ground above Crocket Rapids

is mostly privately owned and has scattered homes and cottages.

Crocket Rapids is an easy Class I series of riffles over gravel and rocks up to bushel size. They should offer little challenge except during very high water, when standing waves develop. In very low water, rocks will need to be avoided.

Access and parking are good at Crocket Bridge, ❷ on South Black River Road. There is public land for about a quarter-mile upstream, with several often-used campsites on the high bank above the river.

CROCKET BRIDGE to TOWER DAM
14 MILES / 5 – 7 HOURS

From Crocket Bridge the river slows and widens somewhat. Width is 40 – 60 feet; depth is 2 – 5 feet. Terrain is mostly lowlands of hardwoods and tag alders.

Milligan Road Bridge has poor access and parking.

There is parking and fair access at the public site at the end of Wigglesworth Road.

Errat Road Bridge has fair access and limited roadside parking.

County Line Road Bridge is immediately below Errat Road and has no access or parking. Watch for large rocks under the bridge—they create a narrow chute that can be easily run at mid-river.

Black River Road Bridge, just above Tower Pond, has fair access and roadside parking.

Tower Pond is about a mile long and quite narrow. Access at the M-68 Bridge is poor, with poor roadside parking. It is better to take out at the public access site on the west side of the pond ❸ (reached via Black River Avenue past the fire department), where parking and access are good. Portage Tower Dam on the left.

TOWER DAM to BLACK LAKE
12.25 MILES / 4 – 6 HOURS (est.)

We have not paddled this section, but we drove the roads to determine access sites. The river appears to be slow to moderate and, generally, 50 to 80 feet wide. The general area is within the Black River State Forest, but much of the bordering land is private. Most of the terrain is lowlands and swamps.

Kleber Pond begins almost immediately below Tower Dam and is a 2.5-mile crossing. Just before the pond is Barkley Avenue Bridge with fair access and roadside parking.

Kleber Dam is a fairly difficult portage on the left, down a steep bank. A public access site with vault toilet is below the dam, on the right. From here to Black Lake the river meanders through continuous lowlands, and there appears to be little or no streamside development.

Shortly before Black Lake there is a bridge at Upper Black River Road. A public access site **4** is located one-tenth of a mile downstream from the bridge, on the right.

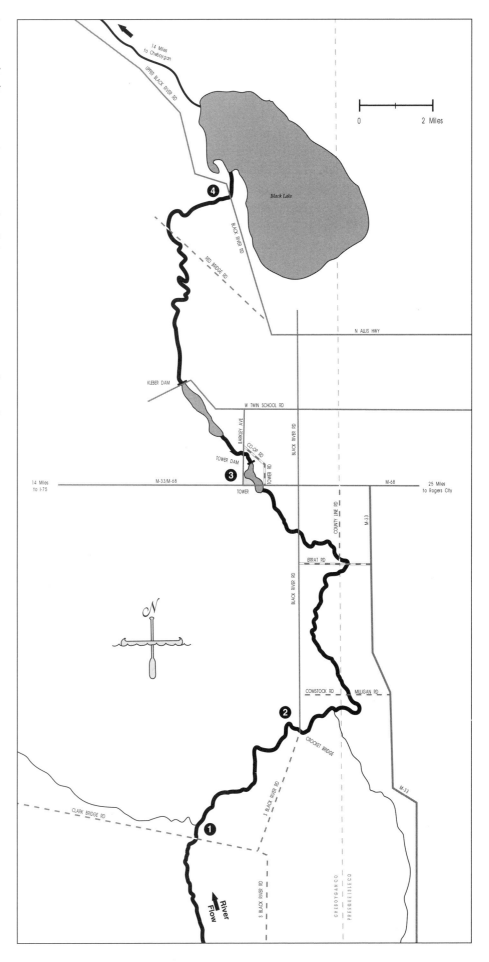

BOARDMAN RIVER

COUNTY: Grand Traverse
START/END: Supply Road Bridge to Traverse City
MILES: 25.25
GRADIENT: Supply Road to Brown Bridge Access—3 ft/mile
                  Brown Bridge Access to Boardman Pond—9.6 ft/mile
PORTAGES: 3 dams, fairly easy; occasional fallen trees in upper section
RAPIDS/FALLS: Beitner Rapids, directly below Beitner Road Bridge—Class I-II
CAMPGROUNDS: Several in upper section
CANOE LIVERIES: Few (see Appendix D)
SKILL REQUIRED: Upper section—I; Lower section to Boardman Pond—I-II

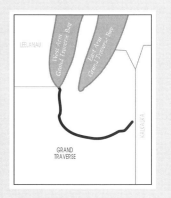

One of Michigan's finest and best-known trout streams, the Boardman is as highly esteemed by canoeists as it is by fishermen. It is not a heavily used river, however, except on summer weekends when crowds of paddlers and tubers use the middle section, especially from Shumsky Road Public Access to Beitner Road Bridge.

Dams for many years divided the river into an upper section, a middle section, and a lower section of slow river and backwaters before the mouth at Grand Traverse Bay in Traverse City. The upper section (and its tributaries), above the former site of Brown Bridge Dam, is designated a Wild-Scenic Michigan Natural River and is the river's remotest and least-developed section. It passes through Fife Lake State Forest and has several stream-side state-forest campgrounds. The river below the site of the former Brown Bridge Dam is designated Country-Scenic but, since it flows through mostly private property, has few camping opportunities. This section is generally faster than the upper and requires slightly more advanced paddling skills. Beitner Rapids, especially, will challenge inexperienced paddlers.

The big news on the Boardman River since 2011 has been the Boardman River Dams Project, which, when it is complete, will be the largest dam removal and river restoration project in Michigan history. The plan calls for removal of the three hydroelectric plants in the river above Boardman Lake and modification of the much smaller dam at Union Street in Traverse City. At present Brown Bridge Dam has been removed and restoration of the river above it is in progress. As of early 2012 there is a temporary ban on paddling within the restoration area, making it necessary to portage 1 mile around the section of river that was previously beneath the pond. Boardman and Sabin dams are slated to be removed and those sections of river restored in 2013 and 2014, though that schedule is dependent upon funding and other factors. At present water drawdown has opened up a quarter-mile of previously drowned river at the site of the former Boardman Pond. For updates and progress reports, go to http://www.theboardman.org.

Fishing in the Boardman River is for brook and brown trout from the headwaters to Boardman Lake. Warmwater species predominate in Boardman Lake and in the river downstream to the mouth. At present, salmon and steelhead are allowed to run only as far upstream as the Union Street Dam in Traverse City.

SUPPLY ROAD BRIDGE to BROWN BRIDGE ACCESS
7 MILES / 3 – 4 HOURS

Originating in Kalkaska County, the North and South Branches of the Boardman are generally too small and brushy for enjoyable canoeing. They meet at the Forks, immediately above Supply Road Bridge in western Grand Traverse County, where the mainstream is large enough for clear passage, although there may be occasional fallen trees to bypass, especially in spring.

Access at Supply Road is fair, with parking limited to the roadside. Instead, many paddlers put in one-half mile downstream at Forks State Forest Campground, ❶ where primitive sites are on the riverbank and access and parking are good. The river in the upper section varies from 20 – 40 feet wide and 1 – 3 feet deep, with some pools over 5 feet. Current varies from moderate to fairly quick over bottom of alternating gravel and sand. The river passes through a largely undeveloped valley of mixed hardwoods and conifers, including many

large pines and hemlocks, especially near Forks Campground. Water levels are usually sufficient, although some stretches of light riffles may be shallow in summer. Cedars line the banks in many places, some leaning or fallen into the river to become the "sweepers" famous as trout habitat in Michigan angling lore. In the close confines of the small upper river, they also create minor hazards to canoeists.

Midway through the section is Ranch Rudolf, the only commercial development along the upper river, with lodging, canoe rental, and private access (there is no access at the bridge on Brown Bridge Road here).

About 1 mile downstream, at the second bridge on Brown Bridge Road, is Scheck's Place State Forest Campground ❷, with rustic facilities and good access to the river. It is the last easy access before the site of the former Brown Bridge Dam, 1 to 2 hours downstream. The mile-long stretch of "new," fairly fast river, at the site of the former Brown Bridge Pond, winds through an open valley studded with the stumps of thousands of trees that were cut before the pond was formed in 1921.

Access and parking are good at the public access located at the old dam site ❸, a quarter mile above Brown Bridge, where access is poor and parking is limited to the roadside.

BROWN BRIDGE ACCESS to BOARDMAN DAM
12.5 MILES / 4 – 5 ½ HOURS

This middle section is generally swift, with gravel and sand bottom and occasional riffles over fist-size to pumpkin-size stones. Width is 30 – 45 feet; depths are 1 – 4 feet, with pools over 5 or 6 feet common. Many submerged and half-buried logs, remnants of early log drives, are visible on the bottom.

Water quality continues to be excellent, with water generally clear. Levels fluctuate moderately except during major storm events. There are scattered stretches of undeveloped land, but cottages and homes are frequent and most streamside property is private. Numerous private bridges, some low enough to require caution, cross to residences. Stands of hardwoods and thickets of cedars and tag alders alternate with occasional meadows and farmlands.

Access and roadside parking are fair at Garfield Road.

Six miles below Brown Bridge Access Site is Shumsky Road Public Access ❹ with the best intermediate access in this section. The two bridges on River Road offer fair access with limited roadside parking.

Beitner Road Bridge ❺ has good access and parking at the roadside park on the right, upstream side of the bridge.

Beitner Rapids begin immediately below the bridge and become more intense a few hundred yards downstream. Although these rapids will never rate more than Class II, standing waves, a few bushel-sized boulders, and several abrupt turns make this half-mile stretch fairly challenging, especially during high water. The best water is at the site of the washed-out Keystone Dam, where the river channel narrows to 15 feet and waves are high enough to surf and can occasionally swamp an open

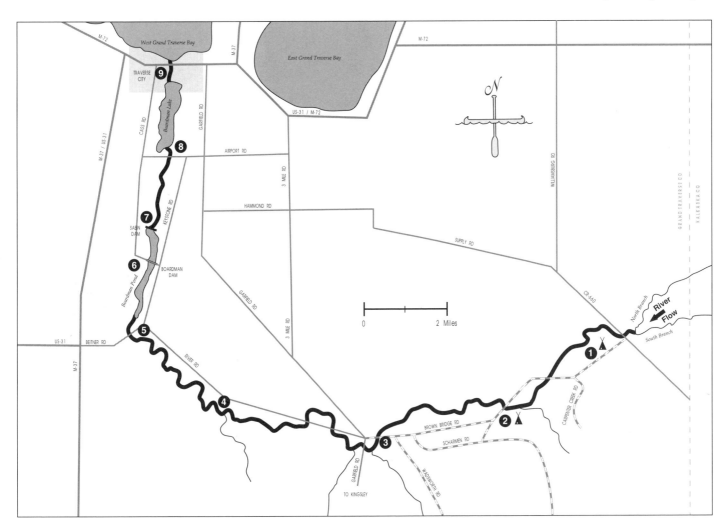

boat. Experienced paddlers will not find Beitner Rapids difficult; beginners may find them well beyond their ability.

A short distance below the fastest water is a footbridge and a 100-yard carry to good parking at a public site reached off Keystone Road. The drawdown of water at Boardman Pond downstream has opened an additional half-mile of fast water from here to the old pond.

Take out at the public site ❻ to the left of Boardman Dam, where parking and access are good. Portage across Cass Road and follow the rather long and steep marked portage trail left of the dam. This portage will of course not be necessary once the dam is removed.

BOARDMAN DAM to THE MOUTH (TRAVERSE CITY)
6 MILES / 2 – 4 HOURS

Sabin Pond begins almost immediately below Boardman Dam. There is good parking and access on the hill above Sabin Dam at Boardman River Nature Center, ❼ although the climb is steep and fairly long. Portage the dam

on the right. The river below passes for 2.5 miles through an undeveloped and, considering its proximity to Traverse City, surprisingly remote valley. Thickets of cedar and tag alders near the bank and mixed stands of hardwoods and conifers away from the river alternate with meadows and grassy banks. Current is slow to moderate over bottom of sand and silt.

Access is prohibited at busy South Airport Road. Immediately downstream is Boardman Lake, ❽ with good access and parking at a public site and picnic area to the right of the river mouth. Boardman Lake is about a 2-mile crossing and leads into Traverse City, where there is a low dam to portage at Union Street. Take out and portage on the left, being careful to avoid the turbulent outflow of the dam.

The final mile of river passes through residential neighborhoods and the downtown area before emptying into West Grand Traverse Bay. Immediately below the Front Street Bridge is a fish weir that blocks the river during the salmon run in September/October.

Portage it on the left and carry around the facility building. Most of the year, when the weir is not in operation, you can paddle between the stanchions.

Good access and (metered) parking are available at a public boat-launching site on the left, a hundred yards before the mouth of the river. ❾

CASS RIVER

COUNTIES: Tuscola, Saginaw
START/END: Cass City to M-13 Bridge
MILES: 59
GRADIENT: 2.5 ft/mile
PORTAGES: Two dams, easy
RAPIDS/FALLS: None
CAMPGROUNDS: None
CANOE LIVERIES: None
SKILL REQUIRED: I

Anyone familiar with the lower Cass River where it crosses M-13 just before joining the Saginaw River—and where it is wide, slow and muddy—is likely to be surprised by the upper river. Rock and gravel bottom, pools of still water alternating with stretches of riffles, and quiet, wooded terrain are reminiscent of northern rivers. Canoeing and fishing pressure is light, and the Cass will seldom be crowded. Water quality is fair to good, with visibility barely reaching three feet in the lower reaches but increasing higher up. After rain, however, the entire river muddies.

In summer, low water will make many short riffles in the upper stretches impassable. Even at the end of a wet September, we did a lot of scraping and bumping, especially in the section between Cass City and Caro. Flow is supplemented by ground springs and tributaries, so midsummer trips are usually possible between Caro and Frankenmuth and are probably never a problem between Frankenmuth and the junction with the Saginaw.

Long stretches of river pass through Defoe, Tuscana and Vassar state game areas, where the chances of sighting deer, beaver and other wildlife are excellent. Camping potential is limited due to wetlands in the game areas and private property elsewhere, but a few good sites can be found. Fishing is for warm-water species, especially smallmouth bass and northern pike.

CEMETERY ROAD BRIDGE (CASS CITY) to CHIPPEWA LANDING (CARO)
17 MILES / 6 – 8 HOURS

A short distance upstream from Cass City, the North, East and Middle branches of the Cass converge, creating a mainstream large enough to be navigable. Cemetery Road Bridge ❶ (Seeger Street in Cass City) is the farthest upstream access to the mainstream; access is fair, and parking is limited to one or two vehicles. The river ranges from 30 – 60 feet wide with depths of 6 inches to 3 feet.

Short runs of moderately fast water spill over reefs of fist-size to bushel-basket-size stones and boulders. In the alternating slow stretches, the bottom

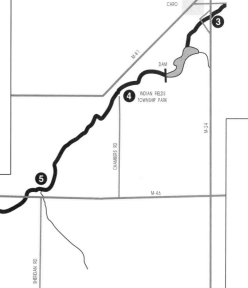

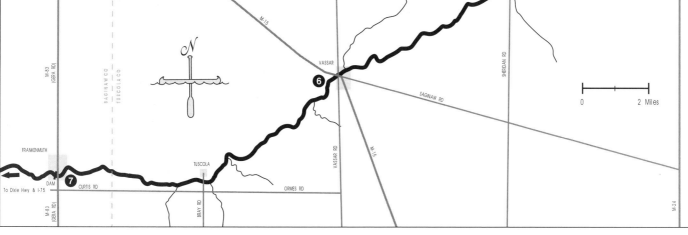

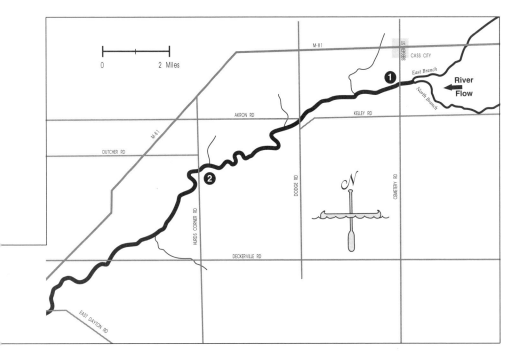

is paved with gravel and stones over bedrock slabs with frequent boulders to dodge. Many stretches require careful maneuvering through rock gardens. Note that when the water is clouded, many submerged rocks, especially in slow water, are difficult to detect. The chutes, riffles, and light rapids should not create problems even for beginning paddlers, although in extremely high water in spring, some could require caution and fairly complex maneuvering.

Hardwoods, poplars, and occasional cedars fill the shallow river valley, and thick beds of aquatic weeds line the water's edges. In this section, as along much of the river to Frankenmuth, there are occasional suitable campsites on public land.

Dodge Road Bridge has poor access and parking.

Hurd's Corner Road Bridge ❷ has poor access and very limited parking.

Deckerville Road Bridge has fair access and roadside parking.

Water volume increases gradually, due to ground springs and small tributaries, so that by Hurd's Corner Road, levels are noticeably increased. Summer passage is easier from here downstream, although there may still be some sections that require walking through. Generally, the stretches of riffles and quick water through rock gardens—although they

are found all the way to Frankenmuth—diminish in frequency and duration the farther downstream you progress. A few larger tributaries—most notably White Creek, just upstream from Deckerville Road—add substantial amounts of water.

Not far below Deckerville Road, slow, deep water precedes the backwaters of Caro Dam. Take out at East Dayton Road Bridge, where access and parking are fair, or, better, go to Chippewa Landing ❸ public park and boat ramp next to the M-24 Bridge in Caro.

The dam is approximately 1.5 miles downstream from Chippewa Landing and can be portaged either right or left; use caution in the vicinity of the dam, where there is no barrier at the spillway. There is very poor access to the dam and river off Wireline Road. Access to the next section is better at Chambers Road Bridge, four miles downstream.

About one-half mile before Chambers Road there is access and parking at Indian Fields Township Park (no camping). ❹

CHAMBERS ROAD BRIDGE to FRANKENMUTH
22 MILES / 7 – 10 HOURS

The topography of this section varies little from that of the section above. A

few scattered homes are visible, especially near bridges, and occasionally the valley deepens and banks become steeper and dense with hardwoods. The river also is similar, although it widens in some stretches to 90 – 100 feet. Shallow, rocky riffles are common, but, as mentioned, they diminish in frequency. Stretches of slow water are longer and deeper.

Access and parking at Chambers Road Bridge are fair.

There is good access and parking at the roadside park at M-46. ❺

In Vassar, there is good access and parking at the community park below Saginaw Road ❻ (Huron Avenue in town). Caution should be used at the old mill dam site here—the 3-foot drop over a concrete spillway is runnable on the right but is potentially hazardous, especially in high water, when the hydraulic at the bottom becomes significant. Portage through the park on the right if in doubt.

The bridge in Tuscola at Bray Road offers poor access and roadside parking.

In Frankenmuth, fair access and parking are found at the park near the bridge on Gera Road ❼ and just downstream at the flood-control dam. The dam must be portaged on right or left.

FRANKENMUTH to M-13 BRIDGE (NOT ON MAP)
16 MILES / 5 – 8 HOURS EST.

We ended our trip in Frankenmuth, but paddlers continuing downstream will find the water becoming consistently slow, deep and turbid, and the terrain low and marshy. There are bridges at Dehmel Road (poor access and parking) and Dixie Highway (no access or parking). Fort Road in Bridgeport has fair access and limited parking at the bridge and good access and parking (no overnight) at the township park immediately below the bridge. Access and parking at Sheridan Road are poor. M-13, the final bridge before the Cass joins the Saginaw River, has good access and parking just below the bridge on the right.

CHIPPEWA RIVER

COUNTIES: Mecosta, Isabella, Midland
START/END: Barryton Dam to Midland
MILES: 88.5
GRADIENT: Barryton Dam to Lake Isabella—4.8 ft/mile
             Lake Isabella to Mt. Pleasant—6 ft/mile
             Mt. Pleasant to Midland—2 ft/mile
PORTAGES: Four dams, easy; occasional fallen trees
RAPIDS/FALLS: Unnamed rapids near Deerfield County Park—Class I
             Unnamed rapids below Chippewa Road—Class I-II
CAMPGROUNDS: Few
CANOE LIVERIES: Several (see Appendix D)
SKILL REQUIRED: I-II

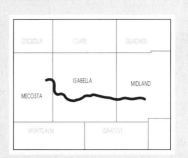

The Chippewa is one of many rivers in the Saginaw Valley that were important during the logging boom that centered around Saginaw in the second half of the 19th century. Canoeists will find the Chippewa the best of the lot. Its clear water, gravel and rock bottom, moderate to fast current, and mostly undeveloped banks make it a pleasant and popular float. Low water can be a problem during dry seasons, especially in the sections above M-20. High water in spring can make some stretches, especially the rapids below Chippewa Road, inadvisable for paddlers without experience and good basic skills.

Camping possibilities are somewhat limited, although there is a good campground about midway on the river at Deerfield County Park. Fishing is excellent for smallmouth bass, walleye, northern pike, and panfish, and for salmon in the fall.

Although some of the river is fairly heavily developed with homes and cottages, in recent years an active watershed conservancy has acquired and protected a significant amount of property near the river, ensuring that at least some portions of this fine river remain in pristine condition.

BARRYTON DAM to COLDWATER ROAD BRIDGE
19.5 MILES / 6 – 9 HOURS

The dam at Barryton ❶ gathers the two upper branches (the North and the West), and only below here is there enough width and depth for easy paddling. Good access and parking are available at the dam. Put in either down the short, steep bank at the tailrace or follow one of several two-tracks a short distance downstream for lower banks and easier access. The river here is 30 – 50 feet wide and 1 – 2 feet deep and flows moderately fast over gravel and stones. The slightly tea-colored river passes through low woodlands of maples and willows with tag alders at the banks. There are few houses and cottages.

Fair access and roadside parking are available at 20th Avenue Bridge, where the river slows and deepens.

Fair access but poor parking are found at 10th Avenue Bridge.

Nineteen Mile Road Bridge has poor access and parking.

Between 10th Avenue and 19 Mile Road, much of the river is lined with cottages on both banks. There are sections of fairly fast water over shallow gravel bottom scattered with occasional large rocks. The riffles alternate with sections of slow water—a pattern repeated through most of the length of the Chippewa. A few spots in this stretch combine quick current with tight bends and obstacles to make good maneuvering abilities an advantage.

After 19 Mile Road Bridge, there is much slow water punctuated by unusual low reefs of rocks and boulders. The current is forced back by the damming action of the reefs, then spills over them into what amounts to tiny rapids. They should present no difficulty, even to inexperienced paddlers, unless low water makes the rocks a hindrance. Some

sections of slow, deep, sand-bottomed river wind through lowlands, woods, and picturesque, well-used cow pastures. Fallen trees and minor logjams have increased in number in the final two miles before Airline Road. John Buckley, of Buckley's Mountainside Canoes, advises paddlers to allow a little extra time and "be prepared to use imagination and good humor to make your way over, under, around, and through the windfalls." Mike Anderson of Chippewa River Outfitters reports that a single strand of wire remains stretched across the river shortly before the bridge at Airline Road.

The river is accessible at Airline Road, but parking is on the roadside and very limited. Access is better at Wyman Road Bridge ❷ where there is roadside parking for several vehicles.

Below Wyman Road is more water similar to above—slow sections alternating with fairly fast riffles and one or two reefs and short drops. Shortly before Drew Road is a stretch of slow, deep, tag-alder-lined water leading to Drew Dam. This is a jumble of large boulders with a narrow chute of fierce water through the center. The drop is severe—5 or 6 feet—and may be runnable by experts in high water, but we strongly recommend portaging on either right or left.

Access and parking are poor and limited at Drew Road. Rolland Road, a short distance downstream, is not much better but is a less-busy road and probably a better choice for access. It is the last access site before Lake Isabella, a large, popular impoundment about 3 miles long. Portage Isabella Dam at the golf course on either the right or the left.

COLDWATER ROAD BRIDGE
to DEERFIELD COUNTY PARK
12.5 MILES / 4 – 7 HOURS

No access is available at Lake Isabella Dam because of private property, but Coldwater Road Bridge, ❸ is a short distance downstream with adequate access and fair roadside parking. The river here is 30 – 50 feet wide and 1 – 3 feet deep and runs slow to moderate over sand and gravel bottom. Not far downstream is Iron Bridge, now closed, at the end of an unnamed gravel road. Because the bridge is quite low, local canoe liveries often put in here during the early season when high water makes passage under the bridge difficult. Access is fair, and parking is not bad but remote.

The river to M-20 flows through low country, with tag alders common along the banks and occasional meadows punctuating forests of young hardwoods. A few scattered houses line the river, with more appearing just before M-20. The streambed is generally gravel and occasionally shallow, especially in summer, with bushel-size rocks common.

Access is fair at River Road Bridge; parking is on the roadside.

Littlefield Road Bridge has good access and roadside parking.

Access and parking are good just downstream on the left of the M-20 Bridge. ❹

Below M-20 are more stretches of slow water alternating with wide, shallow riffles. Not far downstream, the river opens into a wide pond formed by a gravel pit. Paddle nearly straight across to find the outlet. A well-worn access site and parking area known as Majske

Landing are found on the point beside the outlet. Broomfield Road Bridge follows immediately and offers excellent parking and access at the county landing just before the bridge.

Winn Road Bridge has fair access and roadside parking. During periods of low water, liveries often put in here rather than at Lake Isabella to avoid the shallow riffles in that upper section.

From Winn Road to the county campground and picnic area at Deerfield Park are remote, low hills of hardwoods and pines. The river runs somewhat faster and deeper here over a bottom of gravel and rock, with some riffles breaking into light rapids. About half a mile after the swinging foot bridge (part of a network of footpaths in the county park), look for a small sign in a tree on the right bank announcing the Deerfield County Park Campground. ❺ On the bank are ten unnumbered, lightly developed campsites with water and pit toilets.

Downstream from the campground is a covered bridge followed by a short stretch of Class I rapids. The rapids are minor, with some maneuvering around rocks required, but should not be difficult even for inexperienced paddlers. Just downstream, the river enters a natural pond, and there is access and parking at the landing in the bay or the lagoon to the left. Continue to the right, beneath another swinging bridge, to proceed downstream.

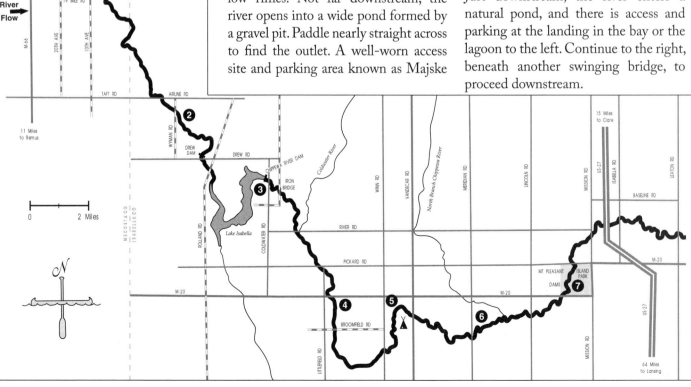

DEERFIELD COUNTY PARK to MT PLEASANT
11 MILES / 3 ½– 5 ½ HOURS

This stretch is similar to the water above, with the slow, deep water near Deerfield Park giving way to sections of riffles. Water levels from here downstream are usually adequate, even in late summer. Slow sections have sand bottom and are more prevalent than above. The river is somewhat larger, with average width 40 to 60 feet. Houses appear in greater numbers—scattered near bridges at first, becoming more prevalent closer to Mt. Pleasant.

Vandecar Road Bridge has access on the left upstream side, but parking is limited to the roadside.

The river is accessible from Meridian Road, but parking is forbidden—use the landing at the park a few hundred yards downstream, ❻ where there is good parking and access.

The North Branch of the Chippewa enters on the left. This sizable tributary drains farmlands and is frequently dredged, and is therefore often discolored.

Good access is available below Lincoln Road at the landing built by Chippewa River Outfitters. The livery is on the right side of the river and offers free parking with permission.

Lincoln Road Bridge has no access or parking.

The river slows as it approaches Mt. Pleasant and winds through a golf course and woodlots choked with underbrush. A city park 15 to 30 minutes below Lincoln Road Bridge has good access and parking.

MT PLEASANT to GENEVA ROAD BRIDGE
23.5 MILES / 6 – 10 HOURS

Several parks in Mt. Pleasant offer good access to the river and good parking, although in most cases overnight parking is forbidden. The dams in the city are scheduled to be removed, but as of this publication, still require portaging. Portage either on the right or continue along a channel to the right until you come to the twin sister of the first dam; portage this one on the right as well.

Approximately in the center of Mt. Pleasant is a large community park appropriately named Island Park. ❼ The river splits to form the island, with the left channel falling into 30-foot rapids that might be runnable during high water. Most paddlers go to the right side of the island, where the current is slow and there are many grassy banks suitable for access or picnicking.

Below Mt. Pleasant the river remains slow and deep as it meanders through an almost entirely undeveloped valley of lowland with large maples, oaks and willows predominating. The water picks up sediment from mud banks here and in the city and is clouded, with visibility about 1½ to 2½ feet. Bottom is sand through the slow stretches below Mt. Pleasant. Fallen trees are common as are well-established logjams at the bends and against fallen trees; expect several short, easy portages.

Access is possible at BR M-27 Bridge (Mission Road), but parking is poor; at Isabella Road Bridge, where parking is poor; at Leaton Road Bridge, where parking is poor; and at Shepherd Road Bridge, where parking is at the roadside and poor. Loomis Road Bridge has fair access and limited roadside parking.

By Loomis Road, the river has gained momentum, current is faster, bottom is gravel and rock, and some sections are shallow. The terrain has opened up into farmlands and low wooded hills. Shallow riffles alternate with long, slow stretches most of the way to Midland.

Just below the bridge at Chippewa Road, where there is no access or parking, is a set of rapids that rates a solid Class II in high water. These rapids, known as Bucks Run, are only about 100 feet long, but the drop is sudden and pronounced and there are surprisingly substantial standing waves at the bottom. Run them straightforward, down the middle.

Coleman Road Bridge has fair access and poor parking.

There is no access or parking at M-20 Bridge. Below here is another long section of slow, winding river through lowlands of hardwoods and underbrush. Expect a few fallen trees and logjams.

Geneva Road Bridge ❽ has fair access with limited roadside parking.

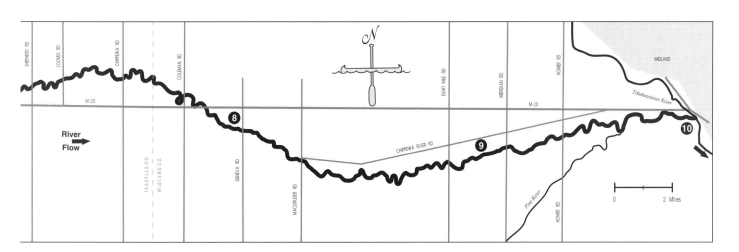

An aluminum hatch on the South Branch of the Au Sable River

GENEVA ROAD BRIDGE to MIDLAND CITY PARK
22 MILES / 5 ½ – 9 ½ HOURS

Most of the river in the lower section is shallow, quite slow, and wide—up to 150 feet. Bottom remains gravel and stone, studded with boulders that rise above the water level most of the year. A few shallow riffles glide around bends. Houses are frequent but scattered.

MacGruder Road Bridge has fair access and roadside parking.

Eight Mile Road Bridge has fair access but poor parking.

Chippewa River Road Public Access ➒ has good access and parking and has restrooms. It is the last good access site before Midland. There are two more bridges, at Meridian Road and Homer Road, but access and parking are so poor we recommend ending the trip at Chippewa River Road or continuing 2 to 3 hours into Midland and ending at the city park at the junction with the Tittabawassee. This final stretch, after the junction with the Pine River, is big water.

The city park ➓ in Midland has good access and parking.

DOWAGIAC RIVER

COUNTIES: Cass, Berrien
START/END: M-62 Bridge (Dowagiac) to Old US-31 Bridge (Niles)
MILES: 13.5
GRADIENT: 4.4 ft/mile
PORTAGES: One dam, fairly easy
RAPIDS/FALLS: None
CAMPGROUNDS: Few
CANOE LIVERIES: Several (see Appendix D)
SKILL REQUIRED: I

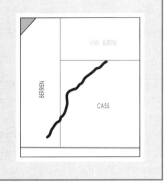

This small, mild-tempered tributary of the St. Joseph River offers one of the most interesting trips in southwest Michigan. It flows through a variety of terrain, much of it wooded and nearly all of it undeveloped and surprisingly remote. As with many rivers in the southern third of the state, camping opportunities are limited, and there are not nearly enough good access sites and parking areas. But, in spite of such limitations, the Dowagiac remains an attractive and pleasant river, well-suited for beginners and families seeking a casual one- or two-day trip. Water quality in the Dowagiac is good—much improved since the first edition of this book—thanks to the efforts of local conservation groups and the new run-of-river regulations at the dam at Pucker Street. The conservation organization MEANDRS (Meeting the Ecological and Agricultural Needs within the Dowagiac River System) is continuing the rather daunting task of restoring the meanders that were removed in the 1920s when much of the river was channelized.

Fishing is good throughout most of the Dowagiac River and Dowagiac Creek for brown trout, and for anadromous steelhead and salmon in the lower river below Niles Dam.

M-62 BRIDGE (DOWAGIAC) to Old US-31 BRIDGE (NILES)
13.5 MILES / 5 – 7 HOURS

The initial put-in at M-62 **❶** presents something of a problem. There are two bridges to consider. The western one is over the Dowagiac River; the eastern structure is over Dowagiac Creek. Neither offers very good access or parking, other than at the roadside. Both streams are about the same size—25 to 30 feet wide—and both are plagued with fallen trees. We put in on Dowagiac Creek, which is clear, shallow and sandy with a moderate but steady current. Trees form an almost continuous canopy overhead; where they have fallen, they reach easily from bank to bank. Don't despair—the downed trees last less than a quarter mile until the junction with the Dowagiac River.

Water volume doubles with the addition of the mainstream, and from here to the end of the river there are few obstructions. The river after the junction of the two branches flows uncannily straight, between banks 12 to 15 feet high. This portion of the river was dredged and channelized in the 1920s in a misguided effort to make it easier to farm the flood plain bordering the river. Dense woods of black willow, silver maple, poplar, sycamore, oak, beech and other hardwoods crowd the banks and form the overhead canopy. Some trees are remarkably large. The bottom is sand with occasional patches of gravel and rocks. Depth at midsummer is 2 to 5 feet, but high-water marks in the trees suggest spring floods of considerable depth.

There is a private bridge and landing shortly below the junction of the river and Dowagiac Creek. The next bridge is at Peavine Road with no access and parking.

Sink Road Bridge, **❷** 1½ – 2½ hours below M-62 Bridge, has good access and parking. County maps show camping both here and at Rogers Lake Recreation Area; the facilities, however, are in private ownership and can be used only by club members. From Sink Road the river continues artificially straight, through a wooded valley. Some of the old river meanders are still visible and might be restored by the time you read this.

Crystal Springs Road Bridge has poor access and parking.

Indian Lake Road Bridge has fair access, but parking is on the roadside only and very limited. Watch for a low-hanging cable below Indian Lake Road Bridge.

One-half mile below the bridge is Arthur Dodd Memorial Park, **❸** with good access, parking and picnic grounds. The river from here increases in current speed, and tight bends, logs, and leaning or fallen trees require basic maneuvering skills to negotiate. This stretch could be tricky for beginners, especially in high water.

At Kinzie Road Bridge, there is fair access and roadside parking. The river previously slowed here and entered the back waters of Niles Dam, ❹ but the drawdown in 1999 to allow run-of-river below the dam drained the backwater. (There is increasing pressure from environmental groups and the DNR to remove the dam but as of 2013 it is still present.) The river is fairly swift here and winds between banks of dense vegetation. Mud flats that once were an inconvenience—and even a bit of a hazard—are now overgrown and firm.

Take out on the right bank just before the bridge. Portage 200 yards over Pucker Street across the circle drive on the right side of the dam to the wooden foot bridge. The trail leads to a small community park with access to the river below the dam.

From the dam to US-31 is a fine 1- to 1½-hour float past the outskirts of the city of Niles. This is one of the best stretches of quick water in southern Michigan. The current is quick, the water clear, and the bottom predominately gravel and stone. Much of the terrain is wooded and undeveloped, giving the river a northern feel.

Access is fair at Old US-31 Bridge, ❺ and parking is limited to the roadside. Better parking and access are available, with permission, at Niles Canoe and Outfitting.

We did not continue the short distance downstream to the St. Joseph but were told it is a popular trip and that the river and terrain are similar to the water above. After the junction with the St. Joseph River, continue 6.5 miles downstream to the town of Buchanan, where good access and parking are available.

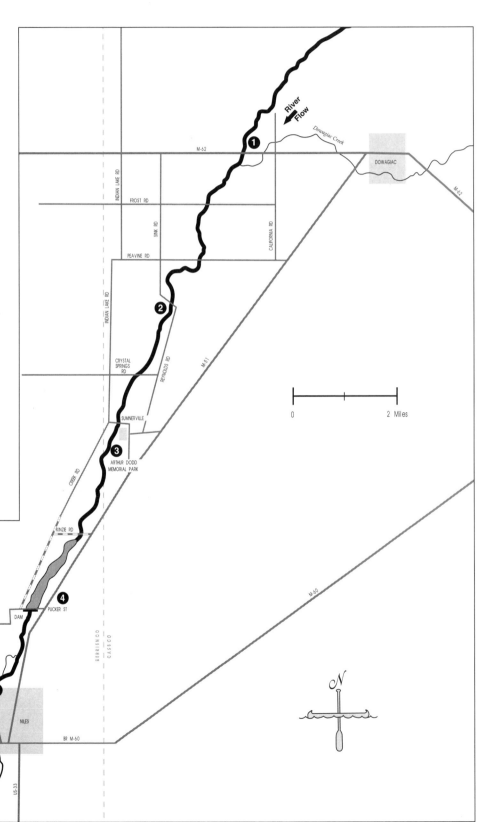

FLAT RIVER

COUNTIES: Montcalm, Ionia, Kent
START/END: Greenville Dam to Lowell
MILES: 32.5
GRADIENT: Greenville to Fallasburg Park—3.2 ft/mile
　　　　　　　Fallasburg Park to Lowell Dam—6.25 ft/mile
PORTAGES: Four dams, fairly easy
RAPIDS/FALLS: Unnamed rapids before Ingalls Bridge (Smyrna)—Class I
CAMPGROUNDS: One (private)
CANOE LIVERIES: One
SKILL REQUIRED: I

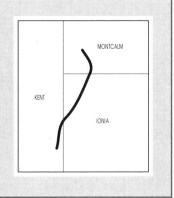

The Flat is one of the many fine tributaries of the Grand River that spread a network across the center of the Lower Peninsula. This serene and gentle river is generally quite wide and shallow with slow to moderate current, and has a more consistent flow than most streams in the area, making it a good choice for families and beginning canoeists. A Michigan Natural River, designated Country-Scenic, it passes through several stretches of state land, where streamside camping is possible. Other camping possibilities are limited to a private campground below the town of Smyrna. Fishing is excellent for smallmouth bass and other warm-water species.

GREENVILLE DAM to BELDING DAM
12.5 MILES / 4 – 6 HOURS

Although there are many miles of river above the city of Greenville, we found the upper sections extremely small, shallow, and obstructed by fallen trees and logjams. We recommend putting in at Greenville, either at the Greenville Dam ❶ (where there is good parking and access at a community park), or at Jackson's Landing, below the M-57 Bridge (where access and parking are good). The river here is 50 – 75 feet wide and 1 – 3 feet deep, with current steady to fairly quick over gravel and rock bottom. The water is often slightly discolored.

Baker Road Bridge has fair access and roadside parking for one or two vehicles. This is the beginning of the Flat River Game Preserve, an uninhabited area of hardwoods and pines, where the river is wide and generally quite slow. It is a pleasant, relaxing 2- to 4-hour float through the preserve and is rightfully considered the prime water on a Flat River canoe trip.

Bricker Road Bridge, a steel truss bridge on a gravel road, has fair access and limited parking. A short distance below it, Long Lake Road Bridge, with fair access and parking, marks the end of the Flat River Game Preserve. There is much slow, somewhat deeper water from here to Belding and the narrow backwaters of Belding Dam.

In Belding, several bridges have no access or parking. Portage the dam ❷—where there is a community park with good access and parking—on either the right or the left. The water below the dam is fairly fast over gravel. Take the right channel around the small island immediately downstream to take advantage of the most water flow.

Main Street Bridge is a few minutes below the dam and has good access and parking downstream on the right.

BELDING DAM to FALLASBURG PARK
12 MILES / 5 – 6 HOURS

Below Belding the river widens to 60 – 80 feet with depths from 3 – 6 feet. It flows through largely uninhabited countryside of low hardwood hills with tag alders at the banks among scattered meadows. There is no access or parking at the M-44 Bridge just below the town. Downstream stretches of gentle riffles alternate with slow water. The riffles flow over gravel with some rocks up to bushel size.

The bridge at Button Road (6 Mile Road) has fair access and roadside parking. Below it is a long stretch of riffles which climax into short rapids at the site of a washed out dam near Smyrna. ❸ Take the rapids through the center to best avoid rocks or portage on the left if in doubt. It is not difficult water by most whitewater standards, but high spring flows could create some fairly high standing waves. There is fair access and good parking at the old dam site before the bridge.

Double-R Ranch Resort is a private campground, resort, and canoe livery beside the river shortly below the rapids.

Riffles continue downstream a short distance before the river enters the backwaters of White's Bridge Dam. The reservoir is fairly long and narrow and winds through wooded hills. Portage the dam on the left.

A short distance below the dam is one of Michigan's few original wooden covered bridges, White's Bridge, **4** with good access and parking downstream on the right. The river here is wide (80 to 150 feet), rocky, and shallow with moderate current. From the covered bridge to Fallasburg Park expect a few scattered homes, but much of the distance is through the low wooded hills and meadows of the Lowell Game Area. The current remains moderate to fairly quick over shallow riffles, where large rocks are frequent and where low-water canoeing is sure to result in some bottom dragging.

McPherson Road Bridge has good access and parking below the bridge on the left. Fallasburg County Park **5** is just downstream and has extensive picnic grounds and good access and parking at the lower end of the park just before Covered Bridge Road—site of the Flat River's second covered bridge.

FALLASBURG PARK to LOWELL
8 MILES / 2 ½ – 4 HOURS

The lower end of the river has two medium-size reservoirs with sections of moderately paced river between. Below Covered Bridge are about two miles of backwater behind the first dam. Houses near the bridge give way to high wooded hills and isolated forests in the Lowell State Game Area. The reservoir is formed by two dams. Paddlers intending to continue downstream to Lowell should bear to the right (west) to reach the dam, which is visible from the wide body of the impoundment. Portage on the right. Access to this dam is poor—limited to two-track dirt trails that circumvent power-company property—making it an inconvenient choice for a put-in or take-out.

The alternative is a channel visible on the left (east) end of the impoundment. The channel there is narrow, and the Sayles Road Bridge is visible from the pond. Take out at the bridge. Fenced power-company property—with a very difficult portage at the small power dam there—is immediately downstream.

Access at the bridge is fair, and parking is limited to the roadside.

Continuing downstream from the west dam, the river is shallow and rocky until below the Borroughs Road Bridge, where there is poor parking and access. Below the bridge the river slows and deepens as it winds through hilly farmlands before entering the backwaters of Lowell Dam.

Take out at the dam in downtown Lowell **6** on the left upstream shore. The junction with the Grand River is less than a mile downstream.

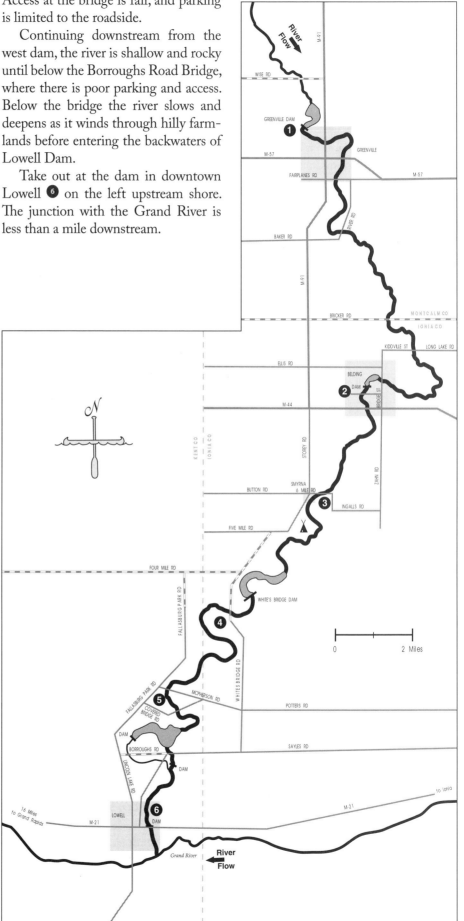

HURON RIVER

COUNTIES: Oakland, Livingston, Washtenaw, Wayne
START/END: Proud Lake to mouth
MILES: 100
GRADIENT: Hudson Mills to Ann Arbor—3.6 ft/mile.
         All other sections—less than 2 ft/mile
PORTAGES: 9 dams, easy; 2 dams, difficult
RAPIDS/FALLS: Unnamed rapids at Territorial Road Bridge—Class I
         Delhi Rapids, above Delhi Road Bridge—Class I-II
CAMPGROUNDS: Several
CANOE LIVERIES: Numerous (see Appendix D)
SKILL REQUIRED: I-II

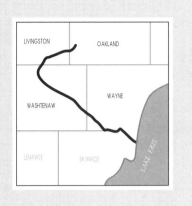

Of all southern Michigan rivers, there is probably none that has been promoted more for canoeing and other recreational uses than the Huron. An extensive system of parks has been arranged to make the river accessible and attractive to large numbers of people in Ann Arbor, Ypsilanti and Detroit. But it is not just the river's proximity to metropolitan areas that has inspired this kind of development.

With its clear water, rock and gravel bottom, and attractive and unspoiled surroundings, this Country-Scenic designated Michigan Natural River would be a favorite with canoeists wherever it happened to be located. Generally, it has slow to moderate current and few hazards or obstructions that cannot be easily avoided. There are, however, several stretches of fast water that can be difficult for beginners. At least one short set of rapids is challenging enough during high-water stages to attract kayakers and other whitewater enthusiasts. Although never quite out of earshot of freeways, the Huron flows through mostly undeveloped country, much of it wooded. Except in the cities, of course, there are few houses on its banks, and wildlife is as abundant as on many far northern rivers. We were surprised to see otters, herons, osprey and a variety of waterfowl.

Fishing is excellent, primarily for smallmouth bass and other warm-water species, although a put-and-take trout fishery has been established in the section below Proud Lake.

Wilderness enthusiasts will perhaps find the large number of reservoirs and the fee-oriented park system too civilized, but the Huron provides local urban dwellers a quick and convenient getaway. Certainly most of them come away, as we did, surprised and delighted by a fine river.

PROUD LAKE to KENT LAKE DAM
13.5 MILES / 4 ½ – 6 ½ HOURS

Proud Lake ❶ is the upstream limit of good canoeing water. Above here is a series of lakes and impoundments threaded together by narrow, shallow river. Access and parking are good at Proud Lake Recreation Area, where there are several boat launch sites and where a state vehicle permit is required. Get used to it, because virtually every service in the state and metropolitan park systems along the Huron requires fees. Proud Lake is small, narrow and bordered by marshlands. Stay to the right to find the outlet. A state park and campground is on the south shore midway down the lake. At the outlet, portage the water-control dam on the right.

The river from here to the dam at Milford is clear and slow, with sand bottom punctuated by stretches of gravel and small stones. It averages 25 – 35 feet wide, with summer depths of 1 – 3 feet Terrain is lowland forests and marshlands. Trout are planted annually, and flies-only fishing regulations are in effect from Proud Lake outlet to Wixom Road. Angling pressure here is very high, especially in April and May.

Access and parking are good at Wixom Road Bridge, ❷ where a motor-vehicle permit is required and parking is prohibited from 10:00 p.m. to 8:00 a.m. Paddlers planning to park overnight should contact the Metropolitan Parks Authority to make arrangements. (See Appendix C: Further Information—Huron River.)

Access is fair at Burns Road Bridge, and roadside parking is very limited.

In Milford, there is a community park next to the bridge on Main Street ❸ (Milford Road). The river is accessible, but parking is allowed only during daylight hours. The river widens here to enter the backwaters of Milford Dam. Portage the dam on the right.

Below Milford, the river continues much as it did above but, just below Dawson Road, widens again and enters Kent Lake. Just downstream from General Motors Road (no access) is a Kensington Metropark canoe campground. ❹

Dawson Road Bridge has good access and parking for half a dozen vehicles and is a good take-out for paddlers who want to avoid large Kent Lake.

There are numerous well-marked parks, picnic areas and access sites on Kent Lake, which is large enough to support a marina and sailboats and is capable of producing high winds and large waves. Just past the I-96 Bridge, portage Kent Dam ❺ on the left, where there is also parking and access. To reach the dam by road, enter Island Lake Recreation Area off Kensington Road.

We bypassed the series of lakes beginning with Strawberry Lake and have only incomplete information about them. Strawberry Lake, especially, is heavily developed, but there are uninhabited marshlands surrounding the channels between the lakes and the shorelines along several of them.

Portage the control dam below Baseline Lake on the left and the rock barrier immediately downstream on the right. (Note: There is a public access site on Portage Lake connected by a channel to the Huron River below Baseline Lake.)

just below Territorial Road. Upstream, fair access and parking are found at Bell Road. The river here is 60 – 90 feet wide and alternates sections of slow water 1 – 4 feet deep with sections of very shallow riffles. Low water in summer will produce some bottom-bumping. Hudson Mills has been the site of a saw mill, grist mill, cider mill and plaster mill, the earliest dating back to 1827. Today, only the ruins of foundations and a short stretch of light rapids mark the spot just below Territorial Road Bridge where the mills were located. The rapids can be run down the chute at left center. Pumpkin- to bushel-size rocks create standing waves that could become fairly high during high water. If in doubt, portage on the left just beyond the bridge.

Light riffles extend well into Hudson Mills Metropark, where there are several

KENT LAKE DAM to BASELINE LAKE DAM
19.5 MILES / 6 – 9 HOURS

Below Kent Lake, through Island Lake Recreation Area, the river is 40 to 60 feet wide and slowly meanders through lowland forests. It is subject to fallen trees that seem to be regularly cleared.

There is no access at Kensington Road Bridge, but there is access and parking at several picnic areas and launch sites as well as at a canoe campground in the park downstream.

McCabe Road Bridge has fair access and parking.

Ricket Road has poor access and parking.

Neither the bridge at Winans Lake Road nor at M-36 has access to the river.

HUDSON MILLS METROPARK to ANN ARBOR PARKS
16.5 MILES / 5 ½ – 8 HOURS

Put in at Hudson Mills Metropark, ❻ where there is good access and parking

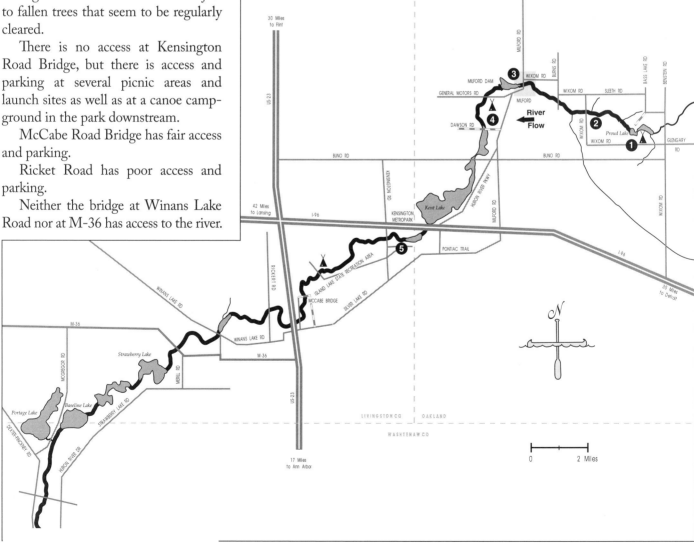

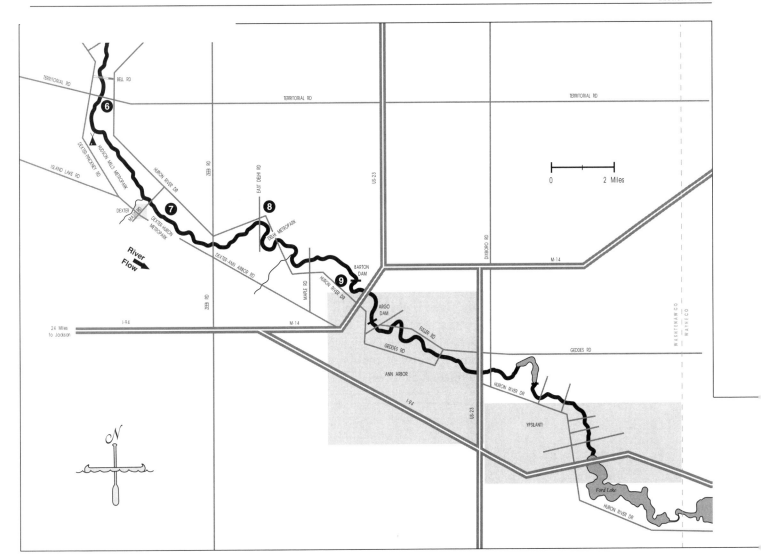

access sites and two overnight canoe campgrounds. This is one of the finest sections of the Huron River. The current alternates from quick to slow, and water is clean and clear as it flows over sand, gravel and rocks up to bushel size. The river passes through low hills of upland forests.

Occasional houses line the river, especially near Dexter, but generally this is a quiet, relatively remote section that supports a variety of wildlife. A runnable drop over a rock barrier just upstream from Dexter should be scouted during high water. Run it through the chute at right center.

Access and parking are poor at Mast Road Bridge in Dexter. A mile downstream is good access and parking at Dexter-Huron Metropark ❼ picnic grounds. Riffles near the park give way to slow water 2 to 5 feet deep. Just above

Zeeb Road is another rock barrier, which can be run on the right.

Zeeb Road Bridge has fair access and fair parking for five or six vehicles along the roadside. From here to Delhi is a 1- to 1½-hour float through wide river with slow to moderate current.

At Delhi ❽ there are locally famous rapids that should be scouted, especially by beginning or intermediate paddlers. Islands divide the river into two main channels, both of which can be run except during low water when exposed rocks prohibit passage. Spring's high water attracts kayakers to this stretch of rare southern Michigan whitewater. Paddlers with any whitewater experience will negotiate these short, straight-forward rapids without difficulty. Descent over jumbled rocks is quick for about 200 feet; jammed logs and other debris may create obstacles. To avoid the

rapids, take out at a good access site on the right or portage either right or left. There is also good access and parking (for a small fee) at Delhi Road Bridge, immediately below the rapids.

From Delhi to Barton Pond, riffles extend about one-half mile, then slow water precedes the reservoir. There is no access at Huron River Drive or at Maple Road Bridge. Good access and parking for several vehicles can be found beside Huron River Drive next to the railroad trestle. These trestles are low and may require portaging during high water.

Portage Barton Dam ❾ at the marker on the right. From here to Argo Pond the river is wide and deep. Take the left channel at Argo Dam, then portage. Island Park, one-half mile below the dam, has good access and parking, as do several parks in Ann Arbor.

ANN ARBOR to LOWER HURON METROPARK
22.5 MILES / 7 ½ – 11 HOURS

This section contains an almost continuous series of backwaters with four dams to portage. Its virtue is that it provides a pleasant and unusual means of viewing Ann Arbor and Ypsilanti. Because the cities are anxious to promote the recreational potential of the river, they've built several large parks along the banks, complete with access sites, parking, picnic areas, drinking water and restrooms. Portages are well marked and obvious, except at Belleville Lake Dam (also known as French Landing), where, on the right side, the portage through an industrial area is unpleasantly long and difficult. (Note that high winds can be a nuisance in the open waters of Ford Lake and Belleville Lake, although more often than not the wind will be from the west.)

LOWER HURON METROPARK to FLAT ROCK DAM
15.5 MILES / 5 – 7 HOURS

There is no access at French Landing; put in one mile downstream at Lower Huron Metropark. ❿ The river from here to Flat Rock passes almost entirely through metropark property and is managed for recreational uses. Current is slow to moderate, similar to much of the river upstream, although the water is not as clear. The river is 75 – 90 feet wide and 2 – 4 feet deep; bottom is sand and gravel with occasional larger stones. Most of the terrain is lowland forests of hardwoods. There is a canoe campground—as well as several picnic areas that provide access to the river—in Lower Huron Metropark. Reservations are required to camp. Call Lower Huron Metropark: 734-697-9181.

Numerous access sites are at Willow Metropark, ⓫ 10 miles below Lower Huron. There is also fair—and free—access, with parking for several vehicles, at the bridge on Willow Road.

Oakwoods Metropark has parking, access, and other facilities and is the last good access before Flat Rock Pond.

To portage Flat Rock Dam requires permission. Call Flat Rock Metal Company at 734-782-4454. Once permission is granted, portage the dam on the right, through the gate in the factory fence. If you choose to end your trip here, a better alternative is to take out at Oakwoods Metropark ⓬ at the west end of Flat Rock Pond.

FLAT ROCK to POINTE MOUILEE (LAKE ERIE) (NOT ON MAP)
9.5 MILES / 3 ½ – 4 ½ HOURS

This final section of the Huron is wide, slow, and discolored and does not equal the quality of the river upstream. The community park in Flat Rock has good access and parking. Fishing pressure is extremely high in the first mile or so below the dam, especially in spring and fall. There are several boat launch sites near the mouth of the river, including Dodge Brothers Park and Labo Park in South Rockwood, and Brownstown Boat Launch off West Jefferson Avenue. Pointe Mouillee State Game Area just north of the mouth at Lake Erie has good access, parking, water and restrooms.

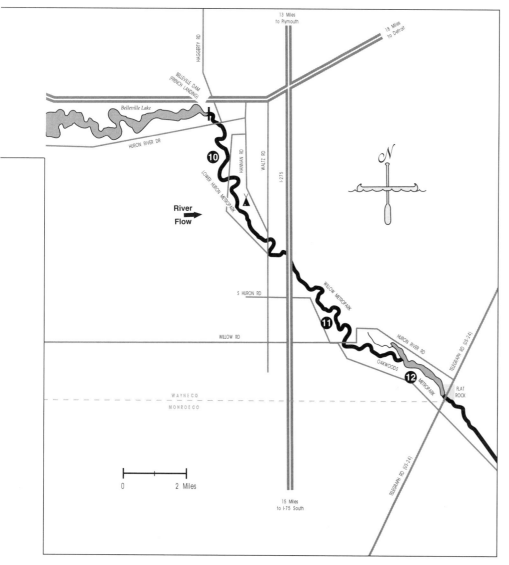

JORDAN RIVER

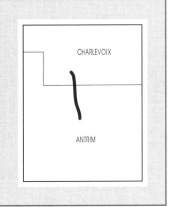

COUNTIES: Antrim, Charlevoix
START/END: Graves Crossing to Lake Charlevoix
MILES: 10.5
GRADIENT: 6.2 ft/mile
PORTAGES: None
RAPIDS/FALLS: None
CAMPGROUNDS: Few
CANOE LIVERIES: Two (see Appendix D)
SKILL: I-II
TOPO. MAPS: Boyne City (15 min.)

This small, lovely Wild-Scenic designated Michigan Natural River has long been considered one of Michigan's finest trout streams. Despite its small size, it attracts many paddlers, especially during summer weekends, when the crowds can be a bit daunting. Recent efforts to limit the number of paddlers and restrict their consumption of alcohol have been unsuccessful. The Jordan's most striking feature is the clarity of its water; in fact, aquatic biologists consider it to have perhaps the purest water of any Lower Peninsula river. Water levels do not fluctuate greatly and will not be excessively low even in dry summers. Generally quick current in the upper section combined with tight bends make basic paddling skills advisable.

Fishing is for resident brook, brown and rainbow trout, as well as lake-run rainbows and browns in the spring and fall, and a few coho salmon in the fall.

Camping is mostly limited to the state-forest campground near Graves Crossing. Although parts of the river flow through state land, most of the shoreline is thickly overgrown with cedars and tag alders, and good riverside campsites are not common.

GRAVES CROSSING to LAKE CHARLEVOIX
10.5 MILES / 3 ½ – 5 HOURS

The river upstream from Graves Crossing ❶ is too small and too choked with fallen trees to be negotiated. About a mile upstream is the junction of a major tributary, the Green River; above that, fallen trees and logjams make the river virtually uncanoeable.

At Graves Crossing—where access is good and where parking is adequate for a dozen or more vehicles—the river is 30 – 50 feet wide and 2 – 5 feet deep. Moderately fast current flows over gravel and stones up to fist size. Water is clear and very cold.

A short distance below the bridge on Graves Crossing Road is a state-forest campground that offers the best camping in the area. Primitive facilities include water, toilets and picnic tables.

Access is fair at Old State Road, with parking limited to the roadside.

Webster Bridge Access Site ❷ is below the bridge on the right and has good access and parking and a vault toilet.

Alba Road Access Site is located off Mount Bliss Road at the end of Alba Road; it has good access and parking and vault toilets.

Expect the river from here to remain moderately quick, narrow and winding most of the way to Rogers Road. Frequent limestone ledges and sudden dropoffs make fishing in waders tricky for such a small river. Fallen trees may be an occasional problem, especially in early spring, but most of the year passage is kept clear.

The public site at Rogers Road Bridge ❸ has good access, parking, and a vault toilet.

The final mile of river between Rogers Road and Lake Charlevoix is flat and slow through marshlands. Continue into the lake beyond the bridge at M-32 and take out on the left at the public boat ramp ❹. Overnight parking is prohibited at the ramp but is allowed across the road at Sportsman's Park.

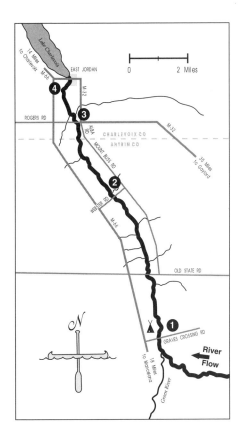

KALAMAZOO RIVER

COUNTIES: Hillsdale, Jackson, Calhoun
START/END: Goose Lake Road Bridge (above Homer) to Battle Creek
MILES: 46.5
GRADIENT: 2.8 ft/mile
PORTAGES: One dam, easy; three dams, difficult;
　　　　　　　occasional fallen trees on South Branch
RAPIDS/FALLS: None
CAMPGROUNDS: Few
CANOE LIVERIES: Several (see Appendix D)
SKILL REQUIRED: I

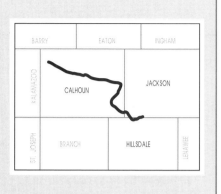

This major southern Michigan river has much to offer canoeists—in spite of certain handicaps—and is zealously supported by local paddlers. In many ways it is a fine river. Much of it flows through forested, uninhabited countryside; current is strong enough to make an enjoyable float, yet is gentle enough for beginners; and water quality, especially in the upper reaches, appears to be good.

There are, however, problems. Access and parking are so difficult in places that we gave up on entire stretches in frustration. There are difficult portages at Marshall, Ceresco, and especially in Battle Creek, where little effort has been made to promote the recreational potential of the river. In the heart of Battle Creek the river has been diverted down a nearly mile-long concrete sluice, where storm fences and city ordinances prevent further progress and force paddlers to arrange shuttles around this barrier or face the unpleasant prospect of a mile portage through busy city streets. Partly because access and passage are deterred at Battle Creek and partly because the river quickly loses velocity and quality below that city, we ended our trip there.

The Enbridge oil spill of July 2010, during which a ruptured pipeline spewed more than a million gallons of crude oil into the river near Marshall, was still being cleaned up more than two years later.

SOUTH BRANCH
GOOSE LAKE ROAD BRIDGE to HOMER
9 MILES / 3 ½ – 5 ½ HOURS

The river as far upstream as Goose Lake Road Bridge ❶ is navigable, although it is very small (10 – 15 feet wide, 1 – 3 feet deep) and is subject to obstruction from fallen trees. Expect to find a few fallen trees most of the way to Homer, although there are fewer below 29 Mile Road Bridge than in the upper stretches. There is a private campground and canoe livery at Good Lake Road Bridge. Access is good, with roadside parking.

Better put-ins are at Folks Road Bridge ❷ or at the private campground just downstream, where there is access, parking and supplies. The river at Folks Road is slow, winding and generally shallow. Water is clear over mostly sand bottom. Fishing is for warm-water species, including smallmouth bass and northern pike. The river averages 25 – 35 feet wide and 6 inches to 2 feet deep. Expect to drag bottom in places during the summer. Terrain is lowland marshes and low hills of mixed hardwoods, much of it state owned. Signs of human habitation are infrequent even though the river is usually within a half-mile of roads.

At Van Wert Road Bridge, access and parking are poor. Twenty-Nine Mile Road Bridge offers better access and is often used to start a short 1- to 2-hour trip to Homer that avoids many of the obstacles upstream.

In Homer, good access and parking are found at the old gristmill. ❸ The low dam just before the mill can be run on the right if there is enough water; otherwise expect to scrape on concrete and on the rocks at the bottom. If in doubt, portage on the right.

SOUTH BRANCH HOMER to ALBION
9 MILES / 3 – 5 HOURS

Below Homer the river varies from 25 to 60 feet wide, with some sections very shallow in summer. Expect an occasional fallen tree, although canoe liveries succeed in keeping passage clear most of the year. There is fair access and limited roadside parking at most of the half-dozen bridges in this section.

Current speed varies from slow to moderate, and bottom is sand or silt with occasional stretches of gravel. Before Albion, a long stretch of slow water meanders through marshland before entering the backwaters of Albion Dam.

Access is good off M-99 at Albion Pond, ❹ or continue to the dam at Haven Road and portage on the right, through a community park. The river is diverted into several channels here, making the portage two- to three-hundred-yards long. Access and parking are good.

MAINSTREAM ALBION to CERESCO DAM
19.5 MILES / 6 – 9 HOURS

In Albion the South Branch is joined by the North Branch to form the Kalamazoo Mainstream. The North Branch is said to be canoeable as far upstream as the town of Concord, but with many obstructions. We found it to be distressingly small and shallow and did not attempt to canoe it.

In Albion, put in either at the dam at Haven Road or downstream at East Cass Street. The river through town is slow to moderate in speed and shallow over gravel, rocks and the usual urban deposits of tires and bottles. Be prepared for the novelty of riding the river beneath the sidewalks and floors of the downtown district.

Below town the river is 40 – 75 feet wide and 1 – 3 feet deep. Water quality—with silt and sand bottom and water that tends to be clouded—is not as good as in the two branches above Albion. Farmlands of rolling hills alternate with patches of hardwoods, where fallen trees may occasionally reach across the river. There are bridges at B Drive North, where access and parking are fair; at 23 Mile Road, where there is no access; and for a second time at B Drive North, where access is good and there is limited roadside parking.

Near Marshall, a long backwater can be a problem during low water when mud flats make passage difficult. Portage the dam ❺ on the right and follow the signs for a 250-yard portage across 17½ Mile Road, then through the gates of an industrial complex to the river.

Below the Marshall Dam is a stretch of fairly fast riffles over rocks and gravel, but most of the river continues slow to moderate over sand and gravel bottom. West of Marshall the river passes beneath I-69 (US-27) and beneath the bridge at 15 Mile Road, where access is poor and there is no parking. From here the river is wide and slow coming into Ceresco Pond. As in the backwaters at Marshall, mud flats may hinder passage during low water. There is no clear portage at Ceresco Dam. ❻ The best chance is to the left, but because you must cross over private property, permission must be granted to pass through, as well as to put in below the dam.

MAINSTREAM
CERESCO DAM to BATTLE CREEK
9 MILES / 3 – 5 HOURS

This short stretch is a popular trip, although even on summer weekends it will probably not be excessively crowded. There is a private campground midway through it, and access is relatively good in several places. Putting in at Ceresco Dam can be difficult due to private property, and permission should be sought at the small office building on the left side of the dam.

The river at Ceresco is 60 – 90 feet wide and 1 – 4 feet deep over gravel and rock. Current ranges from slow to moderately fast, with numerous riffles that are very shallow in summer. Most of the section passes through lowland forests of mixed hardwoods—including oak, maple, sycamore and basswood—with heavy streamside brush. There are occasional houses, but they are widely scattered.

Eleven Mile Road Bridge has fair access and roadside parking and is an alternative to putting in at the dam upstream. Below the bridge is a short stretch of relatively fast water with scattered bushel-size rocks to avoid.

Just below the I-94 and Nine Mile Road bridges is a picnic area and public access site. ❼ Immediately across the river is a private campground. From here until Battle Creek the river continues to alternate slow water with light riffles. Access is available on the outskirts of the city at Raymond Road, but the

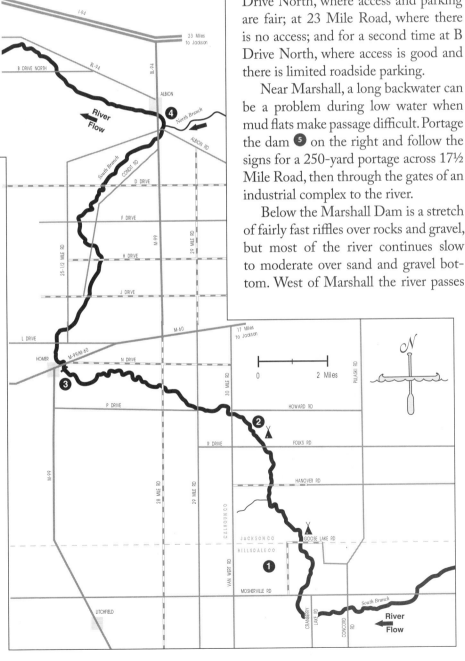

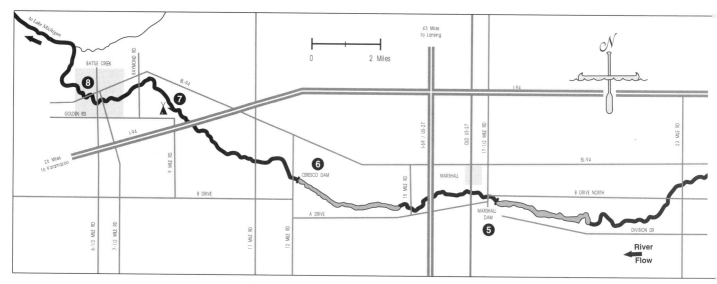

access road has been blocked, making it necessary to park at the roadside and carry a short distance to the river.

Below Raymond Road the river slows to enter the backwaters of a water-control dam 8 in Battle Creek. Fair access to the backwaters is available near the corner of 6½ Mile Road and 7½ Mile Road. This is the last decent access to the river before the dam, and a nearly mile-long concrete sluice below it make further progress difficult. We were told that hardy paddlers sometimes make the long portage through busy Battle Creek streets, but we found the logistics too complicated and ended our trip at Raymond Road.

Paddlers wishing to explore the Kalamazoo downstream from Battle Creek will find it to be a large, generally slow river, winding through a variety of woods and farmlands. Major dams and reservoirs are found at Comstock (Morrow Lake), Otsego, Trowbridge and Allegan (Lake Allegan). The Allegan State Game Area is well worth investigating; it's located west of Allegan and about 10 miles east of Lake Michigan. In this large area of marshlands, the river passes beneath bluffs of pine and oak and branches out into many bayous. Waterfowl and other wildlife are abundant, and fishing is said to be excellent. This section of the river and down to the mouth in Saugatuck is designated a Wild-Scenic Michigan Natural River.

LITTLE MANISTEE RIVER

COUNTIES: Lake, Mason, Manistee
START/END: Indian Bridge (Irons Road) to Stronach Road Bridge
MILES: 30.5
GRADIENT: Indian Bridge to Nine Mile Bridge—6 ft/mile
Nine Mile Bridge to Six Mile Bridge—14 ft/mile
Six Mile Bridge to Stronach Road Bridge—4 ft/mile
PORTAGES: DNR weir below Six Mile Bridge, easy; occasional fallen trees
RAPIDS/FALLS: Unnamed rapids between Nine Mile Bridge and Six Mile Bridge—Class I-II
CAMPGROUNDS: Several
CANOE LIVERIES: Several (see Appendix D)
SKILL REQUIRED: I-II
TOPO. MAPS: Wellston, Freesoil, Manistee (15 min.)

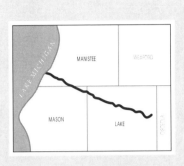

Although the Little Manistee is well known for its trout and salmon fisheries, canoeists have often overlooked it in favor of the nearby Pere Marquette, Pine and Big Manistee rivers. Yet those who have canoed the "Little River" are quick to list it among their favorite trips. Small, quick-spirited, clean and relatively stable, it flows through long stretches of largely undeveloped national forest land with several USFS campgrounds on its banks. Current is moderate to fairly quick along much of the river and suited to paddlers with basic skills. The section between Nine Mile and Six Mile bridges, however, is one of the fastest and most challenging stretches in the Lower Peninsula and requires more advanced ability. Fallen trees can slow progress, especially in the upper reaches, but they appear to be cleared fairly regularly.

Brook, brown and rainbow trout are abundant, as are spring and fall runs of steelhead. Angling pressure can be heavy during the peaks of those runs.

INDIAN BRIDGE (IRONS ROAD) to DRIFTWOOD VALLEY ACCESS
10 MILES / 4 ½ – 5 ½ HOURS

Although there is a campground and access site at Old Grade National Forest Campground on M-37 (and a DNR public access site at Spencer Bridge on Peacock Road), the river that far upstream is too small and choked by fallen trees to be easily navigated.

The most practical access is at the DNR access site upstream on the right above Indian Bridge, ❶ where there is good access down a short set of stairs. The river here is small (15 to 20 feet), shallow, and has its share of logjams and fallen trees. Be prepared to go over and around several obstructions. The current is moderate and steady over sand and gravel bottom. Terrain is hilly with upland hardwood and pine forests; cedars and tag alders line the banks.

The river opens up somewhat after Johnson's Bridge at Johnson Road, where access and parking are poor. Passage is through a continuous series of tight bends with few places to really dig a paddle in for speed. During the early season, there might be enough water volume to make a few tight spots tricky for beginners. Basic paddling and maneuvering skills are sufficient during normal flow.

There is no access at Dewitts Bridge. It is easy to be confused at Dewitts, Fox and Poggensee bridges because of their close proximity and lack of signage. Fox Bridge ❷ (Bass Lake Road) has a designated public access site with good parking upstream on the left.

Poggensee Bridge (Mitchell Road) is unmarked but can be identified by a gravel road and by the wooden bridge, which looks from the river like it could be a low railroad trestle. Access and parking are poor. Immediately downstream the road closely parallels the river, making access possible with roadside parking.

Driftwood Valley USFS Recreation Site ❸ is just downstream on the left. This former campground, now a day-use area, has good access and parking. It is not marked on the river and could easily be missed—look across the river for stones piled into a partial dam with a narrow, quick passage through the center. On the left, there are wooden stairs and hand rails leading up the bank.

From here the river is large enough and open enough for easy passage. Current remains generally moderate, though there are both some slow and some fairly quick stretches; a few tricky bends require good maneuvering skills.

DRIFTWOOD VALLEY ACCESS to NINE MILE BRIDGE
9.5 MILES / 3 – 4 ½ HOURS

This makes a short trip for overnighters not wanting to run the fast water

below Nine Mile Bridge. Those who want to continue can go the additional 2 to 3 hours to Six Mile Bridge and the access there. The stretch to Nine Mile Bridge is typical of northern Lower Peninsula rivers, with its sand and gravel bottom, moderate to moderately fast current, and cedar-lined banks backing up to high ground of hardwoods and occasional pines and hemlocks.

Eighteen Mile Road Bridge has poor access and parking. A short distance below it, there is good access and parking at Bear Track USFS Campground ❹. Like Driftwood Valley Access, it is unmarked from the river but can be recognized by brown painted hand rails on the ridge above the left bank and steps leading down to the river. The best access is from the group camping area.

There is good access and parking at Nine Mile Bridge (Campbell Road). ❺

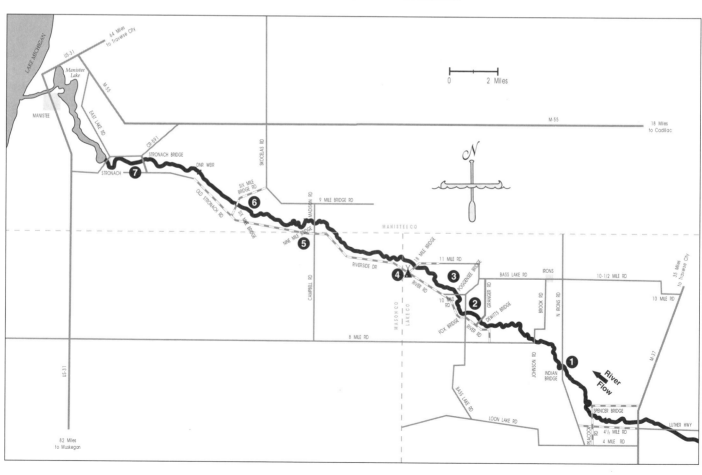

NINE MILE BRIDGE to STRONACH ROAD BRIDGE
11 MILES / 4 ½ – 6 ½ HOURS

After Nine Mile Bridge is a locally famous stretch of fast water. The river speeds noticeably near the bridge; within a mile it drops quickly over bottom of gravel and rocks to pumpkin size. Expect about four miles of very quick, tricky water. The challenge does not come from whitewater, of which there is little, but from extremely tight bends with logjams and leaning trees. The fast, strong current is naturally funneled into the obstructions on the outside of the bends. There is also thick brush of tag alders and willows that narrows passage in places to as little as five feet. Precise maneuvering is necessary, with backstrokes and especially drawstrokes indispensable. This is a delightful and challenging stretch for experienced paddlers and those seeking more experience but is not recommended for beginners or families with small children. The water is not generally deep, but fast-water dredging beneath logjams and fallen trees always creates the potential for hazards.

Near Six Mile Bridge ❻ the river slows and widens somewhat. From here downstream, current is slow and predictable, and there are few obstructions that cannot be easily avoided. Frequent sandbars make excellent picnic and swimming sites. Access is good at Six Mile Bridge, with parking limited to the designated lot 100 yards up the hill to the north on the right side of the river.

One to 1½ hours below Six Mile Bridge is a DNR weir; portage on the right. From here on is slow water and sandy bottom, with stretches of very deep water alternating with stretches of very shallow water. This is a leisurely float through mostly lowland with few houses or other development.

Access and parking are good at the public site at Stronach Road Bridge. ❼ This is the recommended take-out. From here to the final bridge in the village of Stronach (in sight of Manistee Lake) are 2 miles of slow water through marshlands. Parking and access in Stronach are poor.

Au Sable River

LITTLE MUSKEGON RIVER

COUNTIES: Mecosta, Montcalm, Newaygo
START/END: Altona Dam to Croton Pond Junction with the Muskegon River
MILES: 33.75
GRADIENT: Altona to Morley—3.6 ft/mile
       Morley to Croton Pond—6.2 ft/mile
PORTAGES: Two dams, easy; occasional fallen trees
RAPIDS/FALLS: Several unnamed rapids below West County Line Road Bridge—Class I
CAMPGROUNDS: One
CANOE LIVERIES: Few (see Appendix D)
SKILL REQUIRED: I-II

The Little Muskegon is often overlooked by paddlers traveling north to more famous rivers, yet its clear water, quick current and relatively remote surroundings make it one of the most attractive rivers in central Michigan. Rising out of headwaters in northeastern Mecosta County, the Little Muskegon is not large enough to be easily navigated until it reaches the village of Altona, 20 miles downstream. From there to the Muskegon River at Croton Pond is a two-day trip through a variety of terrain, including woodlands and farms. Current velocity varies from moderate to quick, with some stretches, especially in the section below Morley, fast enough to be challenging to beginners. Camping opportunities are limited, unfortunately, due to private property and a lack of established campgrounds. Fishing is primarily for smallmouth bass and, in the upper reaches, some trout.

ALTONA DAM to MORLEY DAM
11 MILES / 4 – 5 HOURS

Altona has a community park, ❶ with fairly good access and parking, just below the small dam at the east end of town. The river is 25 – 30 feet wide, varies from 6 inches to 3 feet deep, and flows over a bottom of mostly gravel and small stones. Current is moderate to fairly quick, with basic paddling skills more than sufficient in the shallow water and meandering turns. Some light riffles are too shallow for free passage during low-water periods and may require walking through. The terrain is fairly open, with stretches of meadows and tag alders interrupted by small woodlots of hardwoods. Occasional houses and farms line the river, but generally expect a quiet, fairly remote trip.

At the end of Three Mile Road is a state-maintained public access site ❷ with good access and parking. A short distance downstream are narrow, short backwaters and a small dam to portage on the right. From here to Morley is water similar to above, with shallow riffles and occasional rocks alternating with slow water and sand bottom. Passage is generally clear, but fallen trees are a possibility. Access at 130th Avenue Bridge is fair with roadside parking.

Fair access and roadside parking are found at 155th Avenue Bridge.

The bridge at Jefferson Road, at the upper end of Morley Pond, has fair access and poor roadside parking. Better access is found at the community park midway on the north shore and at the dam in Morley; access and parking are good at both sites.

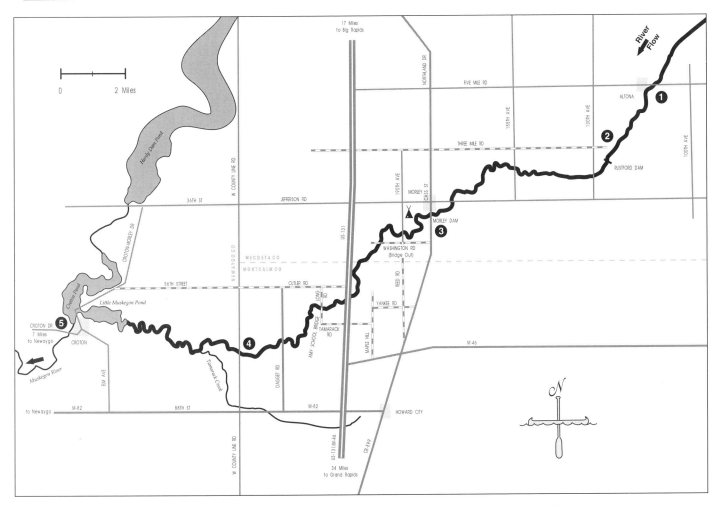

MORLEY DAM to CROTON DAM
(JUNCTION WITH THE MUSKEGON RIVER)
22.75 MILES / 7 ½ – 10 ½ HOURS

In Morley, put in at the Cass Street (CR-599) Bridge ❸ below the dam, where there is good access and parking. The river from here is 25 – 40 feet wide and 1 – 3 feet deep. The bottom is sand, gravel and rock. Water added from Big Creek and other tributaries helps keep levels higher than in the river above Morley, although a few shallow riffles may still be bottom-draggers in dry periods. Minor logjams and occasional fallen trees may require maneuvering through or portaging. A few scattered houses and cottages are found along this section, but it flows mostly through quite remote hills of hardwoods and pines with patches of tag alders at the banks. The current can be surprisingly fast, especially in the final stretch after West County Line Road Bridge, and

tight bends and occasional obstructions make basic maneuvering skills advisable.

The bridge at 190th Avenue has poor access and roadside parking.

No access is available at the bridges at Washington Road and US-131. Stretches of fast riffles in this area alternate with stretches of low, deeper water over sand bottom.

Access is poor with roadside parking at Amy School Bridge (Long Road) and at the steel and wood bridge at Dagget Road.

West County Line Road Bridge (Newcosta Avenue) ❹ has fair access and road-side parking and offers the last access before the landing at Croton Pond. Quite a few houses are clustered in the vicinity of the bridge, but they dwindle quickly. Current is slower than above, and the river meanders through low woods, where windblown trees—some of which may require going over or around—are common.

The final section is a 3- to 3½-hour trip through the most remote—and the fastest—portion of the river. The course twists through high sand and clay banks wooded with maple, oak, birch and pine. Long stretches of riffles and light rapids make a quick descent over gravel, stone and scattered bushel-size and larger rocks. Tamarack Creek increases water volume by half and frequently clouds the water of the mainstream. Riffles and tight bends continue until shortly before Little Muskegon Pond, where current slows, bottom becomes sand, and lowlands and marshes appear.

At the pond, head for the bridge—visible at the west end—and enter Croton Pond. A public landing ❺ is located on the west shore, just north of the power station. Parking and access are good, and several private and township campgrounds are found in the vicinity of the dam and along Croton Drive to Newaygo.

MANISTEE RIVER

COUNTIES: Crawford, Kalkaska, Missaukee, Wexford, Manistee
START/END: Deward to Manistee Lake
MILES: 163
GRADIENT: 4 ft/mile or less
PORTAGES: Two dams, moderately difficult
RAPIDS/FALLS: None
CAMPGROUNDS: Numerous
CANOE LIVERIES: Numerous (see Appendix D)
SKILL REQUIRED: I

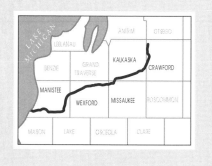

Rising from headwaters in Antrim and Otsego Counties, the Manistee River does not gain significance for canoeists until it enters the northwest corner of Crawford County near the ghost town of Deward. Named after 19th-century lumber baron David Ward, Deward was built in the heart of the last big stand of virgin white pine in the Lower Peninsula. Around the turn of the century it boasted a population of 800 and a daily output of up to a quarter of a million board feet of lumber. Thousands of weathered stumps still dot the surrounding hills and meadows as a reminder of the forests that once made the Manistee one of the most important log-driving rivers in the state.

Canoeists will find the Manistee one of the finest rivers in the Lower Peninsula for expedition canoeing and camping. Numerous campgrounds and access sites are found the entire length of the river. Long stretches of undeveloped countryside and clear, clean water have caused the Manistee to be designated a National Recreational River from Tippy Dam to the M-55 bridge, and a Wild-Scenic River in the Michigan Natural Rivers Program.

Current is slow to moderate, with occasional light riffles that should not challenge paddlers who have basic skills. Because it is largely spring fed, water levels on the Manistee, like those on the nearby Au Sable, are quite stable.

Fishing is for brook and brown trout in the upper reaches and brown trout down as far as the Baxter Bridge area above Hodenpyle Backwaters, and below Hodenpyle and Tippy dams. Walleyes, smallmouth bass and northern pike predominate in the lower reaches; steelhead and salmon runs up to Tippy Dam are among the most prolific in the Great Lakes.

DEWARD to M-72
14.5 MILES / 5½ – 8 HOURS

The river near Deward is barely large enough and open enough for canoeing, and access is uncertain because of private property and poorly marked dirt roads. The best access is on the two-track marked with a "binocular" sign (for wildlife-viewing area), but it requires a quarter-mile carry to the river.

Access is better either 4 miles downstream at Cameron Bridge, ❶ where there is good access and limited roadside parking, or 2 miles farther at Red Bridge (CR-612), where access is good and parking is limited to the roadside.

The river in this upper section is small, meandering, clear, and beautiful. Width averages 30 – 50 feet and depth 1 – 3 feet with deeper holes. The bottom is alternately gravel and sand, with gravel becoming more and more prevalent due to the removal of sand in recent years at "sand traps" built and maintained by Trout Unlimited and other conservation organizations. The river is occasionally congested with stumps and sunken logs, and fallen trees can block the flow. Scattered cottages and houses are interspersed with large parcels of public land. Occasional giant pines shade the river.

Goose Creek State Forest Campground has good access and parking.

Upper Manistee River State Forest Campground is a short distance below Red Bridge and is reached off Goose Creek Road. It has primitive facilities in two camping areas—the drive-in site is for car campers; the less used and more spacious site downstream is reserved for canoeists.

Manistee River Bridge State Forest Campground is on the west side of the river just before the bridge at M-72 and has good access and parking.

There is good access and abundant parking at the access site on the downstream side of the M-72 Bridge. ❷

M-72 BRIDGE to CCC BRIDGE
14.5 MILES / 5 – 7 HOURS

Expect a nice float through this section but with lots of company on summer weekends. This is fly-fishing-only water and can be fairly crowded with anglers. The river averages 40 – 80 feet wide and 1 – 4 feet deep with deeper holes. Bottom is sand with gravel riffles. The current is steady, with some slow stretches. Much of the way is lined with cottages or is posted against trespassing, making it difficult to find resting places.

About halfway to CCC, on the right, is a public site at Yellowtrees Landing. Access and parking are good.

Camping, access, and a picnic area are available at CCC Bridge State Forest Campground, **3**.

CCC BRIDGE to LOWER SHARON BRIDGE (WEST SHARON ROAD)
9.5 MILES / 3 ½ – 5 HOURS

Below CCC, riffles over shallow gravel alternate with stretches of very deep, shaded pools. Cottages appear in clusters. This section is usually less crowded than above, though weekend use can be heavy. The terrain varies from hardwoods and high banks to lowlands of cedar and tag alders. Some stretches through steep valleys of maples and aspen provide outstanding scenery in autumn.

Near Sharon the current increases to moderately fast in places with occasional pumpkin- to bushel-size rocks

to avoid. There is plenty of water volume from here downstream, and many locals seem to prefer outboard-powered boats to canoes.

Upper Sharon Bridge (North Sharon Road) has poor access because of posted private property and limited roadside parking.

Lower Sharon Bridge **4** (West Sharon Road) is 1.5 miles downstream and has good access and parking at a public site.

LOWER SHARON BRIDGE to M-66 BRIDGE
9.5 MILES / 3 ½ – 5 HOURS

Below Sharon the river slows and widens, averaging 60 – 90 feet wide and 3 – 4 feet deep with many pools up to 10 feet deep. It passes through lowlands of cedars, tag alders and dead elm.

A public access site is located about five miles below Sharon on Dutch John Road. It is one of the few suitable rest stops on this section.

Just below M-66 is Smithville Landing, a canoe livery and private campground, with access restricted to canoe-rental customers. Five minutes beyond the bridge is a public access

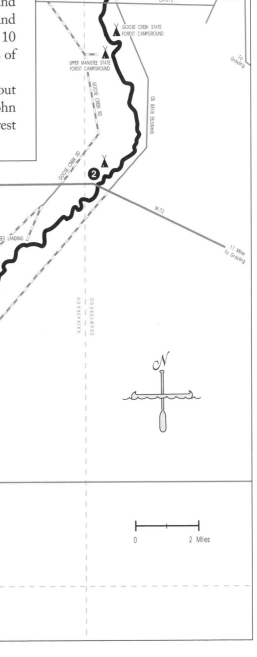

site **5** on the right, with good access and parking. This is the site of a former state-forest campground, now closed.

M-66 BRIDGE to OLD US-131 CAMPGROUND
25 MILES / 8 – 12 HOURS

Immediately below M-66 begins a long series of moderately fast riffles over gravel bottom and some fairly large rocks. High banks of maple, birch, and red and white pine alternate with grass banks and meadows. There are very few cottages through most of this stretch and—at least compared to the popular water upstream—few canoeists. Good campsites can be found along this stretch, and the high wooded banks are spectacular in autumn. Current is steady much of the way, with several stretches of quick water and riffles.

Shortly before Coster Road homes and cottages appear, many with artesian wells spouting from their front yards into the river. The river deepens and slows somewhat, the bottom becomes predominantly sand, and the current is slow and heavy—characteristics typical of the Manistee the remainder of its length. Access and parking are good at the public access site at Rainbow Jim Bridge at Coster Road.

From Coster Road to Lucas Road Bridge is a 4-mile, 1- to 2-hour trip. There are a few more stretches of light riffles with gravel and stone bottom, but they become less frequent. Again there are few cottages and much solitude.

Access and parking are good at Lucas Road.

The site of the now-closed Chase Creek State Forest Campground is on the left side of the river at Chase Creek. It offers access and parking, and, in a pinch, can still serve as a campsite, though the grounds are in disrepair. Take out at the second access site—the first is a steep climb up stairs.

One and a half to 2½ hours below Chase Creek is the US-131 Bridge. There is good access and parking at the roadside park and boat ramp just before the bridge, on the right.

Old US-131 State Forest Campground **6** is one-half mile below US-131 and has primitive facilities and good access and parking.

OLD US-131 CAMPGROUND to BAXTER BRIDGE
10 MILES / 3 – 5 HOURS

Expect much the same water and terrain below US-131 as immediately above it—stretches of moderate current and gravel bottom alternating with long stretches of slow, deep water over sand bottom.

Access and parking are good at Baxter Bridge State Forest Campground and Canoe Camp, at Baxter Bridge. **7** Or take out at the DNR access site at the bridge.

BAXTER BRIDGE to HARVEY BRIDGE
20.5 MILES / 6 – 10 HOURS

The river here meanders tightly and averages 60 – 100 feet wide and 3 – 4 feet deep with very deep holes at the bends. Hills of hardwoods overlook the river valley, with tag alders, cedars, aspen, and maple near the banks. Houses and cottages are infrequent.

Indian Crossing State Forest Campground is closed, but still serves for camping. Bring your own water. Access is good here, though the road turns to gumbo after rain.

Harvey Bridge (N. 19 Road) has good access and parking with vault toilet at the public access site. The bridge itself is closed.

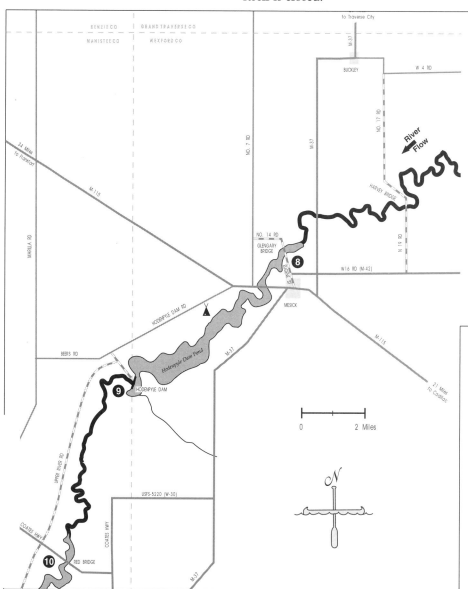

HARVEY BRIDGE to HODENPYLE DAM
16.5 MILES / 6 – 8 HOURS

From Harvey Bridge to the backwaters of Hodenpyle Dam, the water is often murky with sediment and discolors quickly after rain. High clay banks make it hard to get out of the river. The current remains steady; bottom is sand and silt.

Access at the M-37 Bridge is poor, but Wilderness Canoe Trips on the left below the bridge offers access, shuttles, and supplies.

Just below M-37 the river slows and widens as it enters the Hodenpyle Backwaters. Long, shallow sandbars make it necessary to seek deeper channels during low water.

Parking and access are fair at Glengary Bridge, **8** 8.5 miles (3 – 4 hours) below Harvey Bridge. Or continue 1.5 miles downstream to Veterans Memorial Community Park at the M-115 Bridge, where there is a picnic area and restrooms with fair access and no overnight parking.

Hodenpyle Backwaters commences just below M-115 and is a 6.5-mile crossing that can be difficult in windy conditions. Watch for partially submerged logs and drowned stumps, especially when waves obscure the surface. A private campground with access is located at the northwest end of the pond.

At Hodenpyle Dam, **9** the portage trail is to the right (north) of the dam face. It is clearly marked with a large yellow sign. Portage over the dam and

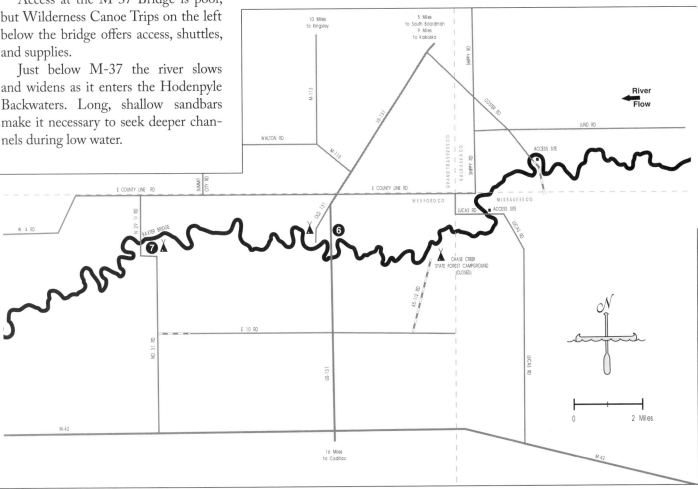

down stairs to a parking area reached via Hodenpyle Dam Road. Past the parking lot is a long set of stairs down the bank to the river.

HODENPYLE DAM to
RED BRIDGE (COATES HIGHWAY)
10 MILES / 3 – 4 HOURS

This is one of the most interesting sections of the Manistee. Water level is controlled by flowage from the Consumers Power Company hydroelectric dam, and was previously subject to rapid change. However, "run of river" regulations have stabilized flow dramatically, reducing erosion and helping to clear the water. During low and normal water levels, expect a leisurely 4-hour float over easy glides, riffles, and calm pools, past gravel and sand bars. During high flow, which usually occurs only during spring run-off and after unusually heavy rain, expect a 3-hour trip, with current moderately fast, heavy, and tricky enough in places to be difficult for beginning paddlers.

The river is 80 – 100 feet wide with depths of 2 – 8 feet. Surrounding land is almost entirely undeveloped and owned by Consumers Power Company. High clay cliffs with seeping springs line the way, and tributaries with waterfalls up to 6 feet high are frequent. Hardwoods predominate on the high banks, and wildlife is abundant and varied. Camping on Consumers Power land is restricted to designated sites scattered along the river.

One-half mile below the dam is a footbridge linking to the North Country Trail (the Manistee River Trail is a 9 mile hike from here to Red Bridge).

A few miles above Red Bridge, the

current slows, and the river channel widens as it enters lowlands before the backwaters of Tippy Dam. Several bays and channels lead into bayous before the bridge and can be confusing.

Access and parking are good at the large public site at Red Bridge ❿, where you'll find drinking water, restrooms, and a few campsites at the edge of the parking area.

Tippy Pond begins immediately downstream from the bridge and is a winding, 6-mile crossing. Shorelines are remote and undeveloped, and wildlife is abundant. Follow the right (north) shore to avoid the possibility of inadvertently bearing south into the lower Pine River. Portage Tippy Dam ⓫ at the boat ramp on the right and follow the road down to the public access site and large parking area below the dam.

TIPPY DAM to BEAR CREEK ACCESS SITE
14.25 MILES / 4 – 7 HOURS

Plenty of parking and good access below Tippy Dam accommodate the crowds of salmon fishermen who congregate here during fall runs. This is a fee area for day use and parking (Michigan residents can purchase an annual permit for $10; all others pay $8 per day). The river is large enough here (up to 200 feet wide) to make it possible to float through during peak fishing, but be prepared to run a gauntlet of hurled lures.

There is a state forest campground on Tippy Pond, north of the dam on Dilling Road. Keep in mind that it is likely to be filled to capacity with anglers in spring and fall.

The river below Tippy Dam is big and deep, with quick, powerful current. The addition of the Pine River in Tippy Pond adds about 50 percent to the flow. It is wider and does not have as many sharp bends as the river upstream, but watch for occasional large rocks, gravel bars, logs, and stumps.

One and a half to two hours below Tippy Dam is the original site of High Bridge, a well-named and now-dismantled railroad trestle. Shortly downstream is the new, not-so-well-named High Bridge, with good access and parking at the National Forest site below the bridge on the right. A $5/day ($15/week) vehicle pass is required to use this and other USFS sites, including Sawdust Hole, Blacksmith Bayou, Bear Creek, and Rainbow Bend. Passes are available at the Manistee USFS Ranger Station and at local vendors.

From High Bridge to the mouth of Bear Creek is an easy 3- to 4-hour trip. The river has slowed and widened to 100 – 200 feet and is generally 3 – 10 feet deep. Houses and other development are rare in this marshy stretch. During high water, there are many backwaters and side channels into broad marshlands to explore; watch especially for waterfowl.

Udell Rollways Campground is a USFS facility with access to the river.

At the mouth of Bear Creek is a USFS public access site ⓬ with restrooms and good parking.

BEAR CREEK to M-55 AND MANISTEE LAKE
13.25 MILES / 4 – 7 HOURS

We recommend ending a Manistee River trip at Bear Creek. Another alternative is 2 miles downstream at the Rainbow Bend Public Access, a fee site where there is excellent access and parking, with restrooms but no overnight parking. Below those sites you can expect lots of wide river and slow water. Predominate headwinds can make this slow going (we've seen whitecaps). The river passes entirely through lowland forests, bayous, and marshlands and is largely undeveloped. It is water better suited to powerboats than canoes, but abundant wildlife and solitude can make it an interesting trip.

Access is poor at M-55 just before Manistee Lake, and no parking is allowed along the highway.

A better alternative is to take the left channel coming into Manistee Lake, and bear left (south) about a mile along the east shore to the public access site ⓭ at the village of East Lake.

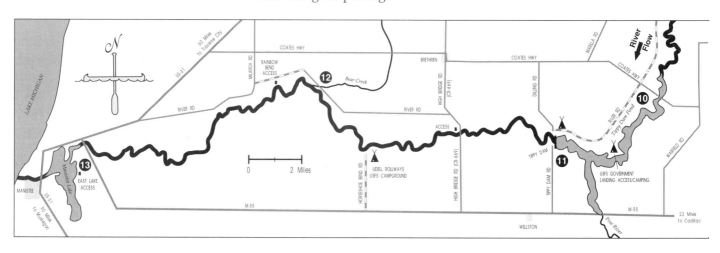

MUSKEGON RIVER

COUNTIES: Missaukee, Roscommon, Clare, Osceola, Mecosta, Newaygo
START/END: Reedsburg Dam to Bridgeton
MILES: 170
GRADIENT: Entire river—4 ft/mile or less
PORTAGES: Four dams, easy to moderately difficult
RAPIDS/FALLS: Big Rapids—Class I-II
CAMPGROUNDS: Numerous
CANOE LIVERIES: Numerous (see Appendix D)
SKILL REQUIRED: I

This second-longest of Michigan rivers (exceeded only by the Grand) is navigable almost from its headwaters, north of Houghton Lake, to its mouth, in Lake Michigan at the city of Muskegon. Except for a popular stretch of fast water at Big Rapids, the entire Muskegon is well-suited for beginners and families. The dams at Rogers, Hardy and Croton ponds are the only major obstacles and their backwaters can be a formidable paddle in a headwind. Like the Au Sable and Manistee, the Muskegon offers interesting opportunities for extended camping and canoeing trips. Yet, in spite of the great variety of water and terrain, good access, lots of state land and many developed campgrounds, only a few popular stretches are paddled with frequency. You can expect to have most of the river to yourself.

Fishing is good throughout most of the river and its tributaries. Rainbow and brown trout are found near Evart and in the stretch below Croton Dam, where a thriving trout fishery has earned fame far beyond Michigan. Bass, walleyes, pike and muskies are found throughout most of the river, and runs of salmon and steelhead up to Croton Dam are exceptionally heavy and attract large numbers of fishermen.

REEDSBURG DAM to CADILLAC ROAD BRIDGE
15 MILES / 6 – 8 HOURS

Put in either at Reedsburg Dam, ❶ just below Houghton Lake, where there is a state-forest campground, or 4 miles downstream at the roadside park near M-55 Bridge, where there is portable, running water. From here downstream the river is slow and meanders through lowland forests, where frequent fallen trees make progress slow. Shortly below M-55, the West Branch of the Muskegon enters, adding significantly to the flow of the mainstream.

Access at the former site of Hi-Lo Bridge at Kelly Road is fair with fair parking.

Just before Cadillac Road Bridge, ❷ where access is fair with roadside parking, is a private campground with all facilities.

CADILLAC ROAD BRIDGE to LEOTA BRIDGE
20.5 MILES / 8 – 10 HOURS

Most of the river in this section is 30 – 60 feet wide and 1 – 6 feet deep, with much deeper pools, and flows with slow to moderate current over sand and very occasional gravel and stone bottom. Terrain is low, though generally dry, with oaks and pines as well as lowland varieties of trees common. Most fallen trees have been cleared, but expect to go around a few. Much of the bordering land is state forest dotted with infrequent cottages.

Lowe Bridge on Dolph Road has fair access and parking. Within 3 or 4 miles is Camp 1, a former state-forest campground, now closed, that has been overrun by dirt bikes and other off-road vehicles. Camping is prohibited, but there are good sites on high ground and state land just downstream.

Below Camp 1 at regular intervals are Camp 2 and Camp 3. These were the sites of "beat camps" established during log drives in the mid- and late-nineteenth century. Each camp based 30 rivermen whose duties were to relay logs through the slow water and break

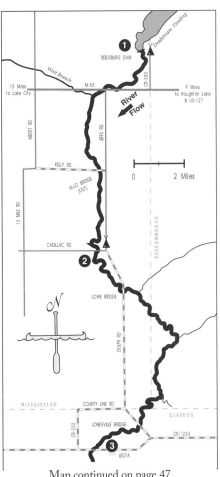

Map continued on page 47

up jams in their assigned stretch of river. Many sunken logs and stumps—further evidence of past logging activities—create minor obstacles for paddlers during low water.

Not far above the Jonesville Bridge is a stretch of gravel bottom with occasional large rocks to avoid. Moderate to Moderately fast current is still far from challenging, even to beginners, although winding around obstacles will be less eventful with basic paddling skills. Jonesville Bridge is closed to automobile traffic (but open to ATVs). Continue 2 miles on to Leota ❸ where access and parking are good at a small park with a canoe dock and picnic area. Supplies are available one-half mile west of the CR-1233 bridge.

LEOTA BRIDGE to M-61
23 MILES / 8 – 12 HOURS

Below Leota the river remains generally slow with sand bottom. Fed by frequent springs and small streams, it is fairly clear and cold. Width is 40 – 75 feet; depth is 1 – 5 feet. The terrain remains low, with maple, basswood and

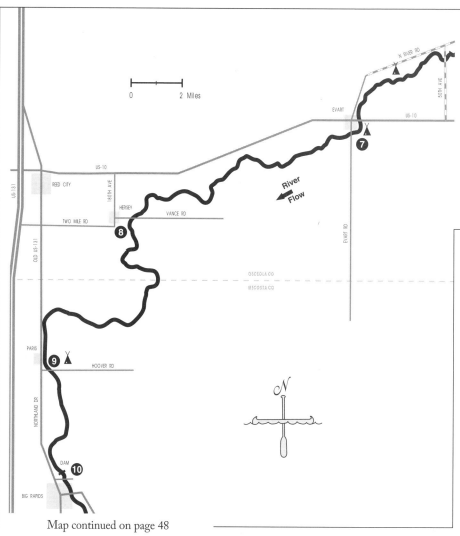

Map continued on page 48

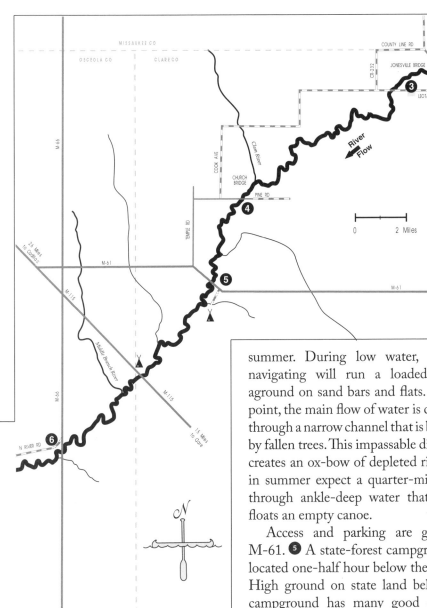

Map continued from page 45

Access and parking are good at the M-66 Bridge. ❻

M-66 BRIDGE to EVART
10 MILES / 3 – 5 HOURS

The river in this section becomes quicker, with light riffles occurring more often than above, and bottom becoming predominately gravel and cobble-stone. Brown and rainbow trout are regularly planted and are caught along with smallmouth bass and occasional northern pike.

Between Sears Road (50th Avenue) and Evart is a private campground with supplies and good access. In Evart, good access and parking are available at the municipal park and campground ❼ located between the first and second bridges in town.

EVART to BIG RAPIDS
28 MILES / 10 – 14 HOURS

Below Evart the river slows and deepens and flows through mostly un-inhabited lowlands of thick underbrush and hardwoods. Slow sections alternate with light riffles. Water levels are usually sufficient for enjoyable floating.

In Hersey, fair access and poor parking are found at the bridge on Vance Road (Fourth Street). ❽ Supplies are available one-half mile west.

In Paris, there is camping, supplies, access and parking at the county park ❾ just before the bridge at Hoover Road. A small fee is charged for use of the access at the park.

Hoover Road has no access or parking. The river to Big Rapids continues to alternate slow pools with long, gentle riffles. Width averages 150 – 200 feet and depth 2 – 8 feet.

In Big Rapids, good access and parking are available at several sites. The Big Rapids Portage Park runs the length of the rapids and offers an excellent, paved portage trail for those who choose not to run the rapids. A low-head dam that was the site of several drownings in the

summer. During low water, careless navigating will run a loaded canoe aground on sand bars and flats. At one point, the main flow of water is diverted through a narrow channel that is blocked by fallen trees. This impassable diversion creates an ox-bow of depleted riverbed; in summer expect a quarter-mile walk through ankle-deep water that barely floats an empty canoe.

Access and parking are good at M-61. ❺ A state-forest campground is located one-half hour below the bridge. High ground on state land below the campground has many good sites as well.

M-61 BRIDGE to M-66
15.5 MILES / 5 – 8 HOURS

The river remains up to 200 feet wide and, in places, is very shallow from M-61 to M-115. Clusters of houses and cottages near the bridge dwindle in number as you move downstream.

At the M-115 Bridge is a private campground and canoe livery. Access is good, with a small fee required for use.

Between M-115 and M-66 the river is slow enough that head winds can halt progress. Most of the bordering land is private, and cottages are scattered much of the way.

ash common. There are few suitable campsites, although much of the section is quiet and secluded, with only a few scattered cottages.

Several tributaries join the Muskegon below Leota. Most significant is the Clam River, a fairly fast, cold trout stream that is small but can be canoed from as far upstream as the town of Falmouth.

Access and parking are good at Church Bridge, ❹ on Pine Road. From here to M-115 is a 5- to 6-hour trip that is quite popular and may be relatively crowded on summer weekends. Below the bridge the river widens to 100 feet or more, with very shallow water in

past has been removed, opening up a longer stretch of rapids. The take-out to the park and portage trail is marked with a sign 200 feet in advance. The park has drinking water, picnic pavilions, and toilets.

Light rapids begin above Baldwin Street ⑩ and are continuous downstream. Several hundred yards below the bridge is a stretch of Class I-II rapids. An island splits the river into two channels. The left is smaller and too shallow for passage except in very high water. In the right channel the bulk of the flow slides close to the right bank, creating several hundred feet of standing waves. Descent is quite steep but there are few obstructions. During high water, waves can be substantial enough to swamp an open canoe, and good judgment should be used.

Another access is at Highbanks Park ⑪ just south of Big Rapids off M-20.

Access is good, though the climb is fairly long; parking is also good. Picnic grounds, water and toilets are available.

River Bend Bluffs ⑫ is a public access site about 5 miles below Big Rapids. It is a small site nestled between rows of cottages that line the wide, shallow river near Rogers Pond. Take out here or at the access site off Northland Drive just west of Rogers Dam. ⑬

ROGERS DAM to CROTON DAM
22.5 MILES / 8 – 12 HOURS

We chose not to paddle this section of virtually continuous backwaters, which includes the smallish Rogers Dam Impoundment, as well as much larger Hardy Dam Pond and Croton Dam Pond.

The portage at Rogers Dam is on the left—opposite the public access site—and is not particularly long or difficult.

Several miles of slow, winding river lead to Hardy Pond. Just before the pond, off Polk Road, is Brewers Park County Campground.

Hardy Pond is the largest and most formidable of the Muskegon River reservoirs. The approximately 18-mile crossing (about half of which is on big water) can be difficult or dangerous due

Map continued from page 46

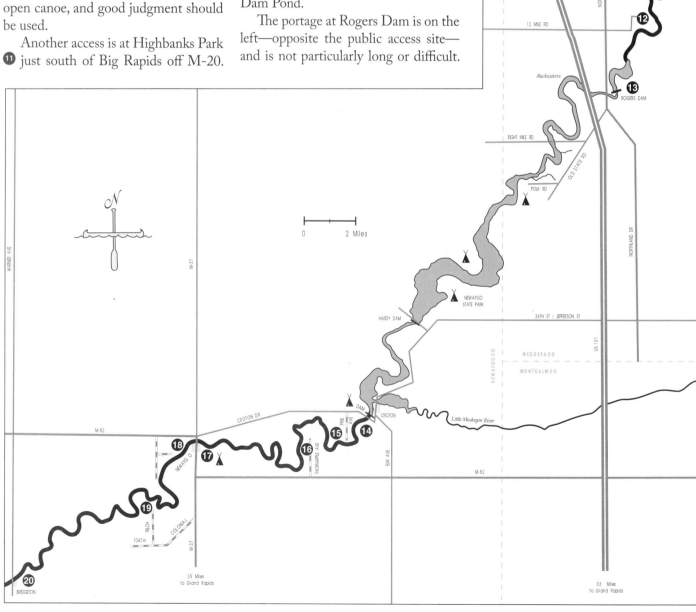

to large waves and power-boat traffic. Several county parks and campgrounds are located along its shores, including Newaygo County State Park.

Portage Hardy Dam on the left, at Consumer Energy's Operators Village Park, where there is drinking water, toilets, a swimming beach, and picnic tables. Follow the "Portage" sign through the gate, across 36th Street, about 120 yards toward the dam. Enter a second, larger gate to a lane leading about 240 yards down the hill to the put-in.

Croton Pond is almost immediately downstream. Although much smaller than Hardy, it adds up to about ten miles of slow water. Because it is quite narrow, wind and waves are seldom the problem they are on the larger impoundment. Take out at the public access site to the right of the power station and portage across Croton Drive to the access site below the dam.

CROTON DAM to NEWAYGO
13 MILES / 4 – 6 HOURS

Access and parking are good at the county-run site below Croton Dam. **14** Day-use stickers must be purchased for parking. A canoe livery and private campground with toilets, water and other facilities is located just west of the dam above the access site.

Below Croton, the Muskegon is wide and, at least until Newaygo, moderately fast. The confluence with the Little Muskegon River in Croton Pond adds significantly to water flow, creating (below the dam) an average annual discharge of nearly 2,000 cfs. The river below the dam flows over a bottom of gravel and stone and averages 150 – 200 feet wide and 2 – 6 feet deep with much deeper pools. Water level is consistent, thanks to run-of-the-river operation of the hydro dam.

The river passes through a valley with high banks wooded with oak, maple and pine. Sections of fairly quick riffles alternate with pools of still, deep water. Houses and cottages—dense concentrations in several places—are scattered throughout much of the section.

As an alternative to the county park below Croton Dam, use the state-maintained public access site **15** 10 minutes downstream on Pine Avenue. Parking and access are good.

One to two hours below Croton on the left, reached off Thornapple Avenue, is a public access known as High Rollaway or Carmichal. **16**

On the right, shortly before the M-37 Bridge in Newaygo is a county park **17** with good access and parking for a fee. There is also fairly good access and parking on the right bank just before the bridge. Underneath the bridge is a short stretch of broken water that can be tricky for inexperienced paddlers, especially in high water. Moderately quick water continues for a mile or so, then slows and deepens. Take out at the public access site on the right, off North River Drive **18** below Newaygo.

The public access site **19** on the left, off Felch Road, has good access and parking.

NEWAYGO to BRIDGETON
14 MILES / 4½ – 6½ HOURS

From Newaygo to Bridgeton the river remains wide and slow, with much of the bordering land uninhabited and alternating between lowland forests and high, wooded banks. Access and parking are good at the public site in Bridgeton. **20**

Below Bridgeton are 19 miles of river, then Muskegon Lake, the city of Muskegon and Lake Michigan. Maple Island Bridge is approximately 5 hours below Newaygo. Access and parking are good at the public site before the bridge, just after the junction with the Maple River. This is the last reliable access site before the river passes into expansive marshes and enters Muskegon Lake.

OCQUEOC RIVER

COUNTY: Presque Isle
START/END: Lake Emma to US-23 Bridge
MILES: 30
GRADIENT: CR-638 Bridge to Ocqueoc Falls—14.8 ft/mile
Ocqueoc Falls to US-23 Bridge—4.7 ft/mile
PORTAGES: Two dams, easy; Ocqueoc Falls, fairly difficult;
DNR weir, easy; occasional fallen trees and minor logjams
RAPIDS/FALLS: Numerous unnamed rapids below CR-638—Class I-II Ocqueoc Falls
CAMPGROUNDS: Few
CANOE LIVERIES: None
SKILL REQUIRED: I-II
TOPO. MAPS: Hawks (7.5 min.), Onaway (15 min.)

The Ocqueoc (pronounced OCK-ee-ock) is one of the most interesting and frequently overlooked rivers in the Lower Peninsula. It is best known for Ocqueoc Falls, a series of 2- to 6-foot drops and ledges that are considered the only Lower Peninsula falls of consequence.

For our purposes, the river divides conveniently into three sections. The upper section includes a series of lakes connected by narrow, slow channels and is well-suited to beginning paddlers or those looking for remote, expedition-like trips. The middle section ends at Ocqueoc Falls State Forest Campground, just before a fairly strenuous half-mile portage around the essentially unnavigable falls area. The difficulty of that portage and numerous shallow rapids below CR-638 make this section a poor choice for inexperienced paddlers. The final section, from the falls to the US-23 Bridge near the mouth of the river, is a better choice. However, occasional deadfalls and logjams and lack of good access could be a problem for beginners.

Fishing is good in the entire river, with bass and northern pike predominating in the upper and lower sections and brook trout found in the Ocqueoc Falls area and most tributaries. Spring and fall runs of steelhead and salmon are quite heavy, and attract significant numbers of wading anglers.

LAKE EMMA to CR-638 BRIDGE (MILLERSBURG ROAD)
10.5 MILES / 4 – 5 HOURS

In previous editions we recommended putting it at Sportsmen Dam Reservoir, however access there is now restricted due to private property. Much better access and parking are found at the DNR public site on Lake Emma ❶ reached via 634 Hwy.

This is beautiful, uncivilized country. Lake Emma and other headwater lakes and ponds are bordered by forests of pine and hardwoods and rimmed with lily pads. The water is remarkably clear, and fishing is excellent for largemouth bass and northern pike. Much of the shoreline is privately owned, which limits camping opportunities.

With depths of 2 to 6 feet, the river below Lake Emma is nearly as deep as it is wide, but passage is easier than it looks. Tight bends might seem to bring the bow-man back to meet the stern-man, but we made it through without much difficulty in our 17-foot, 9-inch Sawyer. The current is almost imperceptible—just strong enough to point aquatic weeds downstream. Expect to pass through a long stretch of marshes as the river gradually widens and gains depth. Signs of civilization begin to appear near Lake Nettie, and the shoreline of the lake is spotted with cottages.

Once on Lake Nettie, bear right—around the first point to the public access site ❷ on the southeast shore—or continue the length of the lake and portage the small water-control dam at CR-638 Bridge. Downstream are several smaller lakes plus a stretch of slow, fairly shallow river before Millersburg.

At Millersburg there is good access and parking just south of the village at the bridge at CR-638 (Millersburg Road) ❸.

CR-638 BRIDGE to OCQUEOC FALLS FOREST CAMPGROUND
6.75 MILES / 2 ½ – 3 ½ HOURS

From Millersburg to Ocqueoc Falls expect a lively trip through a variety of water. Average descent through this section is among the fastest of any Lower Peninsula river. At the CR-638 Bridge, the river is narrow (15 to 25 feet) and fairly slow until past the first bends, where stretches of quite-fast water begin. Riffles and light rapids alternate with slow pools the remainder of the distance to Ocqueoc Falls, with some narrow chutes requiring precise maneuvering and occasional fallen trees needing to be negotiated. This section is best run in spring or early summer during high water; low water exposes shallow riffles and rock gardens, some of which will have to be walked through. Rocks on the Ocqueoc are irregular, sharp and hard on canoe hulls. An abrupt 4-foot falls, locally known as Chipmunk Falls, follows a stretch of slow water. It can be run, we found, but only at the price of a battered boat. The terrain is largely upland forest of mixed hardwoods and conifers with cedars and aspens near the banks. The bottom is generally rocky, with sand predominating in the slow stretches.

Access is poor at M-68 Bridge.

A few bends below the arched concrete bridge on River Road, watch for the picnic tables of Ocqueoc Falls Forest Campground ❹ on the right bank above the river. Take out here or continue with caution a short distance downstream to where the concrete abutments of an old mill dam crowd the river just above Ocqueoc Falls Hwy. Do not go beyond the abutments—Ocqueoc Falls are immediately downstream and are preceded by very heavy current. Take out through the underbrush on the right to reach the highway, then find the trail on the right side of the river to portage the falls. The half-mile trail is an easy carry, much of it paved, through the falls viewing area.

Put in well below the second (lower) set of falls. Fast, shallow riffles give way to slower, deeper water and sand bottom. Expect occasional fallen trees.

OCQUEOC FALLS to US-23 BRIDGE
12.75 MILES / 5 – 6 HOURS

Finding access below Ocqueoc Falls is a bit of a problem. Other than portaging the falls, the only recourse is poor access at bridges on Pomeranke, North Ocqueoc and Domke highways. There is no parking at Pomeranke and only limited roadside parking at the other bridges. The river is steady, with moderate but heavy current. The water is dark—stained by passage through swamps and water depths vary from 3 to 8 feet. The bottom is generally sand. Meadows, farmlands and cedar swamps alternate, and there are occasional short stretches of rock bottom and light riffles.

Be alert for farmers' low wires stretched across the river.

From North Ocqueoc Highway is a 1-hour float through thick cedars and tag alders to Ocqueoc Lake. The current is stronger than it looks, and a few tricky eddies at bends, as well as at least one logjam, require attention. Just before Ocqueoc Lake the river divides into channels. During low water, portage the sandbars that form at the mouth. Follow the right shoreline of the lake to the public access site on Domke Road, ❺ where there is good access and parking.

Just below the lake, portage the DNR lamprey control station at Ocqueoc Lake Road Bridge—get out on the left side and take the trail around the fence. The river here is 35 to 50 feet wide with strong current and deep holes. It widens

and slows the final mile or two before US-23 and the mouth.

At US-23 Bridge, ❻ there is a large public launch site, with good access and parking below the bridge on the left.

PERE MARQUETTE RIVER

COUNTIES: Lake, Mason

START/END: M-37 Bridge to P.M. Highway Bridge at Ludington

MILES: 56

GRADIENT: M-37 to Sulak Landing—5 ft/mile

Sulak Landing to Ludington—2 ft/mile

PORTAGES: Occasional fallen trees in upper sections

RAPIDS/FALLS: Rainbow Rapids below Rainbow Rapids Landing—Class I

CAMPGROUNDS: Numerous

CANOE LIVERIES: Numerous (see Appendix D)

SKILL REQUIRED: I

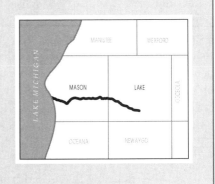

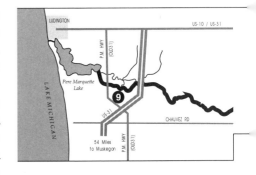

The Pere Marquette is one of Michigan's finest and best-known rivers. It is a very popular river with fishermen and canoeists and can be crowded on summer weekends as well as during spring and fall runs of anadromous fish. Concentrations of canoes, kayaks, drift boats, and other watercraft are heavy enough to create problems on occasion. In an effort to monitor watercraft and relieve congestion on the Pere Marquette, the U.S. Forest Service requires that anyone who launches or retrieves a boat on national forest land have a permit. Unfortunately, this is a fairly complicated process. There is a $2 per watercraft per day fee for the permits, which are required from approximately the middle of May to the first week of September (depending on where the weekends fall in the calendar), and reservations must be made and paid for at least 14 days in advance. Permits may be purchased in person on site at the ranger stations (checks or cash only), but there is no guarantee of a reservation. Because the number of permits per day is limited the USFS recommends making reservations as early as January 1 each year. Beginning in 2014, permits can be reserved and paid for online; until then, contact the Baldwin or White Cloud Ranger stations for more information: http://www.fs.usda.gov/main/hmnf/about-forest. Or call the Huron-Manistee National Forest Headquarters in Cadillac: 231-775-2421.

The Forest Service also requires that watercraft not be launched or retrieved before 9 a.m. or after 6 p.m. during the May to September period. Vehicle permits and day-use fees are required at many of the USFS access sites. They can be purchased at pay stations on site.

The Pere Marquette from the junction of the Middle and Little South Branches to the US-31 Bridge is designated a Scenic River by the National Wild and Scenic Rivers Program, and Wild-Scenic by the Michigan Natural Rivers Program. Although it is, for the most part, a fairly gentle river, water fluctuations are quite extreme with high levels common in early spring. Low water will seldom be a problem. The opposite is more likely to be true, with heavy rains sometimes raising water levels and current speed to a degree that beginning paddlers might find challenges their abilities.

In 1884 the Pere Marquette was the site of the first planting of brown trout in North America, and it has been first-class trout water ever since. Spring and fall runs of steelhead and salmon are some of the heaviest in the state and attract large numbers of anglers. Many special regulations are in place; see a current DNR angling guide for details.

Much of the river passes through national forest land, where good campsites and developed campgrounds are plentiful.

M-37 BRIDGE to BOWMAN BRIDGE
(CARR'S ROAD)
11 MILES / 3 ½ – 5 HOURS

Put in at the M-37 Bridge ❶ south of Baldwin or go upstream one-half mile to Forks Landing. Both are fine, well maintained DNR access sites with restrooms and plenty of parking. No fees are required to use DNR sites.

This first section is quite representative of the entire upper river. The current is steady, moderately fast and not difficult during normal water levels for paddlers with basic skills. The river follows a winding course of switchbacks and sharp bends that makes for many more river miles than expected. Terrain is largely wooded and hilly, with white and red oak predominating and tag alders and cedars near the water. High banks on the bends were often used as high rollaways during the logging era. There are occasional fallen trees, stumps and minor logjams to avoid. The river averages 40 – 60 feet wide and 1 – 3 feet

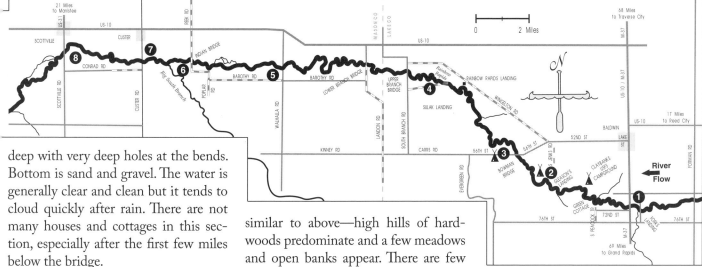

deep with very deep holes at the bends. Bottom is sand and gravel. The water is generally clear and clean but it tends to cloud quickly after rain. There are not many houses and cottages in this section, especially after the first few miles below the bridge.

Green Cottage is a walk-in access site on the left, a mile or so below M-37; a vehicle pass and fee are required to park there. Like all the fee-sites from here downstream, you must take a form/receipt/envelope from the self-serve paystation, fill it out, put the receipt on your dashboard where it can be seen, seal the $5 per day fee in the envelope, and place it in the fee tube.

A few bends downstream, on the right up the high steps, is Claybanks Public Access. Claybanks USFS Campground is a long climb ½ mile inland through the woods.

Gleason's Landing USFS Campground ❷ has primitive facilities and good access and parking; permit and fee are required. From here downstream the river slows and deepens somewhat as it flows through mostly uninhabited upland forests.

There is good access and parking, with restrooms and drinking water, at the fee-site below Bowman Bridge ❸. Bowman Bridge USFS Campground is a short climb up the hill above the access site.

BOWMAN BRIDGE to SULAK LANDING
10.5 MILES / 3 – 4 HOURS

Below Bowman Bridge the current remains moderate with many stretches of slow, deep water. Shortly before Rainbow Rapids Landing the current quickens until it runs fairly fast over gravel and stone riffles. Terrain remains

similar to above—high hills of hardwoods predominate and a few meadows and open banks appear. There are few houses, but much of the bordering land is private, including a very large private holding in the middle of the section, where access to the banks is prohibited.

Rainbow Rapids are a short distance below the access and parking site at Rainbow Rapids Landing, where permit and fee are required and parking is allowed only on top of the hill. The rapids are a short, fast Class I run over gravel and rock, with two or three easy bends to negotiate. Although not recommended for absolute beginners, they should present no real challenge for anyone with moderate paddling experience. From here to Sulak the river remains relatively fast with numerous riffles over gravel bars and occasional pumpkin-size rocks. Terrain is high banks and hardwoods. There are a few scattered cottages and occasional secluded campsites on national forest land.

Access and parking are good at the public site at Sulak Landing ❹ (permit and fee required; vault toilets; camping is permitted at sites one-quarter mile up the hill).

SULAK LANDING to CUSTER BRIDGE
20 MILES / 7 – 10 HOURS

Below Sulak the river slows and widens into the large water typical of the lower Pere Marquette. Current is slow to moderate, bottom is consistently sand, and water is deep and often

clouded.

Good access and parking are found at Upper Branch Bridge (South Branch Road), where permits and fees are required.

Access is fair at Lower Branch Bridge (Landon Road), with limited roadside parking.

Access and parking are good at the free public site downstream on the left of Walhalla Road Bridge. ❺ Below here the river is 60 to 75 feet wide and is slow and deep. Terrain is largely lowlands of hardwoods and tag alders down to swamps of drowned timber. Shortly below Walhalla Bridge is the "spreads": an area of marshlands where the river divides into channels and sub-channels that meander around sandbars and islands of cattails and tag alders. There seems to be no single best way through; some channels, however, are more congested than others. Be prepared to walk through some shallows in summer. The river gathers itself together again for a time, enters lowland forests, then—a half-mile or so before Indian Bridge—divides again through a swamp of cedar, tag alder and drowned timber. Here the channels are narrow and deep; all seem negotiable and lead to the bridge.

Access and parking are good at the USFS fee site at Indian Bridge (Reek Road). ❻ From Indian Bridge to Custer Road Bridge is a 2.5-mile stretch of wide, slow water. The Big South Branch of the Pere Marquette joins here and swells the mainstream by half again. This major tributary can be canoed from as far upstream as Huntley Bridge (Dickerson Road) in Newaygo County. From there to the junction with the mainstream is a 10- to 12-hour trip through a variety of lowlands and wooded hills. Current is generally slow with a few stretches of moderately fast water over gravel and stone bottom. Fallen trees create frequent obstructions.

About a mile below the junction with the Big South Branch is Custer Bridge ❼ with good access and parking above the bridge on the left.

CUSTER BRIDGE TO P.M. HIGHWAY BRIDGE (LUDINGTON)
18 MILES/6 – 9 HOURS

This final section remains wide and slow and passes mostly through lowland forests. It is more often navigated in powerboats than in canoes.

There is camping at Scottville Riverside Park ❽ (all facilities), before the bridge in Scottville. Access and parking are available at two private parks on the downstream side of the bridge as well as at Scottville Riverside Park, but neither allows overnight parking. We suggest negotiating for a secure parking spot at Riverside Park.

Access and parking are good at the P.M. Highway Bridge (Old US-31) ❾ south of Ludington. Here the river is slow, wide, and often split into channels that pass through extensive marshlands. Pere Marquette Lake is immediately downstream.

Pigeon River

PIGEON RIVER

COUNTIES: Otsego, Cheboygan
START/END: Sturgeon River Valley Road Bridge to Mullet Lake
MILES: 28.5
GRADIENT: Pigeon River Road to below M-68—14.3 ft/mile
             All other sections average—9.3 ft/mile
PORTAGES: Numerous fallen trees, logjams and beaver dams—easy to difficult
RAPIDS/FALLS: Numerous unnamed rapids from Pigeon River Road to below M-68—Class I-II
CAMPGROUNDS: Several
CANOE LIVERIES: Few (see Appendix D)
SKILL REQUIRED: I-II
TOPO. MAPS: Heatherton, Tower, Wolverine (15 min.)

Flowing through the heart of the Pigeon River Country State Forest, the Pigeon is one of the Lower Peninsula's most beautiful and remote rivers. It has faced challenges, however. Twice in the past two decades a private dam on the upper river has failed, releasing surges of silt that have decimated the trout population. There are also periodic calls to open the state forest to oil and gas exploration, a move that would open many new roads and potentially compromise the ecological health of the region.

Purist wilderness paddlers will be pleased to note that the Pigeon remains largely unspoiled and continues to maintain large numbers of fallen trees, logjams, beaver dams and other challenges. One of Michigan's Wild-Scenic Rivers, the Pigeon is well within the range of the only elk herd in the state.

Remote sections and fast current make this river a poor choice for inexperienced paddlers. The swift current and extremely sharp and narrow bends—especially during periods of high water—will test maneuvering skills of even experienced paddlers. Low water can make much of the river difficult or impassable, so it is best to avoid it during drought years.

Abundant public land and several developed campgrounds make camping opportunities excellent. Fishing is very good for brook, brown and rainbow trout.

STURGEON RIVER VALLEY ROAD BRIDGE to RED BRIDGE (WEBB ROAD)
12 MILES / 5 – 7 HOURS

A short distance upstream from the Sturgeon River Valley Road Bridge ❶ is a dam and private pond at the Song of the Morning Ranch. (Many county maps label it "Lansing Club Pond.") Although the Pigeon is navigable for a short distance above the pond, the river there is small, fallen trees are common, and the portage around the dam is a nuisance.

Sturgeon River Valley Road is a more convenient starting point, with the river entering the Pigeon River Country State Forest a short distance downstream. The river here is 25 – 40 feet wide and 1 – 3 feet deep and flows fairly quickly over gravel and pumpkin-size rocks. Tag alders, poplars, spruce and pines line the banks. There is fair to good access at the bridge, with parking limited to a few vehicles at the roadside; better parking is found in a lot 100 yards east. Quality of the clear to slightly tea-colored water is excellent, even after heavy rains have turned other nearby rivers and creeks to chocolate.

Pigeon Bridge State Forest Campground is a short distance downstream on the right. It is unmarked at the river and recognized only by the sand-scarred trail to the water.

Passage is fairly easy through the beginning of the section, with only a few sweepers and downed trees to avoid. However, tight turns in the quick current, make basic maneuvering skills necessary. Even competent paddlers, especially in loaded canoes, will find themselves being swept into the brush at the river's edge. The terrain continues to be wooded low hills but alternates occasionally with small open meadows and marshes.

About 3 miles downstream from Sturgeon River Valley Road is Pigeon River State Forest Campground ❷ with good access to the river, primitive facilities, and drinking water (from an artesian well). Just downstream at an unmarked road is a bridge with fair access and parking near the DNR State Forest Headquarters, which is accessed off Twin Lakes Road. Take the left culvert under the bridge and stay left to negotiate a short drop over jumbled rocks and boulders.

Not far downstream is a stretch of very old logjams that have caused the river to divide into channels. Passage is difficult. We got through by combining portaging, lining, paddling and cussing. Chest waders are a definite advantage.

Fast current in places compounds the difficulty, and some channels that can be negotiated require draw strokes, pry strokes and back strokes.

When the river comes together into a single channel again, the respite is brief thanks to beavers that have, at least at the time of this writing, placed a large dam across the entire width of the river. Portage is difficult but possible through the thick and partially flooded woods on the right. We found a partial break in the dam and ran it like any whitewater chute, with tree trunks and face-slapping branches adding an air of novelty. The river from here alternates tight bends and fast, boulder-studded riffles with stretches of slow, deep water.

By Tin Bridge at Cornwall Flooding Road ❸, the current, though moderately strong in places, is generally slower than above. Access and parking are fair. The terrain becomes mostly lowlands, which edge many drowned trees. Between Tin Bridge and Pine Grove State Forest Campground, we encountered one narrow chute through a logjam that required lining or portaging.

Pine Grove State Forest Campground ❹ is recognized by a trail down a short, steep bank on the right and a small wooden landing. Facilities are primitive and drinking water is available at an artesian well.

Red Bridge ❺ is on Webb Road about an hour downstream from the campground. Shortly before the bridge the current increases, with riffles over gravel and rock bottom. Low hills and upland forests predominate. At the bridge, access is good and parking is limited.

RED BRIDGE to EAST MULLETT LAKE ROAD BRIDGE AT MULLETT LAKE
16.5 MILES / 6 – 8 HOURS

From Red Bridge to M-68 the river increases in size due to tributaries like the Little Pigeon River, and is more likely to be navigable in periods of low water. This section is better suited to beginning canoeists than the water

above. Although there is mostly private property in the vicinity of Red Bridge, a quarter-mile downstream the river again enters state forest, where camping potential is good. An often-used clearing and campsite beside the river is known as McIntosh Landing (we tried without success to find a road to it). Beyond here is a long stretch of lowlands and thick brush with very few possible campsites. Plan to end a day-long trip no farther than McIntosh Landing unless there is time to make the 2- to 3-hour trip to Pigeon River Bridge (Pigeon River Road). Much of this stretch is very slow, sand-bottomed and lined with thickets of tag alders.

Pigeon River Road Bridge ❻ has good access and fair roadside parking. From here the current increases dramatically; expect 5 to 6 miles of nearly continuous riffles and light rapids. The bottom is composed of bedrock, gravel and rocks to bushel size. Descent is steep enough that high water in the spring and after heavy rains makes this one of the longest and most interesting fast-water stretches in the Lower Peninsula. Summer levels are apt to be low enough that some bottom-scraping will occur. Paddlers with basic maneuvering skills should not have difficulty except in the stretch below M-68 or during very high water.

Afton Road Bridge, one-half hour below Pigeon River Road, has good access and good, though limited, parking.

Fifteen minutes downstream is the M-68 ❼ Bridge, with good parking and access downstream on the right. The fast water to here contains few serious obstructions—other than scattered boulders—through rock gardens and shallow riffles. It is an easy, relaxing run that can easily lull a paddler into overconfidence.

Below M-68 the current continues fast, but the riverbed changes character: bends suddenly become very sharp, and fallen trees, sweepers, and beaver dams may create unexpected hazards. Inexperienced paddlers will find this water frustrating and potentially

dangerous, especially during high-water periods. Except for houses and cottages near M-68, there is no access—in case of emergency—for seven miles until Mullett Lake. Much of this section is within the state forest, but lowlands make good campsites infrequent.

In the final miles before Mullett Lake, the river divides into spreads, with some channels blocked by logjams and some too shallow to float through. The bottom is sand, and the current is steady to slow until the final stretch of reeds and cattails, when it slows to enter Mullett Lake.

Access ❽ at East Mullett Lake Road is at the bridge on the right. Parking is limited to the roadside off the bridge approach. Supplies are available one-eighth mile east.

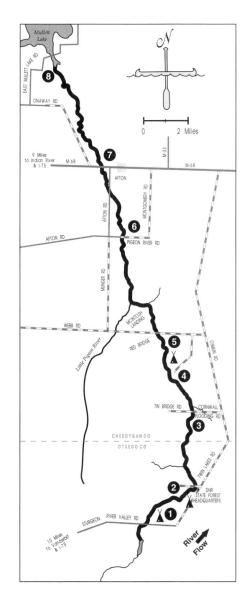

PINE RIVER

COUNTIES: Lake, Wexford, Manistee
START/END: Briar Patch Access Site to Low Bridge (Tower Line Road)
MILES: 38.5
GRADIENT: 9.9 ft/mile
PORTAGES: One dam, easy; occasional fallen trees and minor logjams
RAPIDS/FALLS: Numerous unnamed rapids above and below Peterson Bridge—Class I-II
CAMPGROUNDS: Several
CANOE LIVERIES: Numerous (see Appendix D)
SKILL REQUIRED: I-II

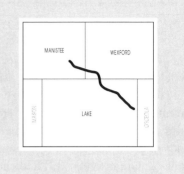

Besides being a beautiful and largely unspoiled river—a National Scenic River for 26 miles below Lincoln Bridge Campground and a Michigan Natural River for its entire length—the Pine also has one of the fastest average flows of any Lower Peninsula river. In the past, the Pine's major problem was that it was sometimes too popular. Summer weekends demonstrated the irony implicit in a such a river:

The virtues that make it appealing in the first place can sometimes lead to its misuse. In an effort to prevent the river from suffering from over-use, the U.S. Forest Service has implemented a permit system in the national forest waters of the river, which includes most of the middle and lower sections of the river in Wexford and Manistee counties; the state-forest sites on the upper river require no fee, but you'll still need a permit to take out at the national forest sites downstream. Permits are required to be displayed on any craft that enters or leaves the river on national forest land in the river "corridor" between May 15 and September 10. The corridor is defined as the land one-quarter mile on each side of the river in the last 26 miles of river, roughly from Lincoln Bridge to the mouth at Tippy Pond. Camping is allowed at designated sites within the corridor, and at Peterson Bridge Campground.

Reserved river permits are $2 per watercraft per day, and reservations must be made and paid for at least 14 days in advance. Permits may be purchased on site at the ranger stations or at area canoe liveries at no cost, but there is no guarantee of a reservation. Because the number of permits per day is limited the USFS recommends making reservations as early as January 1 each year. Beginning in 2014, permits can be reserved and paid for online. Until then, contact the Baldwin or White Cloud Ranger stations for more information: http://www.fs.usda.gov/main/hmnf/about-forest. Or call the Huron-Manistee National Forest Headquarters in Cadillac: 231-775-2421. Vehicle passes are required to use any USFS access site; they cost $5/day and can be purchased at any USFS office or at many local businesses.

In spite of the inconvenience of the permits and vehicle passes, the Pine remains one of Michigan's most popular rivers. For canoeists and kayakers, much of the appeal is undoubtedly the fast water and light rapids in the Peterson Bridge area. For fishermen, the appeal is healthy populations of brook, brown and rainbow trout.

BRIAR PATCH ACCESS SITE (FIVE MILE ROAD) to ELM FLATS
18 MILES / 5 – 7 HOURS

Because the DNR access site at Edgetts Bridge is now closed and access at the bridge is poor, we recommend starting a trip no farther upstream than Briar Patch Access Site ❶ at the end of Five Mile Road (Sportsmen Drive). No vehicle pass is required to use this or other state-forest access sites on the upper river.

The river in this section averages 25 – 40 feet wide and 1 – 4 feet deep with pools up to 6 feet. It passes through mostly wooded hills of hardwoods and pines with cedars and tag alders near the river. Fallen trees and minor logjams occasionally block the river, especially in the spring before the liveries have cleared the way. Current is moderate to fairly quick over sand and gravel. There are occasional houses and cottages.

Meadowbrook Bridge on Six Mile Road has fair access and good parking.

Private property prevents access or parking at Skookum Bridge. However, Skookum South Public Access Site ❷ has good access, parking, and vault toilets one-half mile downstream. A short distance below the access site begins an 8-mile stretch of private property belonging to the Ne-bo-shone Club, where access to the banks is prohibited. The area is clearly posted.

There is no access at Walker Bridge (State Road), but Silver Creek State Forest Campground ❸ has good access with drinking water and vault toilets just downstream on the right.

Lincoln Bridge ❹ (10 Mile Road) is out, replaced by a foot bridge. Lincoln Bridge State Forest Campground has good access and parking. From here downstream, USFS regulations are in effect, with self-service pay stations available for purchasing vehicle passes.

Elm Flats ❺ (off State Road) is a USFS access site with good access and parking, plus restrooms.

ELM FLATS to PETERSON BRIDGE (M-37)
12.5 MILES / 3 ½ – 5 HOURS

Below Elm Flats, expect some stretches of quick water, though the current most of the way remains steady and moderately strong with many tight bends and switchbacks. High banks at the bends are often eroded and should not be disturbed.

Dobson Bridge (50 Road) ❻ has a designated launch site with good parking and vault toilets. From here the current speed increases slightly, and light riffles become more frequent. Some tight bends are tricky for beginners and will pull unwary paddlers into trees and logs.

Hoxeyville High Bridge has no access or parking, and launching of canoes is prohibited.

From here to below Peterson Bridge, fast water and light rapids predominate. While the rapids don't amount to much by most whitewater standards, scattered bushel-size and larger rocks and bedrock ledges create small standing waves and require a fair amount of maneuvering. Usually rated Class I or Class II in high water, these moderately challenging rapids create their share of mischief. Although we do not recommend the Pine for anyone without basic maneuvering skills, beginners often float it and often come away telling stories that serve to enhance the Pine's reputation for being a difficult river. We have heard of no drownings or serious injuries, but the potential for them certainly exists for careless or inexperienced paddlers. Generally, stay to the inside of bends and avoid the larger rocks. No rapids require scouting, but go slowly and wear flotation devices. In spring, standing waves will occasionally reach 2 feet but will not be dangerous except in unusually high flood conditions.

Access and parking are good at the USFS site on the right, upstream of Peterson Bridge ❼ at M-37. The site has restrooms, water, and a picnic area, as well as a USFS campground.

PETERSON BRIDGE to LOW BRIDGE LANDING
8 MILES / 2 ½ – 3 ½ HOURS

Fast water extends much of the way between Peterson Bridge and Stronach Dam. Many narrow chutes formed by underwater rock ledges can simply be ruddered through. Some tight bends require more strenuous paddling techniques, especially draw strokes. Nowhere, however, are there hazards that paddlers with basic skills can't handle.

There is little streamside development in this section. High banks, up to 100 feet, line the river, and hardwoods and pines predominate, with scattered thickets of willows, cedars and tag alders near the water.

Stronach Dam has been removed, after many years of being gradually dismantled. The river through the former site is now a lively and unobstructed run, with a few standing waves. One new wave, which is large enough to surf, has been christened "Mikey's Roller" by a group that regularly paddles the Pine.

Low Bridge is 10 – 15 minutes below the dam on Tower Line Road but the bridge itself has no access or parking. Take out instead at the large, developed USFS site just upstream, ❽ where access is good and there's plenty of parking, as well as a picnic area and vault toilets.

Just downstream from Low Bridge is the lofty bridge at M-55, with poor access and no parking. Below this final bridge the river enters Tippy Pond, as does the Manistee River to the north.

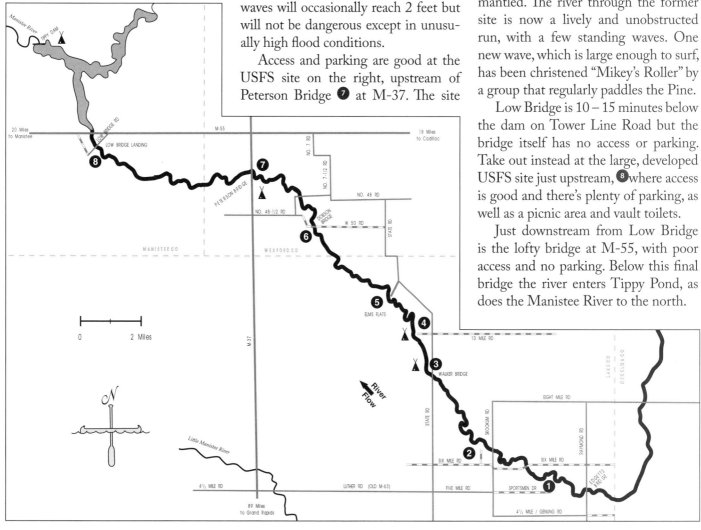

PLATTE RIVER

COUNTY: Benzie
START/END: US-31 Bridge to Lake Michigan
MILES: 16
GRADIENT: US-31 Bridge to Platte Lake—12.9 ft/mile
                     Platte Lake to mouth—2.7 ft/mile
PORTAGES: DNR weir, easy; occasional fallen trees and logjams
RAPIDS/FALLS: None
CAMPGROUNDS: Several
CANOE LIVERIES: One (see Appendix D)
SKILL REQUIRED: I

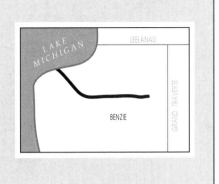

The Platte is a lovely little river with a reputation that far exceeds its small size. Known for decades as a fine trout stream, it became famous in the late 1960s as the site of the first successful plantings of Pacific salmon in the Great Lakes. Since then, salmon runs in the river have been so heavy that paddlers attempting autumn trips will literally be bumping the backs of cohos and Chinooks. Intense fishing pressure for salmon in September and October, and for steelhead in March and April, makes those months poor choices for paddling.

Platte Lake divides the river into upper and lower sections, with the upper tending to be shallow and quick and the lower being slow and serene. Summer canoeing, kayaking, and tubing is extremely popular in the section from M-22 to the mouth of the river. The upper section is very small and shallow and will rarely be crowded. The small size makes it environmentally sensitive. Paddlers are urged not to disrupt vegetation and erosion-prone banks.

State-forest campgrounds are found along both the upper and lower reaches.

US-31 BRIDGE to M-22 BRIDGE
BELOW PLATTE LAKE
12 MILES / 4 – 5 HOURS

Although some sources claim the Platte is navigable from its source in Lake Ann, in northeast Benzie County, that upper water is very small and frequently blocked by fallen trees. We recommend starting no farther upstream than the US-31 bridge east of Honor.

Access and parking are good at the US-31 ❶ Bridge at Veteran's Memorial State Forest Campground, which has toilets, water and a picnic area. A quarter mile upstream is a weir and the DNR fish hatchery where the majority of Michigan's salmon are raised.

The river here is small—20 – 40 feet wide and 1 – 2½ feet deep—and flows quickly over gravel and small stones. Water is clear and clean. Shallow riffles will not float a loaded canoe during low-water periods. Logs and fallen trees often obstruct the upper reaches of this section. Passage becomes clearer and the river wider below the state forest campground on Goose Road.

The terrain through the upper reaches to the village of Honor consists of rolling hills of upland forests, with cedars common on the valley floor near the river. Banks are consistently wooded, as high as 100 to 150 feet and quite steep in places. Much of the bordering land is state owned, although there are intervals of private property with scattered cottages as well as several concentrations of houses and cottages.

Haze Road has fair access and limited roadside parking.

Platte River State Forest Campground, ❷ off Goose Road, has parking, primitive camping facilities and good access to the river.

Pioneer Road Bridge has fair access and limited roadside parking.

In Honor, there are bridges at South Street and at Henry Street, but access and parking are poor at both sites.

Just west of Honor the river crosses beneath US-31 again, but neither access nor parking are allowed along this busy highway.

There is no access or parking at Indian Hill Road Bridge.

Below Indian Hill Road the river slows and deepens somewhat as it enters Deadstream Swamp before Platte Lake. This remote stretch of river is interesting and difficult to reach except by river. Deep holes on the bends alternate with shallow riffles and sand flats.

To avoid the 3-mile crossing of Platte Lake (which is usually made more difficult by prevailing west winds), take out at the small access site ❸ on the North Branch of the Platte on Deadstream Road. This tributary is sluggish, shallow and silt bottomed, but flows unimpeded a short distance to the mainstream of the Platte, joining it on river-right, just upstream from Platte Lake.

Alternative access is available at an unmarked (and possibly private) landing at the extreme northeast end of Platte Lake, 100 yards west of the

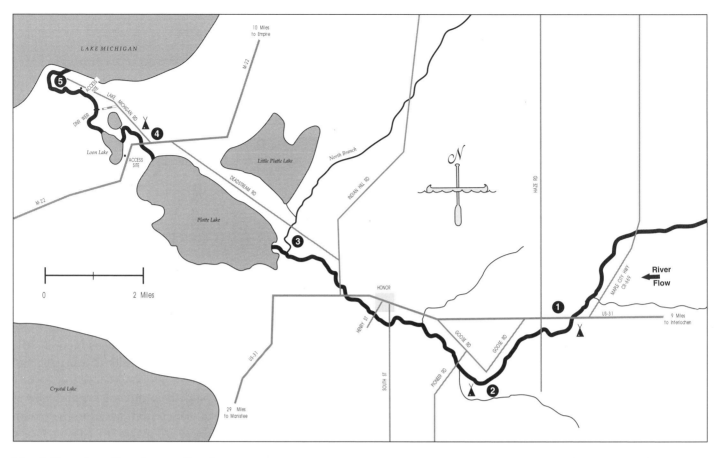

North Branch on Deadstream Road.

A quarter-mile below Platte Lake is the M-22 Bridge, where Riverside Canoe Trips has a store and private access. Good public access, parking, restrooms, water, and phone access are available at the canoe launch ❹ and picnic area below the bridge on the right. Platte River National Park Service Campground is a short hike north, across Lake Michigan Road.

Note that the access site, picnic area, and campground are all fee areas, administered by the National Park Service. Permits are available at the ranger stations at the Platte River campground and the visitor center at Park Headquarters in the village of Empire, 10 miles north on M-22.

M-22 BRIDGE to RIVERMOUTH AT LAKE MICHIGAN
4 MILES / 1 ½ – 3 HOURS

This short trip through the Sleeping Bear Dunes National Lakeshore is a popular summer float and ideal for beginners and families with small children. The river is 50 – 70 feet wide and 2 – 5 feet deep, with consistently slow to moderate current over sand and gravel bottom. The river valley is shallow and wooded with assorted pines and hardwoods and with cedars crowding the water. All the bordering land is within the national park, but there remain a number of widely spaced houses and cottages. Camping is prohibited along the river.

After a dogleg south, the river enters Loon Lake. Bear along the right (northeast shore) to find the outlet. A public access site with boat launch, parking, and restrooms is located on the south shore of the lake, just south of the river's inlet.

Below Loon Lake, the river flows through terrain of low, wooded hills and an increasing number of open sand dunes. Junipers and other dune flora are abundant. A half mile below Loon Lake, a fish weir (with picnic area and restrooms) requires a short portage when in operation. The access road to the weir is open to automobiles during the fall salmon run; the rest of the year it is open to pedestrians only.

A public launch ramp (with parking and restrooms) is located one mile from the mouth of the river.

Access ❺ is excellent at the boat launch at the mouth, where there is good access and parking, as well as restrooms, water, and a picnic area.

RIFLE RIVER

COUNTIES: Ogemaw, Arenac
START/END: Sage Lake Road Bridge to Stover Road Bridge
MILES: 47
GRADIENT: Sage Lake Road to Maple Ridge Road—5.7 ft/mile
　　　　　　　Other sections—3 ft/mile or less
PORTAGES: Occasional fallen trees
RAPIDS/FALLS: Overhead Pipeline Rapids, below M-55—Class I-II
　　　　　　　　　Unnamed rapids below Greenwood Road—Class I
CAMPGROUNDS: Several
CANOE LIVERIES: Numerous (see Appendix D)
SKILL REQUIRED: I

Emerging from a cluster of lakes and small streams in the Rifle River Recreation Area, near the town of Lupton in northeast Ogemaw County, the Rifle begins as a small, clear, sand and gravel bottom trout stream. Attractive surroundings, generally clear water flowing through pools and riffles, and two locally acclaimed rapids are reasons the Rifle ranks with the AuSable, Manistee and other high-quality Michigan rivers. A designated Michigan Wild-Scenic Natural River, it is popular and well suited to either short trips or expeditions of several days. Summer weekends can be crowded.

Water levels seem to fluctuate greatly—spring flooding is common; summer levels are sometimes so low that canoes must be walked through some shallow riffles and rock gardens. Paddlers with basic skills should have no problem negotiating both sets of Rifle River rapids during normal water levels.

Campgrounds and public land in the upper section provide abundant camping possibilities; in the lower sections camping is limited to commercial facilities. Fishing is good throughout the river for resident trout in summer and, in spring and fall, for anadromous salmon and steelhead.

SAGE LAKE ROAD BRIDGE (WHITE ASH BRIDGE) to MAPLE RIDGE RD BRIDGE (MOFFATT BRIDGE)
24 MILES / 8 – 11 HOURS

It's possible to put in above Sage Lake Road in the Rifle River Recreation Area and work down the small river to Sage Lake Road, ❶ where parking and access are good, but we chose to begin our trip at the bridge. Here the river is small—25 – 40 feet wide and 1 – 2 feet deep—with rock-strewn bottom and moderate current. Terrain is lowland forests with thickets of poplars and tag alders at the banks.

The state-forest campground located half an hour below Sage Lake Road is closed. There are several state forest campgrounds in the Rifle River Recreation Area; only private campgrounds are found downstream along the river.

About halfway to Selkirk Bridge is an access site at Klacking Creek. This site, on river left, requires a 100-foot carry down a path through the woods.

The river here is clear and quick, with stretches of riffles over gravel and rock alternating with smooth glides and pools. Water volume has increased as a result of tributaries and springs, and width has increased to 30 to 50 feet. Low hills of hardwoods, with some pines and cedars, border the river, and there are occasional low areas and open banks. Much of the bordering land from here downstream is private property with scattered houses and cottages. Some shallow riffles are bottom-bumpers in low water. Also, pick your way around rocks in boulder gardens and over the artificial reefs of stones and boulders that property owners have erected.

Selkirk Bridge on State Road is surrounded by private land and has no access or parking. Trespassers here are definitely prosecuted.

Access at the M-55 bridge—where there is a steep trail to the river—is poor and parking is very limited along the highway. Below here, pools and riffles continue to alternate, the water is generally deeper, and there are several long stretches of nearly still water. Some tight bends may be tricky in high water.

About two miles below M-55 the West Branch of the Rifle enters from the right. Near the junction of the two rivers, on the left bank, is Highbanks Overlook, a developed state access site with a canoe slide leading down to the river.

Approximately 4 miles below M-55 are Overhead Pipeline Rapids, the first of two sets of rapids on the Rifle. Descent is quick for about one-quarter mile and culminates in a 100-yard stretch of very fast water over layers of bedrock slabs and ledges. Standing waves during high

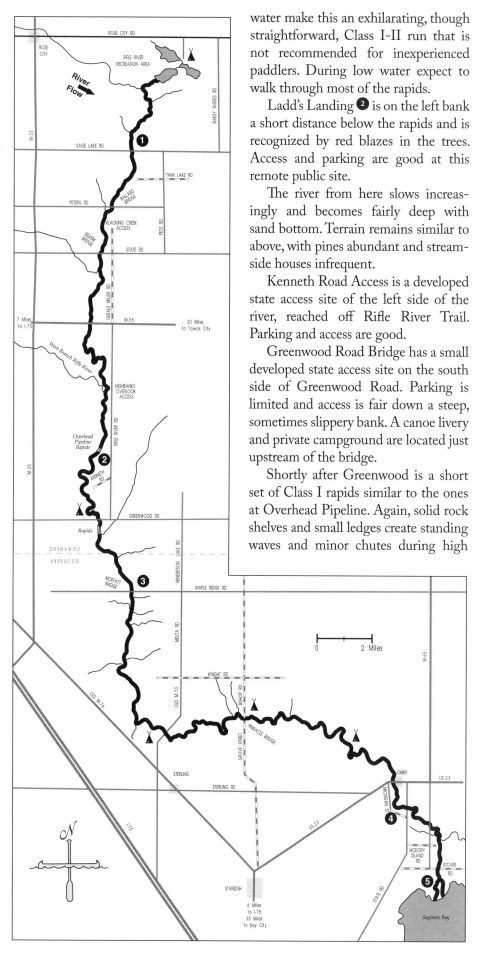

water make this an exhilarating, though straightforward, Class I-II run that is not recommended for inexperienced paddlers. During low water expect to walk through most of the rapids.

Ladd's Landing ❷ is on the left bank a short distance below the rapids and is recognized by red blazes in the trees. Access and parking are good at this remote public site.

The river from here slows increasingly and becomes fairly deep with sand bottom. Terrain remains similar to above, with pines abundant and streamside houses infrequent.

Kenneth Road Access is a developed state access site of the left side of the river, reached off Rifle River Trail. Parking and access are good.

Greenwood Road Bridge has a small developed state access site on the south side of Greenwood Road. Parking is limited and access is fair down a steep, sometimes slippery bank. A canoe livery and private campground are located just upstream of the bridge.

Shortly after Greenwood is a short set of Class I rapids similar to the ones at Overhead Pipeline. Again, solid rock shelves and small ledges create standing waves and minor chutes during high

water. In summer we walked through in our tennis shoes.

From here to Moffatt Bridge, on Maple Ridge Road, the river is wide and shallow with frequent, shallow riffles studded with sizeable rocks. The current is slow to moderate; the water tends toward murkiness. Cottages are scattered along the banks much of the way.

Access and parking are good at the large state access site at Moffatt Bridge. ❸

MOFFATT BRIDGE (MAPLE RIDGE ROAD) to STOVER ROAD BRIDGE
22.5 MILES / 6 ½ – 10 HOURS

From Moffatt Bridge to Old M-70 (Melita Road) the river remains wide (to 100 feet) and alternates slow pools with shallow riffles. During low water you'll need to pick your way around rocks and through the deeper channels.

Old M-70 (Melita Road) no longer has public access (the site was sold to private landholders). Access and parking are available for a fee at the canoe livery and campground near the bridge. From here to Omer, riffles over gravel and stone bottom alternate with sand bottom and slow water.

At Pinnacle Bridge, on Grove Road, is a private campground. Access at the bridge is private.

Near Omer the best access is at the public site ❹ on River Road downstream from US-23. A few light riffles here give way finally to slow, discolored water over sand and clay bottom.

Hickory Island Bridge has poor access and parking.

Stover Road Bridge ❺ has fair access and roadside parking. This is the last access before the Rifle opens into marshlands and empties into Saginaw Bay.

SHIAWASSEE RIVER

COUNTIES: Shiawassee, Saginaw

START/END: Byron to Fergus Road Bridge

MILES: 65.5

GRADIENT: Byron to Owosso—2.9 ft/mile

Owosso to Fergus Road—3.8 ft/mile

PORTAGES: Two dams, easy

RAPIDS/FALLS: Short rapids at old dam sites near Martin Road and Ditch Road—Class I-II

Two runnable dams in the city of Owosso—Class I-II

CAMPGROUNDS: Few

CANOE LIVERIES: Few (see Appendix D)

SKILL REQUIRED: I

A generally quiet, moderately paced river, the Shiawassee rambles through farmlands and woodlots while draining the southern Saginaw Valley. Occasional riffles, especially in the Owosso area, add variety to a river that is slow to moderate most of its length. Except for several dams and old mill-sites that may need portaging, the entire river is well suited to beginning paddlers. Water fluctuations are quite extreme—early spring levels are too high for safe paddling some years, while some riffles will be quite low during dry summers.

Streamside camping is limited to one private campground, making extended trips difficult but possible. Fishing is for bass, pike and other warm-water species.

BYRON to GEECK ROAD PARK
13 MILES / 4 – 6 HOURS

During high water, there is canoeable river as far upstream as Holly, in Oakland County. Fish Lake Road Bridge in Holly has fair access, but the river is small—15 to 25 feet wide—and even after a wet September, we found it too shallow and choked with fallen trees to be easily navigated. Likewise, at the mill dam in Linden—where the river is slightly larger—shallow water and the lowland woodlots it passes through below town convinced us to begin our trip in Byron, where the junction of the South Branch makes the mainstream consistently large enough to navigate.

From Byron, the Shiawassee is 45 – 60 feet wide and 1 – 4 feet deep with water that tends to be slightly clouded. Current is slow to moderate and flows over sand and gravel bottom. Terrain is lowland forests in a narrow valley surrounded by pastures and fields.

Access and parking are good at the new city park on Bath Road in Byron. ❶

Access is fair at New Lothrop Road Bridge.

At Lehring Road, access is prohibited at the bridge, but the canoe livery and private campground there have a landing and picnic area available with permission.

Cole Road Bridge has fair access and limited roadside parking.

Access and parking are good at the township park and picnic area just downstream from the Geeck Road Bridge. ❷

GEECK ROAD to CORUNNA PARK
16 MILES / 5 – 8 HOURS

From Geeck Road the river continues through terrain much like that above, although the banks are somewhat higher in many places. Current is mostly slow to moderate, with depths of 1 to 4 feet over sand and gravel and occasional rocks up to bushel size. Some light riffles may be bottom-bumpers during low-water periods.

Access is fair, with roadside parking at both Business 69 Bridge and downstream at Newburg Road Bridge.

Before the dam at the village of Shiawassee are long, narrow, and marshy backwaters. Portage Shiatown Dam ❸ on the right. The county park and picnic area at the dam offer good access and parking.

Access at M-71 is fair with very limited roadside parking. The river from here is noticeably larger and more clouded due to the addition of the Maple River and other tributaries.

Goodal Road below Vernon has no access.

At Martin Road, where access is poor, there are light rapids at the site of a washed-out mill dam. It should create no difficulty except during very high water, when standing waves might develop.

Lytle Road Bridge has good access but limited parking.

In Corunna, there is good access and parking ❹ at the city park below the downtown district. A low-head dam at State Road requires portaging.

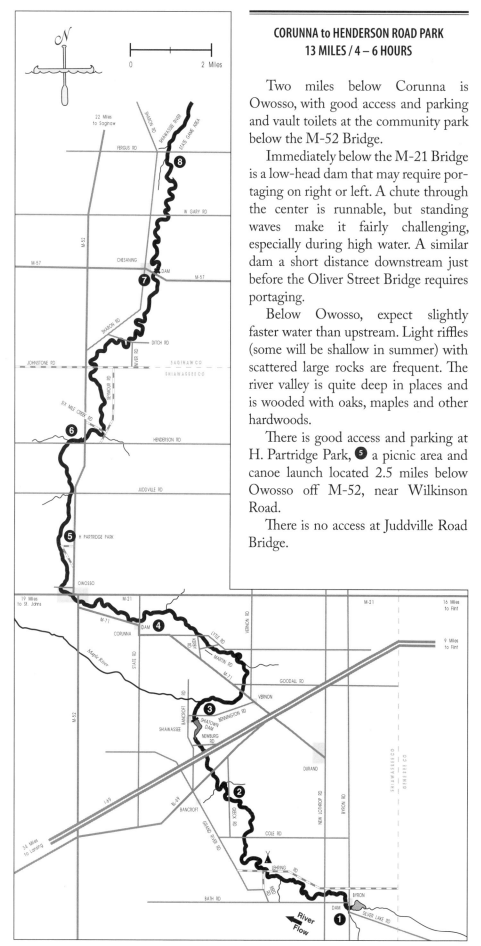

CORUNNA to HENDERSON ROAD PARK
13 MILES / 4 – 6 HOURS

Two miles below Corunna is Owosso, with good access and parking and vault toilets at the community park below the M-52 Bridge.

Immediately below the M-21 Bridge is a low-head dam that may require portaging on right or left. A chute through the center is runnable, but standing waves make it fairly challenging, especially during high water. A similar dam a short distance downstream just before the Oliver Street Bridge requires portaging.

Below Owosso, expect slightly faster water than upstream. Light riffles (some will be shallow in summer) with scattered large rocks are frequent. The river valley is quite deep in places and is wooded with oaks, maples and other hardwoods.

There is good access and parking at H. Partridge Park, ❺ a picnic area and canoe launch located 2.5 miles below Owosso off M-52, near Wilkinson Road.

There is no access at Juddville Road Bridge.

Henderson Road Bridge ❻ has poor access and parking, but the county park just downstream has good access. Note that the park is open only during the summer.

HENDERSON PARK to FERGUS ROAD
23.5 MILES / 6 ½ – 11 HOURS

Below Henderson Park the river averages 80 to 100 feet wide as it flows through a fairly steep-sided valley. Deep water and strong, moderately fast current alternate with shallow riffles. During high water, some riffles will create standing waves and become light rapids.

M-52 Bridge has no access.

Access and parking are fair at Six Mile Creek Road Bridge.

Johnstone Road Bridge is out and has no access or parking.

Ditch Road Bridge has fair access and parking. There is a washed-out dam just upstream, with fast water spilling through several channels. Take the left channel but watch for concrete slabs and reinforcing rod. Also, high standing waves develop during high water.

In Chesaning, ❼ good access and parking are available at two city parks, one above the bridge at M-57, the other below it. Just below M-57 is a 6-foot dam that must be portaged on the right. Use caution near the spillway, where there is no barrier.

Below Chesaning at West Gary Road Bridge, access is fair with roadside parking. The river is slow to moderate, is deeply discolored, and passes through continuous lowlands until the junction with the Flint River. From Chesaning to the state game area starting at Fergus Road, the river valley is quite shallow, and the narrow border of silver maples and willows backs up mostly to pastures and cultivated fields.

Fergus Road Bridge ❽ has good access and limited roadside parking.

Escanaba River

FERGUS ROAD BRIDGE to SOUTH MILLER ROAD (FLINT RIVER)
9 MILES / 3 – 5 HOURS (est.) (NOT ON MAP)

We have not paddled through the Shiawassee State Game Area below Fergus Road and have not included it on the map. It is an area of lowlands, bayous and flooded woods and is popular enough with duck hunters to be crowded during that season. Camping possibilities are limited due to wet ground, and mosquitoes can be overwhelming in summer. Access at the lower end of the game area is not easy.

About 3.5 miles below Fergus Road is the junction with the wide, slow-moving and discolored Bad River. Good access and parking are available at a public site on Hulein Road one mile upstream on the Bad. Take out here or continue downstream to the South Miller Road Bridge boat launch. This access site is located a quarter mile upstream on Marsh Creek. Use caution in this area—expansive marshlands and slow currents on the Shiawassee and Flint rivers and Marsh Creek make it difficult to tell upstream from down and even to discern one watercourse from another.

STURGEON RIVER

COUNTY: Cheboygan
START/END: Trowbridge Road Bridge to Indian River
MILES: 16
GRADIENT: 13.8 ft/mile
PORTAGES: Occasional fallen trees
RAPIDS/FALLS: Numerous unnamed rapids
CAMPGROUNDS: Few
CANOE LIVERIES: Several (see Appendix D)
SKILL REQUIRED: I-II
TOPO. MAPS: Gaylord NE (7.5 min.), Wolverine (15 min.)

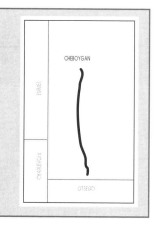

Though its headwaters are in Otsego County near Gaylord, the Sturgeon is not wide enough nor open enough for enjoyable canoeing until it reaches the town of Wolverine, 20 miles downstream. The Sturgeon—considered a premier trout stream—is also one of the Lower Peninsula's most beautiful and challenging canoeing rivers. Consistently quick current and average descent of almost 14 feet per mile make it one of the fastest Lower Peninsula rivers. That, combined with tight turns, leaning trees and occasional obstructions, also make the Sturgeon a river not recommended for absolute beginners, although paddlers with basic maneuvering skills should have little trouble.

Much of the river flows through state forest, where there is an abundance of suitable campsites. In addition, a state-forest campground is located on the river about two miles downstream from Wolverine.

TROWBRIDGE ROAD BRIDGE to M-68 BRIDGE OR BURT LAKE
16 MILES / 5 – 7 HOURS

Most paddlers put in at Wolverine, near the junction of the West Branch and the mainstream of the Sturgeon, but it is possible to begin a trip on the mainstream four miles upstream between the Trowbridge Road bridges, at the DNR access site ❶, where access and parking are good. The river in this section, near I-75, is 15 to 30 feet wide and varies from quick-flowing and very shallow over gravel to slow and 1 to 3 feet deep over sand and rocks. Tight bends, frequent fallen trees and minor logjams make slow going in places; several short portages or lift-overs are usually necessary. Thickets of poplar and tag alders alternate with stretches of open meadows. Expect a 1- to 2-hour trip from the upper Trowbridge Road Bridge to the park in Wolverine.

Below the junction with the West Branch, the mainstream widens to 30 to 50 feet. Current is moderately quick over gravel and cobble-size rocks.

Access and parking are good at Wolverine Park and Campground, ❷ where there are toilets, picnic tables and water. Giant poplars and willows line the river below the park.

One or two chutes create light rapids and standing waves within the first half mile below the park, then the current slows, the water deepens, and the river winds through an area of open meadows and cedar clumps. There are no houses or cottages immediately below Wolverine and few along the entire river until near Indian River.

Meadows Boating Access Site ❸, with good access and parking, is on the right, about a mile below Wolverine. From here the current increases in speed and remains relatively fast through numerous tight bends that require basic maneuvering skills.

❹ Haakwood State Forest Campground is identified by a sand trail visible on the left bank just below

a railroad trestle with a U.S.G.S. water-gauging station beside it. Other sandy trails downstream on the left also lead to the campground.

Rondo Road Bridge has no access, but there is good access, parking, and a vault toilet one-half mile downstream at Rondo Boating Access Site ❺ at the railroad trestle reached off South Straits Highway (Old 27).

From Haakwood Campground to the first White Road Bridge, locally known as Midway, the river remains fast, with riffles and pools alternating with light Class I-II rapids over fist- to bushel-size rocks. Descent is quick— sometimes through long, straight lanes between cedars and other times through series of bends. Occasional chutes between large rocks and ledges require fairly precise maneuvering, especially during high water when standing waves develop. Water levels, even during dry seasons, should be sufficient for clear passage. Fallen trees, stumps and logs are present but seem to be regularly cleared by canoe liveries and paddlers.

Access and parking are fair at the first White Road Bridge.

The second bridge is about 2 miles downstream and has fair access with roadside parking. By the second bridge the current has slowed gradually and continues at moderate speed over gravel and sand. Topography changes to low-land forests, with cedars near the water, and occasional small meadows.

From the access site ❻ at the end of Fisher Woods Road, where access and parking are good, the river continues moderately fast, but houses appear and traffic from M-68 becomes audible.

Continue past the M-68 Bridge in Indian River to Burt Lake. Follow the shore left (west) one-quarter mile to the boat-launching site at Burt Lake State Park. ❼ Camping and all facilities are available at the park; a vehicle permit is required to camp and to use the access site.

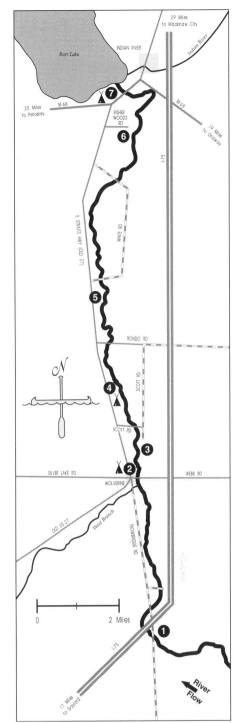

THORNAPPLE RIVER

COUNTY: Barry
START/END: Nashville Dam to Irving Dam
MILES: 25.5
GRADIENT: 2 ft/mile
PORTAGES: Occasional fallen trees
RAPIDS/FALLS: Ruehs Rapids in Alaska (not on map)—Class I
CAMPGROUNDS: Few
CANOE LIVERIES: Several (see Appendix D)
SKILL REQUIRED: I

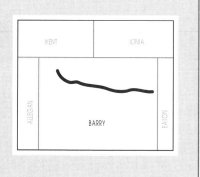

The Thornapple, like most tributaries in the Grand River system, is a gentle river with moderate current flowing over sand and gravel bottom. It passes primarily through lowlands and low hills of hardwoods and in the upper half is not heavily developed. Camping is severely limited due to private property and a lack of developed campgrounds. Fishing is primarily for warm-water species, especially smallmouth bass, but some trout are found in the upper reaches. The lower end of the river, below the village of Irving, consists of a series of dams and impoundments. We confined our trip to the upper reaches.

NASHVILLE DAM to THORNAPPLE LAKE
7 MILES / 3 ½ – 4 ½ HOURS

This is essentially the upper limit of canoeable river. Above Nashville the river is heavily choked with aquatic weeds and is too small and shallow to be easily canoed.

Access and parking are good below the Nashville Dam ❶ on the left. The river here is 30 to 50 feet wide, with a bottom of sand and gravel. The water is discolored, with visibility of 2 to 3 feet. Current is slow to moderate.

Below Nashville, the Thornapple enters a low valley of farmlands and lowland forests. Silver maples predominate and often form an overhead canopy. Some open meadows come to the bank, but the dominant feature is hardwoods above tangles of underbrush and vines. Fallen trees can be a problem. The canoe liveries clear them annually, but there are always new ones, especially in the spring. We made the trip in April and encountered half a dozen trees and logjams that had to be lifted over.

An hour below Nashville is a small bridge at Gregg's Crossing. The bridge is closed and access is poor.

Thornapple Lake Road Bridge is 2 to 3 hours below Nashville and has fair access from the little bay on the right upstream side of the bridge. Parking is limited to the roadside. From here to Thornapple Lake is water similar to above, with slow current and frequent fallen trees.

Barger Road Bridge is about 1.5 miles below Thornapple Road and has good access and roadside parking.

Just below Barger Road is Thornapple Lake. This is a natural lake, not a reservoir, and is quite popular as a resort and recreation area. Expect lots of power boat traffic in summer. Two private campgrounds are found on its shores, one on the left shore about midway down the lake, the other at the outlet.

Charlton County Park ❷—with a museum, picnic grounds, good access and parking—is on the right, before the bridge. There is camping for a fee at the commercial campground across the channel from the county park.

CHARLTON PARK to HASTINGS CITY PARK
6.5 MILES / 2 – 3½ HOURS

The lake outlet beneath Charlton Park Road is a wide, deep channel that remains slow and wide, with depths of 2 to 8 feet, for a mile or more. Banks are quite heavily developed with cottages.

McKeown Road Bridge has poor access and parking. By here the river has increased in velocity, with the water shallow over gravel and small rocks and the current moderate to fairly quick. From here to Hastings, light riffles alternate with slower water. Some of the riffles are shallow and will be bottom-draggers during low water. Cottages diminish in frequency. Terrain is low hills of hardwoods and large sycamores. Generally, the river below Thornapple Lake is wide enough, at 40 to 65 feet, that fallen trees do not obstruct the entire river.

Fair access and roadside parking are found at River Road Bridge and at Center Road Bridge. The remainder of the trip to Tyden Park in Hastings ❸ is through the backyards of the city.

Access and parking are good at the park, where there are restrooms, drinking water, and picnic grounds.

HASTINGS CITY PARK to IRVING DAM
12 MILES / 4 – 6 HOURS

The river from Hastings to Irving is similar to the section above Hastings— mild riffles with gravel and rock bottom

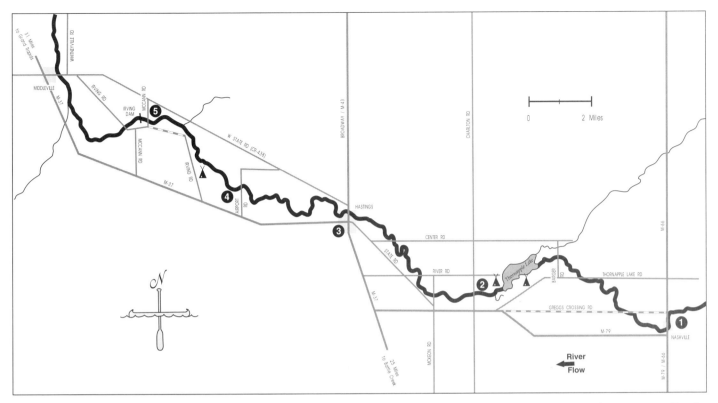

alternate with stretches of slower water. Expect quite a few streamside cottages and houses, and at least one golf course, but otherwise much of the bordering land is low hills of hardwoods. Fallen trees are not uncommon here, and can partially obstruct the river.

Airport Road Bridge ❹ is 2 to 3 hours below Hastings. A couple of hundred yards downstream on the left is a public access site with good access and parking. From here to the backwaters of Irving Dam are more riffles—some fairly fast—and a few houses and cottages. A couple miles above Irving Dam is a private campground and canoe livery on the left.

Well before the town of Irving the river slows and widens, then enters the narrow backwaters of Irving Dam. ❺ Access and parking are good at the dam. Stay to the left and portage the dam on the left. A second dam is located on the right shore of the reservoir, but water levels below it are often extremely low, and there are likely to be obstructions downstream.

Below the dam on the left is a slow channel leading to yet another dam (a power generator), that is best portaged on the left, though it is not an easy or well-marked take-out. Use caution climbing down the steep bank.

We ended our trip at Irving Pond. Much of the remainder of the distance to the junction with the Grand River consists of backwaters and wide, slow sections of river between them. Most of the impoundments seem to be heavily developed and used for recreational purposes.

One stretch worth noting is at Ruehs Park in the town of Alaska, where a 75-foot-long run of fast water is found just before the 68th Street Bridge. These are basic, straightforward rapids that, though not challenging by most whitewater standards, could be tricky during high water when standing waves develop. If in doubt, portage on the left, through the park.

Manistee River

THUNDER BAY RIVER

COUNTIES: Montmorency, Alpena
START/END: Atlanta Dam to Alpena
MILES: 57.25
GRADIENT: Atlanta to Hillman—6.4 ft/mile
Hillman to Seven Mile Pond—4.2 ft/mile
PORTAGES: Four dams, moderately difficult; occasional fallen trees
RAPIDS/FALLS: Speehley Rapids, below M-65 Bridge—Class I
CAMPGROUNDS: Few
CANOE LIVERIES: Few (see Appendix D)
SKILL REQUIRED: I

From its headwaters in McCormick Lake southwest of Atlanta, to its mouth in Lake Huron's Thunder Bay, the Thunder Bay River is a moderately paced river that is well suited to paddlers of all abilities. Though shallow and fairly quick in the upper reaches, most of it winds slowly through a variety of woodlands. The final ten miles is composed of a series of dams and reservoirs. Water level fluctuations are quite extreme, making early season trips inadvisable, especially at Speehley Rapids, below Long Rapids Park on M-65. Low water is seldom a problem except in the section from Atlanta to Hunt Creek Bridge (Hall Road), where some shallow riffles will slow progress.

Much of the river passes through the Thunder Bay State Forest, but good campsites are hard to find and the only developed campground is at the municipal park on Hillman Pond. Fishing is primarily for warm-water species, including smallmouth bass and northern pike. The short stretch of river below the Ninth Avenue Dam in Alpena receives heavy runs of trout and salmon in spring and fall, and attracts much angling pressure.

ATLANTA DAM to HUNT CREEK BRIDGE (HALL ROAD)
11.5 MILES / 3 ½ – 6 HOURS

Access and parking are good at the Atlanta Dam. ❶ The river here is small—15 – 25 feet wide and 1 – 2 feet deep—and flows slowly over sand bottom. Water is remarkably clear. Thickets of tag alders and other underbrush line the banks, and development is light, with only occasional cottages.

Airport Road Bridge has fair access and poor parking. Not far downstream, slow water gives way to riffles over gravel bottom and scattered larger rocks. Some stretches are fairly quick and moderately challenging during high water. Occasional rock reefs usually have a clear chute near the center. During low-water periods expect to drag bottom.

Access is good at Eichorn Bridge (McMurphy Road), but parking is limited and on the roadside. From here, current slows and the river deepens and widens. Average width is 30 – 50 feet

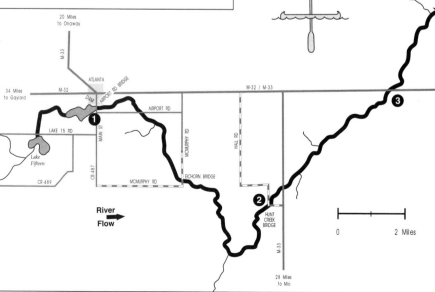

and depth, 2 – 5 feet. Bottom becomes predominantly sand. Terrain is lowland forests. Fallen trees are common but seem to be regularly cleared.

Hunt Creek Bridge **2** (Hall Road) has fair access and very limited roadside parking.

HUNT CREEK BRIDGE to HILLMAN DAM
10.5 MILES / 4 – 5 HOURS

Shortly below Hunt Creek Bridge is M-33 Bridge, with poor access and parking. From here, current remains steady and moderate, and water is usually murky. Lowland forests alternate with hills of hardwoods; cedars and tag alders commonly border the river.

M-32 Bridge **3** has fair access and limited parking. Slow, deep, and discolored water is typical of most of the remainder of the river. Bottom is sand, and banks are thickly overgrown.

The backwaters of Hillman Dam **4** consist of a long and narrow reservoir lined with stumps. Hillman Park is a municipal park and campground on the right shore of the reservoir within sight of the dam. There are both primitive and modern campsites, and supplies are within walking distance.

Portage Hillman Dam on the right.

HILLMAN DAM to SALINA ROAD BRIDGE
10 MILES / 4 – 5 HOURS

Much of the bordering land in this section is within the Thunder Bay State Forest. Good campsites are not abundant but can be found. Current is slow to moderate through constant tight bends and switchbacks. The river remains about 50 feet wide, and up to 3 feet deep over a substrate that varies from rock and gravel to silt and sand.

The Upper South Branch enters on the right a few bends before Salina Road.

Salina Road Bridge **5** has good access and limited roadside parking.

SALINA ROAD BRIDGE to SEVEN MILE POND
19.25 MILES / 7 – 9 HOURS

Long Rapids County Park **6** at the M-65 Bridge, about 5 miles below Salina Road, has good access and parking.

The 7.75-mile section from here to Orchard Bridge, on Herron Road, includes the Thunder Bay's only rapids, called Long Rapids or Speehley Rapids. Beginning 1.5 miles below the bridge, they are a series of cascading riffles that will not challenge paddlers who have

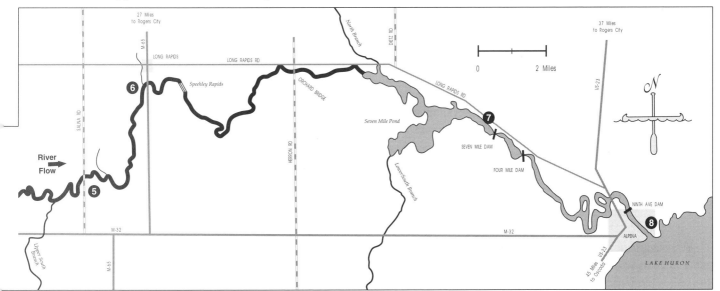

whitewater experience, although they are an exhilarating run after the miles of slow water upstream. Rapids extend for about 1,200 feet over fist- to pumpkin-size rocks. Descent is not very steep, passage is straightforward, and only during high water will there be substantial standing waves and other hazards. Streamside banks are 10 to 20 feet high and slope gradually away from the river.

Orchard Bridge (Herron Road) has fair access and parking.

Shortly below Herron Road, the backwaters of Seven Mile Dam begin, where

the mainstream is joined by the Lower South Branch. It is a 4-mile crossing to the dam. Access and parking are good at the public access site **7** about 100 yards west of the dam on the left bank. This is also the take-out for the long portage around the left side of the dam.

SEVEN MILE POND to ALPENA
6 MILES / 3 – 4 HOURS

We bypassed this section of almost continuous backwaters. There are

portages at Seven Mile Dam, 1 mile downstream at Four Mile Dam, and 5 miles downstream at the Ninth Avenue Dam in Alpena. Shorelines of the impoundments are heavily developed with cottages and houses. Portage the Ninth Avenue Dam on the right. There is a short stretch of steep fast rapids immediately below the dam.

At the mouth of the river take out at the municipal park and marina, **8** where parking and access are good.

WHITE RIVER

COUNTIES: Oceana, Muskegon
START/END: Hesperia to BR-31 Bridge in Whitehall
MILES: 32.5
GRADIENT: Hesperia to Pines Point Campground—11.7 ft/mile
                 Other sections—2.5 ft/mile
PORTAGES: None
RAPIDS/FALLS: None
CAMPGROUNDS: Several
CANOE LIVERIES: Two (see Appendix D)
SKILL REQUIRED: I

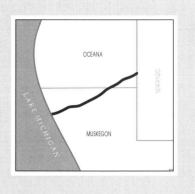

Because it is between two well-known and popular rivers—the Muskegon, to the south, and the Pere Marquette, to the north—the White River tends to be overlooked by many canoeists and anglers. Although it has fewer access sites than its more famous neighbors, an abundance of quiet and solitude on this Country-Scenic designated Michigan Natural River make it very appealing.

The White is a relatively small river that divides conveniently into upper and lower sections, each with a distinct personality. The upper reach, from Hesperia to Pines Point Campground, is generally shallow and rocky with many riffles, while the lower section tends to be slower and deeper and have sand bottom. Except during spring and other periods of high water (when the upper river, especially, may be rather challenging), the entire river is suitable for beginning paddlers and families with small children. Much of the river passes through the Manistee National Forest, where well-spaced U.S. Forest Service campgrounds and access sites make overnight trips easy to plan.

Fishing is primarily for brown trout and smallmouth bass in the upper river; bass and northern pike are found in the lower section. Spring and fall runs of steelhead and salmon are heavy, though fishing pressure is relatively light once you get downstream from the hotspot near the Hesperia Dam. A locally famous run of walleye also occurs in the spring.

HESPERIA DAM to PINES POINT USFS CAMPGROUND
8.5 MILES / 3 – 4 HOURS

We began our trip in Hesperia because the river above it seems too small for enjoyable paddling. This upper section is actually the South Branch of the White. It joins with the North Branch a short distance downstream from Pines Point USFS Campground to form the mainstream.

Below the low-head dam in Hesperia, low water is common in summer, and some shallow riffles may require walking through. Parking and access are good at Hesperia Dam ❶ and at Vida Weaver Park, a short distance downstream.

The river through this section averages 40 – 60 feet wide and 6 inches to 3 feet deep. Gravel and rock bottom predominates, with many shallow riffles.

Current is moderate to fairly quick. Frequent sharp bends, some quite tricky, require basic maneuvering skills. Terrain is low hills and upland hardwood and pine forests. Most bordering land is private with cabins frequent.

Access and parking at Taylor Bridge (Garfield Road) are good at the township park, called Taylor Landing. No overnight parking is allowed. Fairly quick descent and rock and gravel bottom make the river to here a challenging trip during high water.

Pines Point ❷ is a U.S. Forest Service Campground with good access and parking, picnic grounds and primitive camping facilities.

PINES POINT CAMPGROUND to DIAMOND POINT USFS CAMPGROUND
12 MILES / 4 – 6 HOURS

Below Pines Point the river tends to widen and deepen, although not far below the campground is a 1-mile stretch that can be very low in summer. The bottom changes to predominantly sand. Most of this section flows through the Manistee National Forest, but much of the bordering land is low and swampy, making good campsites infrequent. Abundant wildlife and a sense of seclusion are the main appeal of the lower White.

The conjunction with the North Branch adds considerably to river flow. Several minor tributaries in this stretch are often discolored, and the White from here downstream tends to be murkier than above.

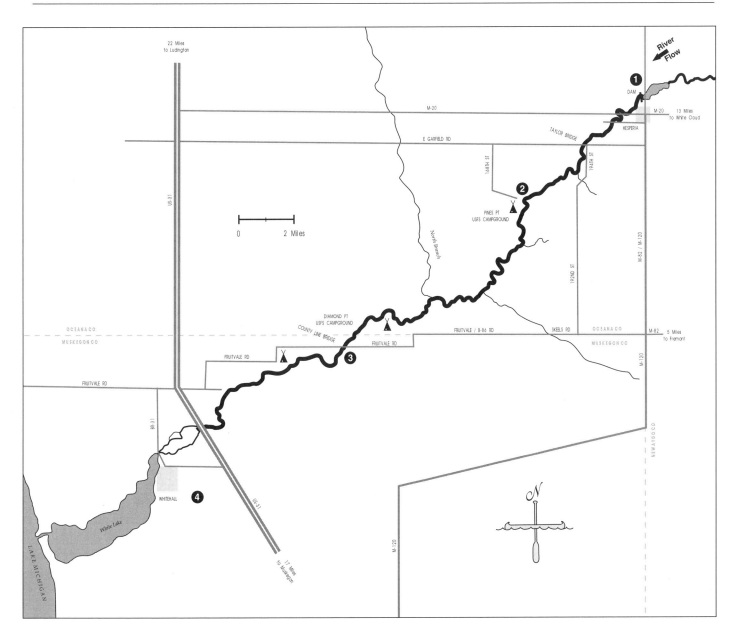

A USFS access site is located at Cisco Rollaway, with good access and parking. Diamond Point USFS Campground has five campsites, primitive facilities, and good access and parking.

DIAMOND POINT CAMPGROUND to BR-31 IN WHITEHALL
12 MILES / 5 – 6 HOURS

About an hour below Diamond Point is County Line Bridge **3** (Fruitvale Road), with fair access and roadside parking. Take out on the left.

From here the river remains slow and deep. Width is 60 – 70 feet, and depth is 3 – 6 feet with deeper holes. There is mostly private land with occasional scattered cabins in this area of lowland forests and marshes.

One-half hour below County Line Bridge, the river spreads through extensive marshlands, with channels branching in many directions. Stay to the right and follow the widest, deepest route.

One hour below County Line Bridge is a private campground with all facilities and some supplies. Most of the remaining river is slow and murky and passes through marshlands. About 2 hours below County Line Bridge is a private canoe landing that should be used only with permission. Shortly below the landing, the river enters a delta area of wide marshes.

There is no access at the US-31 Bridge, but BR-31 Bridge **4** in Whitehall just before White Lake has a good public access site with parking and nearby supplies.

Portaging the gorge, Presque Isle River

UPPER PENINSULA

BLACK RIVER

COUNTY: Gogebic
START/END: CR-513 Bridge to Black River County Park at Lake Superior
MILES: 28.5
GRADIENT: CR-513 to US-2—17.5 ft/mile
      Covered Bridge to Narrows Park—8.4 ft/mile
      Narrows Park to unnamed road—25 ft/mile
      Unnamed road to Lake Superior—48.6 ft/mile
PORTAGES: Numerous falls
RAPIDS/FALLS: Granite Rapids below CR-513—Class II
      Numerous unnamed rapids above and below Ramsay—Class I-II
      Several unnamed rapids below Covered Bridge—Class I-II
      Numerous unnamed rapids below Narrows Park—Class II-III
      Eight major falls—essentially unrunnable
CAMPGROUNDS: Few
CANOE LIVERIES: None
SKILL REQUIRED: II-III
TOPO. MAPS: Ironwood, Wakefield, North Ironwood (15 min.)

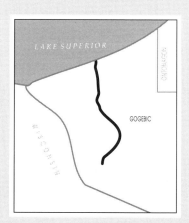

Renowned as one of Michigan's finest whitewater rivers, the Black is designated a National Wild and Scenic River in its lower reaches, from the Ottawa National Forest Boundary to Lake Superior. It is a challenging river and is not recommended for paddlers without whitewater experience. At least eight impassable falls limit passage and make extended expeditions extremely difficult.

Like most western Upper Peninsula rivers, the Black is subject to extreme flow fluctuations, with levels varying even more than on the neighboring Montreal and Presque Isle rivers. Levels are somewhat dependent on discharges from Black River Dam, five miles above the CR-513 put-in, but late summer and fall often find this river a virtual trickle. We paddled it in late May—usually an ideal time—but spring rains had been light, and we found many sections quite low. Most of the major rapids and drops that have given the Black the reputation of being one of the best Class II-III rivers in the Upper Peninsula were lowered a full degree by low water. On the other hand, a day and night of solid rain brought the river up to blood-pressure-raising levels, and some of the same rapids we had traipsed through with impunity became challenging runs capable of swamping open canoes.

Generally, consider the month of May for the best chance of finding ideal levels; go in April if you're equipped (and dressed) for cold and can handle very heavy, very fast water and technical maneuvering around numerous rock and log obstructions. At all times, phone calls to various agencies and businesses in Ironwood, Bessemer, Ramsay and Wakefield can give up-to-the-minute reports. (See Appendix C: Further Information.)

CR-513 BRIDGE to US-2
8 MILES / 3 – 5 HOURS

This upper section of the Black is small—with current varying from very slow to very fast—and is suitable for paddlers with basic skills and experience. In addition to numerous Class I rapids, there is one short Class II drop at Granite Rapids.

Access ❶ is fair from the bridge at CR-513, with parking limited to the roadside. The river is 15 – 30 feet wide—as it is through most of the section to US-2—with depths of 1 – 6 feet during early summer. Current is slow over rock and sand bottom and beds of aquatic vegetation. The water is dark enough to make the river's name seem apt.

Just downstream is a private bridge with no access. From here the river winds through lowlands of spruce and tamarack with tag alders at the banks. Occasional short, light riffles punctuate stretches of slow water.

Granite Rapids ❷ can be heard before they are seen. Their approach is also marked by a house on the bluff to the left. Take out on the left to scout or portage. The rapids are a run of about 50 feet over a series of low ledges and a 3-foot drop. At the drop, take the main chute at right-center. The primary hazards are large standing waves during high water and exposed rock during low water. There is access and room to park at the dead-end road beside the rapids.

From Granite Rapids to the town of Ramsay, Class I rapids through rock gardens and over minor chutes and ledge drops alternate with stretches of slower, deeper water. Several pine-covered knolls make good campsites. Just before Ramsay, a USGS water gauge is on the right, next to a gauge station.

In Ramsay, there is good access and parking ❸ at a community park above the old keystone bridge, the first of three bridges in the town. The sluice dam here can be run through either the left or right spillways, but the left side of the dam has been dismantled, leaving an open channel that necessitates a sharp dogleg to the right; it can be tricky in high water. From the dam to the US-2 Bridge is three-quarters of a mile of continuous Class II rapids. This is a difficult run for inexperienced paddlers. The river's small size—25 to 35 feet wide—makes it susceptible to blockage by fallen trees and debris. Infrequent eddies and continuous, very fast water make it difficult to stop for obstructions or to scout, and high, steep, heavily overgrown banks make it difficult to get out. Precise maneuvering is demanded to avoid obstructions and reach clear chutes and channels.

Do not proceed beyond the US-2 Bridge. Neepikon Falls and Gabro Falls are a short distance downstream and are impassable and extremely dangerous. Portage trails are indistinct and difficult. We recommend shuttling the 2 miles of river from US-2 to the covered bridge at Blackjack Ski Area.

Access ❹ at US-2 is difficult, with a long, steep climb up an embankment and no clear trail through the underbrush. Parking is on the wide shoulder of the highway.

BLACKJACK BRIDGE to THE NARROWS ROADSIDE PARK
9.5 MILES / 3 – 4 HOURS

This meandering, relatively peaceful section is suitable for most paddlers. However, the risk of missing the access at the Narrows Park and being swept into the rapids below causes us to not recommend it to beginners. Inexperienced paddlers should plan to take out at either Bessemer Road Bridge or the unnamed bridge below it. Float times for this abbreviated trip are 1½ to 3 hours.

Good access and abundant parking are available at the bridge ❺ at the entrance to Blackjack Ski Resort. Just downstream, the conjunctions with the Little Black River, Jackson Creek and other tributaries swell the mainstream to 40 to 80 feet wide. Rapids in this section are light and alternate with long stretches of slow and nearly still water. Some slow pools culminate in short drops over light, boulder-strewn rapids that require only basic maneuvering skills. Watch for unseen rocks in slow water. Terrain is low woodlands of underbrush and hardwoods including silver maples. Most bordering land is in the Ottawa National Forest, and there are no houses or cabins.

At Bessemer Road Bridge, ❻ access is fair and there is plenty of roadside parking. Class I rapids at the bridge can produce large waves during high water. From here, rapids intensify somewhat but continue to alternate with slow water.

The bridge at Hedberg Road just off Black River Road has fair access and limited roadside parking. Through the next 4 to 5 miles, pools and light rapids continue as above, although descent continues to increase. Terrain changes gradually to upland forests of hardwoods and hemlocks.

After 4 miles, watch for a gravel-road ford across a shallow riffle. About three-quarters of a mile past the ford is the take-out at the Narrows Roadside Park. ❼ Access is up a high, steep, slippery bank on the left. There is a trail, but it is poor and nearly invisible from the river. Also, watch for the island that splits the river immediately below the Narrows. One way or another, stop before the island and get out on the left (west) to Black River Road (CR-513). Narrows Roadside Park has toilets, picnic tables, limited parking and several very basic campsites.

NARROWS ROADSIDE PARK to BLACK RIVER COUNTY PARK (at Lake Superior)
11 MILES / 7 – 10 HOURS (est.)

Below the Narrows are 4 miles of nearly continuous Class II-III rapids to an alternate take-out that involves some minor bushwhacking. In the first edition of this book we mentioned the possibility of taking out upstream of Algonquin Falls (the first of the six major falls on the lower Black) at a private two-track road with a gate and no trespassing sign at Black River Road. Recently, a section of the North Country Trail has been constructed along the west shore of the river here, offering a fairly good alternative take-out for advanced paddlers wanting to run this challenging and interesting section. Eventually, the North Country Trail will extend 3,200 miles from the Lewis and Clark Trail in North Dakota to the Appalachian Trail in New York state, crossing the entire length of the U.P. The 5-mile section along the Black is accessed from a trailhead and small parking lot on Copper Peak Road, not far north of the base of Copper Peak Ski Jump, and about 500 feet south of the junction where the road rejoins CR-513. From here the trail leads through the woods about a half mile to a low wooded bank above the river. (Note that the trail cannot be seen from the water.)

Plan on 2½ – 3½ hours paddling time from the Narrows to the take-out at the unnamed road or the North Country Trail downstream of it. This leaves ample time to scout the numerous ledge-drops and rapids in this section. The rapids are nearly continuous and are composed of bedrock slabs studded with pumpkin- to Volkswagen-size boulders. Descent is approximately 25 feet per mile. Expect standing waves and backrollers substantial enough to swamp open canoes during high water. During low water, hazards still exist, but finding the deepest, clearest channels and avoiding rocks are the primary challenges. Terrain in this section is

upland forests of hardwoods, pines, and hemlocks on high and very steep hills. Banks along the river range from 20 to 120 feet high and are extremely steep. Copper Peak Ski Jump is visible on Chippewa Hill, to the west of the river. Chippewa Falls—a short series of steep, runnable drops among boulders and ledges leading to a sharp bend to the right—are one half mile before the take-out at the unnamed road. The falls are preceded by long, boulder-strewn rapids. During high water they rate a solid Class III and are runnable but should not be attempted by anyone other than very advanced whitewater paddlers with covered boats. We ran them successfully in low water by keeping to the main chutes at the center. If in doubt, portage on the right. Scouting is easiest on the left.

Below Chippewa Falls is one-half mile of straightforward Class I-II rapids and riffles. Toward the end of the long straight stretch that runs northeast, watch for a shallow ford and narrow two-track road on the left. It is very easy to miss. There are no certain distinguishing marks except for a slight gap in the hemlocks that opens into the road away from the river. The North Country Trail parallels the river on the left, beginning one-half mile below the two-track road. ❽

We have not attempted the vigorous 7-mile trip from the unmarked road to Lake Superior, and in fact, have heard of no one who has. Our information, therefore, is incomplete. For instance, Algonquin Falls are a mystery. Steep 120-foot-high banks line both sides of the river, but the size of the falls and possibilities for portage are uncertain.

Portage Conglomerate, Potawatomi and Gorge falls on the left. Boardwalks and stairs simplify the three-quarter-mile portage.

We have not seen Sandstone Falls and do not know whether they can be run or easily portaged.

Rainbow Falls can be portaged on the left. Trails are clear but tortuous. Put in below the falls and paddle one-half mile

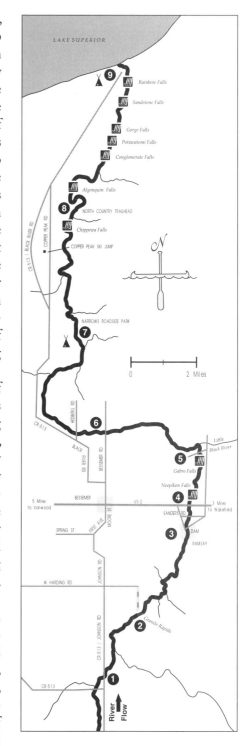

of slow water to Black River County Park, near the rivermouth. ❾Parking and access are good, and there are toilets, drinking water, and picnic facilities. A U.S. Forest Service Campground with most facilities is located one-quarter mile south of the county park on Black River Road.

Brule River

COUNTY: Iron

START/END: M-73 Bridge to Menominee River (with Menominee rapids)

MILES: 43

GRADIENT: M-73 to Pentoga—6.4 ft/mile

Pentoga to US-2—10.4 ft/ mile

US-2 to Brule River Flowage—8.9 ft/mile

PORTAGES: One dam, moderately difficult

RAPIDS/FALLS: Several unnamed rapids above Pentoga—Class I-II

Unnamed rapids below Pentoga—Class II

La Chapelle Rapids, above Washburn Bridge—Class I-II

CAMPGROUNDS: Few, but much of river flows through state and national forests with occasional primitive campsites.

CANOE LIVERIES: Two (see Appendix D)

SKILL REQUIRED: I-II

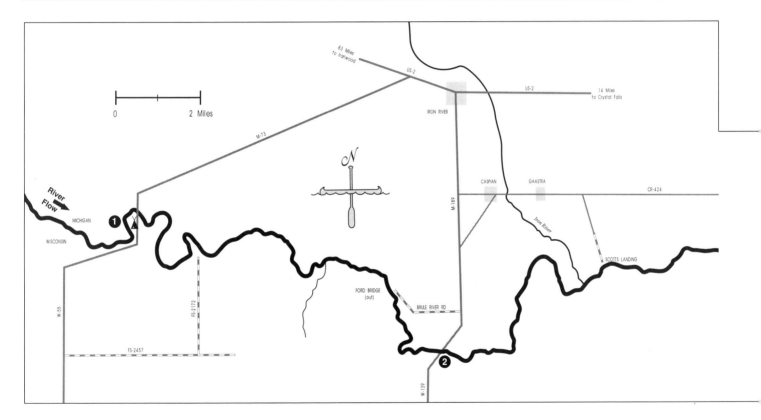

Wisconsin and Michigan paddlers alike claim title to this river that forms about 45 miles of border between the two states. Beginning at Brule Lake, just inside the Michigan border, it winds southeast until it joins the Paint and Michigamme rivers to form the Menominee.

Although numerous Class I rapids occur at intervals along most of its length, it is generally a mild-tempered river that will not prove difficult for most paddlers in normal water conditions. Rapids above and below the town of Pentoga rate Class I or II, as do La Chapelle Rapids, before the Washburn Bridge near the end of the river. Inexperienced paddlers should approach these stretches with caution, especially during high water, and should, perhaps, portage. The Brule's flow is more reliable than many other area rivers. Midsummer trips can be accomplished with only a minimum of bumping and scraping, and most of that will be in the upper section above M-189.

Much of the land bordering both sides of the river is public, with good campsites abundant. Fishing is fair to good for brook and brown trout in the upper reaches and tributaries as well as for smallmouth bass and northern pike in the lower sections.

M-73 BRIDGE to M-189 BRIDGE
13 MILES / 4 – 6 HOURS

This uppermost section of navigable river is a little more than 2 miles below the source at Brule Lake. There is no access or parking at the M-73 Bridge, but just inside the Wisconsin border, a U.S. Forest Service Campground 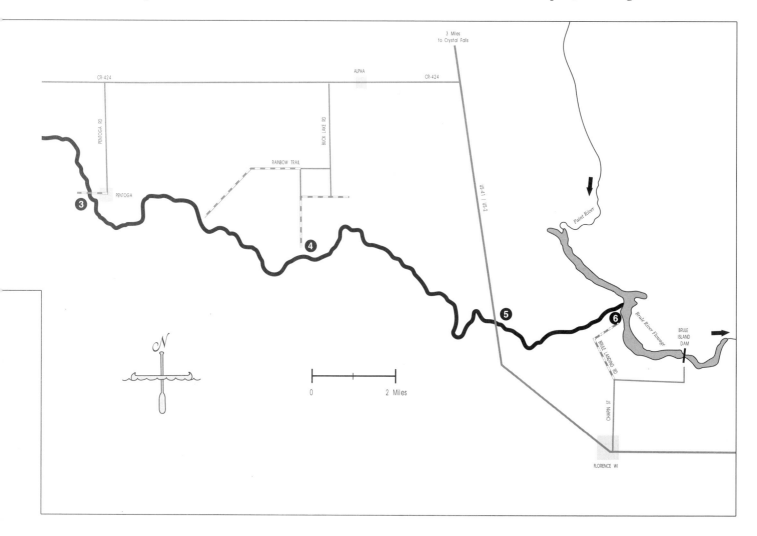 has campsites a short carry to the river. As an alternative, continue south on M-73 (Wisconsin-55) about 5 miles into Wisconsin to FS-2457, then take 5 miles of good dirt road to the FS-2172 landing. There is good access and limited parking at this site, on the Wisconsin side of the river.

The Brule through this section is 30 – 50 feet wide and 1 – 2 feet deep over sand, gravel and small-stone bottom. Water is clean but stained dark. Shallow, light rapids and riffles alternate with slower, deeper water here and throughout much of the river's length. In the upper section during periods of low water, expect to scrape frequently. Terrain is low hills of mixed hardwoods and conifers with tag alders at the banks.

There is a possible access site at the washed-out Ford Bridge, reached by Brule River Road, but the road is narrow and brushy, and parking is limited and remote. The river immediately below the bridge is narrow and fairly tricky at tight bends and at short, Class-I rapids.

At M-189 Bridge ❷ (Wisconsin-139) take out on the right downstream side. Access and parking are good at a small site beside the highway.

M-189 BRIDGE to PENTOGA BRIDGE
12 MILES / 4 – 6 HOURS

In this section the river becomes noticeably deeper and faster after being joined by several tributaries, most notably the Iron River. From here downstream, there should be enough water even during dry seasons for pleasurable paddling. The Iron River contributes some cloudiness to the Brule, but it is considerably cleaner than when we saw it in 1985.

Don't look for a bridge at Scott's Landing; it washed out years ago. Fairly good access and limited parking are found on the Michigan side. Most of the Scott Lake area is farmlands, with pastures and meadows to the river in several stretches. Otherwise, occasional hardwood stands and patches of tag alder and cedar border the river.

Below Scott's Landing are several stretches of fairly easy Class I rapids with medium-size boulders to avoid. Fisherman's Eddy Rapids is a Class I rock garden where the river makes a sharp right bend; a deep pool and Fisherman's Eddy are at the bottom of the rapids, on the right. These and other

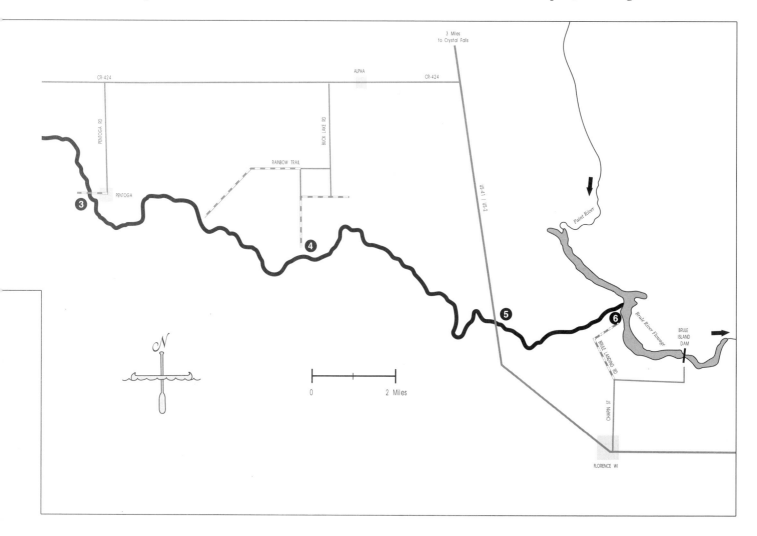

rapids from here to Pentoga should not be difficult for moderately experienced paddlers during normal water levels; use caution during high water. Steep, overgrown banks—mostly wooded with hardwoods and tag alders in this stretch—make access to shore difficult. An abandoned railroad bed that follows the left shore the entire distance to Pentoga can be utilized in emergencies.

At Pentoga, ❸ the one-lane bridge is below several channels and islands as well as a large eddy at the site of an old dam. Take out on the right (Wisconsin) side, upstream from the bridge. Use caution if you choose to continue beneath the bridge—low clearance and quick water can be tricky. Access at the bridge is good on the Wisconsin side, but parking is very limited.

PENTOGA BRIDGE to US-2 BRIDGE
13.5 MILES / 4 – 6 HOURS

Below Pentoga the character of the river and terrain alters little. About 2 miles downstream, watch for a 2-foot ledge drop that can be tricky and is usually rated Class II. It can be run on the right-center at the most prominent chute. However, during heavy flow high waves develop that are capable of swamping an open canoe. If in doubt, portage on the right. Light rapids and riffles continue downstream.

Rainbow Trail (FS-2150) has fair access and parking on both the Michigan and Wisconsin sides of the river. The bridge is out. Current is generally fairly quick in this area, with some shallow riffles requiring careful navigating in low water.

Carney Dam Public Access Site ❹ has good access, parking, and a vault toilet on the Michigan side. There is no existing dam. Below here the river tends to slow, but there are still intervals of quick rocky runs and small riffles. Width averages 75 – 100 feet, and depths vary from 1 – 6 feet. There are very few acceptable campsites in this section.

Access at US-2 ❺ is on the left,

downstream side of the bridge. Parking is good but limited.

US-2 BRIDGE to BRULE RIVER FLOWAGE
4.5 MILES / 1 ½ – 3 HOURS

Below US-2, riffles and stretches of consistent, steady current continue 2 miles to La Chapelle Rapids. These rocky rapids extend for several hundred feet and generally rate Class I-II. In high water, inexperienced paddlers may wish to avoid the standing waves. Scout or portage on the right. Light rapids and riffles extend most of the way to Brule River Flowage.

On the Wisconsin shore, a short distance after the river enters Brule River Flowage (and past the site of the former Washburn Bridge, which is now out) is Wisconsin Electric Recreation Area 28, ❻ with good access, plenty of parking, and vault toilets.

To continue to the dam, follow the right shore for 2 miles. The broad inlet to the north is the Paint River. At the dam, portage on the right and follow the "Canoe Portage" signs, but expect a long hike. The final leg down to the river below the dam is very steep and the trail is full of loose gravel. Wisconsin Electric has provided several benches along the way, with cross-tees for leaning canoes against while you rest.

Because of the steep climb and the long trail to the road, Brule Island Dam is not a good choice for taking out of the Brule or for putting in for a trip downstream on the Menominee.

BRULE ISLAND DAM to MENOMINEE RIVER
RAPIDS (not on map)

Although the Menominee River does not actually begin until about 2 miles below the Brule Dam, where the Michigamme River joins the Brule, this entire section of river is big water and deserves to be treated with caution. Inexperienced paddlers should end their trip at the Brule River Flowage.

We have chosen not to include the

Menominee River proper—which is generally wide, slow water better suited to powerboats than paddlecraft—but two major sets of rapids deserve to be mentioned. The first of these are Big Bull Rapids, 1 mile below the junction with the Michigamme River. These rapids are rated Class III, but in the Menominee's large water volume, they are much more difficult and dangerous than Class III rapids on smaller rivers. Use caution and sound judgment. There is a landing on the Wisconsin side about 1 mile below the rapids.

The second notable rapids are at Piers Gorge, located south of the town of Norway, in Dickinson County, 28 miles below the junction of the Brule and the Michigamme rivers. These half-mile rapids are some of Michigan's fiercest stretches of river and rate Class III-IV. They follow Class II-III rapids called Sand Portage Falls, a few miles below Little Quinnesac Falls Dam. There is good access to the Piers Gorge area at a public site reached off US-8 before it crosses the river into Wisconsin.

The rapids at Piers Gorge are a series of drops and chutes—beginning with 8-foot-high Misicot Falls—with backrollers, souse holes and other hazards present in large numbers, even in low water. This entire stretch should be carefully scouted from the left bank and should be run only by advanced whitewater paddlers in kayaks, inflatable rafts, or covered canoes. All others will probably be content to view the rapids from the safety of the trails and observation points on the Michigan side of the river.

ESCANABA RIVER

COUNTIES: Marquette, Delta
START/END: Gwinn Community Park to CR-420 Bridge
MILES: 46
GRADIENT: Gwinn to Boney Falls—5.9 ft/mile
          Boney Falls to CR-420 —10.6 ft/mile
RAPIDS/FALLS: Unnamed rapids below Gwinn—Class I-II
          Unnamed rapids before the junction with the West Branch—Class I-II
          Unnamed rapids before Boney Falls Basin—Class I-II
          Unnamed rapids below Boney Falls Dam—Class II-IV
CAMPGROUNDS: Few
CANOE LIVERIES: None
SKILL REQUIRED: II

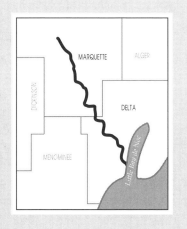

The Escanaba is among the Upper Peninsula's finest and longest river systems, as well as one of the most important for both recreation and power production. Much of its popularity is due to location: It flows between Marquette and Escanaba, the two largest Upper Peninsula cities, and runs roughly parallel with M-35, the major north/south highway in the central U.P.

The Middle Branch begins in lakes north of the town of Champion, about 20 miles west of Marquette. Although we have heard that the many miles of river between Champion and Gwinn are navigable by canoe, we chose to bypass that section because of long stretches of shallow rock ledges, falls, and extremely narrow gorges that appear impassable, and also because of reports of extensive logjams and fallen trees. Below Gwinn the river is quite large and flows through remote country with a variety of forests and terrain before ending at a series of dams and reservoirs in Escanaba. The entire Escanaba system is prone to low water, and there are many shallow riffles that will need to be walked through in summer. Remote country and several rapids make it a poor choice for inexperienced paddlers, and during high water, rapids—especially below Boney Falls Dam—will prove difficult even for those with much experience.

Campgrounds and abundant public land make long expeditions possible. Fishing is for brook and brown trout in most of the mainstream and its tributaries, and smallmouth bass and pike in the lower river and impoundments.

GWINN COMMUNITY PARK (East Branch) to OLD CAMPGROUND
19 MILES / 6 – 8 HOURS

In Gwinn, there is good access and parking at the M-35 Bridge on the west side of town or on the East Branch of the Escanaba at the community park ❶ adjacent to downtown. If you put in on the East Branch expect a short paddle down this small rock and gravel trout stream to the Middle Branch, which from this point is officially considered the mainstream, or Big Escanaba. A mile or so upstream, there is camping at the Gwinn Tourist Park, on Iron Street.

Fishing for brown and brook trout is quite good below Gwinn, with brook trout perhaps predominating. This section requires a full day of fishing and casual paddling. We made it in eight hours of drifting and fishing with a few stops to cast to especially attractive pools.

The river below the junction of the East Branch is 60 – 80 feet wide, with depths of 1 – 4 and 3 – 6 feet, depending on season and dam discharges upstream. The current alternates between very slow and very fast. Immediately below Gwinn all streamside development disappears and the river takes on a wilderness aura. Terrain is largely hilly, with upland forests of pines, spruce, and hardwoods. The bottom is almost entirely rock and gravel, with some sections of fast water studded with boulders.

Shortly below Gwinn is a stretch of rapids with boulders to dodge, but they should present few problems for moderately experienced paddlers, except during very high water. Another set of rapids is located just before the junction with the West Branch. Like most Escanaba rapids, these flow over smooth bedrock, with few rocks to create surface disturbance, yet they can create surprisingly large standing waves. During high water the waves can swamp an open canoe and should be given careful consideration.

Much of this section flows through the Escanaba State Forest, and there are suitable campsites found the entire length. Though no longer maintained, a former DNR access site still serves as access ❷ at the mouth of Sawmill Creek (the first tributary below the Big West Branch). The site is a little difficult to see from the river, so watch for the creek mouth on the left (east) bank.

It is worth noting that the Big West Branch of the Escanaba is sometimes canoed starting at the town of Ralph. Remote country and a series of state-forest campgrounds along the way make this an appealing trip, and trout fishing is said to be good. However, we found it to be a terribly small stream—8 to 15 feet wide in the upper reaches—and prone to blockage by fallen trees. Also, there are stretches of light rapids where jumbles of large, very jagged boulders threaten to batter boats. It is not recommended for leisurely paddling. The final 7 or 8 miles of the Big West is nearly doubled in size by the addition of Bryan Creek near Bridge One on Ross Grade Road. This might be a more navigable stretch, although the shallow ledge-drops visible at the junction of the mainstream look like sure bottom-busters.

Below the mouth of the Big West Branch, the mainstream widens to 100 to 150 feet. From here to Boney Falls Basin, many shallow riffles are found flowing over slab bedrock. In places, the entire river is spread so thinly over the wide river channel that the average depth is measured only in inches. Passage can be maddeningly slow during summer's low water. Even in late spring some years, water levels are low enough to force paddlers to look carefully for the deepest channels.

Access ❸ and parking are good at the site of the old state forest campground at the mouth of Swimming Hole Creek just off River Road. Although the site has no facilities, it still serves as a convenient access point.

OLD CAMPGROUND to BONEY FALLS DAM
10 MILES / 3 ½ – 4 ½ HOURS

Below the old state-forest campground is a long stretch of very shallow riffles—in some places as wide as 250 feet—lined with many cottages or "camps." Some riffles escalate to light rapids over the typical sandwiched ledges. The final mile or two before the backwaters of Boney Falls Basin is one

of the most interesting and beautiful stretches on the Escanaba. It flows between ledges that rise in layers—like patios and verandas—that step from the river to grassy slopes backing up to a forest of spruce, pine, poplar, and hardwoods. The ledges make streamside passage so convenient that it is possible to walk leisurely along the entire length of this stretch. Ideal campsites are plentiful. The river is quick, with several short rapids that can create large standing waves in high water.

The Basin is about a 2-mile crossing. Paddlers intending to end their trip here should take out at the public access site ❹ and Upper Peninsula Power Company (UPPC) campground on the right (west) shore, halfway down the impoundment, where there is excellent access and parking, with drinking water and vault toilets. No fees or permits are required.

To continue, portage the dam at the marked trail on the left. The portage is moderately difficult down a steep trail and ledge steps.

Access to the parking area at the right side of Boney Falls Dam is extremely difficult from the river due to 8- to 10-foot-high sheer cliffs, but good access is available at a narrow landing on river right one-tenth of a mile below the dam, where a narrow two-track ends at the river.

BONEY FALLS DAM to CR-420 PUBLIC ACCESS
17 MILES / 5-6 HOURS

To begin a trip at Boney Falls put in at the narrow, unmarked landing on river right, one-tenth of a mile below the dam. An alternative is to put in at the UPPC campground on the west side of Boney Falls Basin and portage the dam on the left.

The river immediately below the dam contains a set of potentially dangerous rapids over ledges and some boulders. Even in low water, the standing waves are capable of swamping an open canoe; during high water when all the turbines

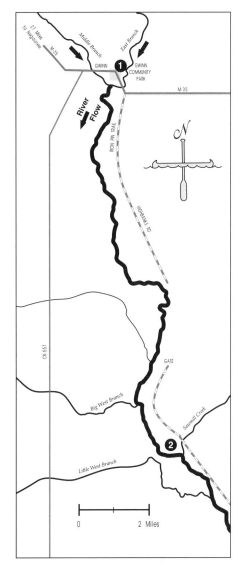

in the powerhouse are operating, awesome waves are sometimes created, raising the rapids to a potential Class IV rating. There is also a danger of sudden discharges, which occur at no set schedule. A warning horn sounds moments before each release, and the resulting rush of water, we were told, is sufficient to overtake and swamp a canoe.

In spite of the hazards, however, this is a breathtaking stretch of river. It flows for almost 2 miles through a gorge framed by sheer 8- to 20-foot-high rock sides and past numerous waterfalls—some quite spectacular—descending from small creeks and streams. In the event of mishap, rescue would be difficult.

Access is virtually impossible at CR-430 Bridge (Robin G. Road), about a mile below the dam. A mile below that

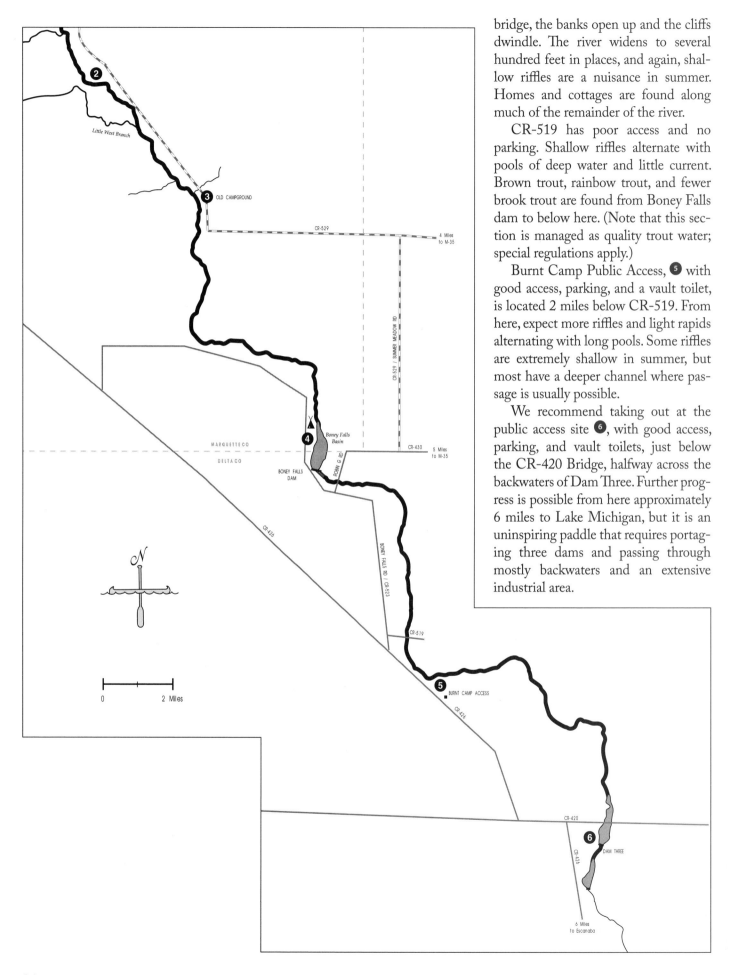

bridge, the banks open up and the cliffs dwindle. The river widens to several hundred feet in places, and again, shallow riffles are a nuisance in summer. Homes and cottages are found along much of the remainder of the river.

CR-519 has poor access and no parking. Shallow riffles alternate with pools of deep water and little current. Brown trout, rainbow trout, and fewer brook trout are found from Boney Falls dam to below here. (Note that this section is managed as quality trout water; special regulations apply.)

Burnt Camp Public Access, ❺ with good access, parking, and a vault toilet, is located 2 miles below CR-519. From here, expect more riffles and light rapids alternating with long pools. Some riffles are extremely shallow in summer, but most have a deeper channel where passage is usually possible.

We recommend taking out at the public access site ❻, with good access, parking, and vault toilets, just below the CR-420 Bridge, halfway across the backwaters of Dam Three. Further progress is possible from here approximately 6 miles to Lake Michigan, but it is an uninspiring paddle that requires portaging three dams and passing through mostly backwaters and an extensive industrial area.

FORD RIVER

COUNTY: Delta
START/END: CR-414 Bridge to M-35 Bridge (mouth of river)
MILES: 14.75
GRADIENT: CR-414 to US-2—7.9 ft/mile
US-2 to mouth—10.9 ft/mile
PORTAGES: None
RAPIDS/FALLS: Unnamed rapids below US-2—Class II-III
               Several unnamed rapids below US-2—Class I-II
CAMPGROUNDS: None
CANOE LIVERIES: None
SKILL REQUIRED: I-II
TOPO. MAPS: Gladstone, Escanaba (15 min.)

Like many Upper Peninsula rivers, the Ford is quite seasonal, and midsummer paddlers should be prepared to walk through shallow riffles and rock gardens. Generally, it is a quick-spirited, riffle-and-pool river with slightly tea-colored water. Most of it flows through private land with limited camping opportunities. Fishing is for brook trout in the upper reaches, and smallmouth bass and occasional northern pike in the lower.

The most remote section of the Ford can only be paddled during periods of high water. It is reached by a bridge on an unnamed gravel road that runs west of a railroad siding called Woodlawn, on CR-426 north of Cornell. The river here flows quickly over gravel and rock, but even by the beginning of June, when we were there, water levels are often insufficient to float a canoe. That, coupled with difficulty of access and parking at the bridge because of private property, caused us to begin our trip 17 miles downstream.

CR-414 to US-2 BRIDGE
7.5 MILES / 3 – 4 HOURS

Access ❶ is fairly good at CR-414 at an often-used parking area on the upstream, right side of the bridge, on private property. The owners, who live in the house adjacent, allow paddlers to use the site and park overnight; please respect their property.

From here the current is quick over mostly gravel bottom, but it gives way soon to slow water over sand bottom. In the slow stretches, the river meanders through lowland forests punctuated by a few open meadows. Occasional fallen trees and minor logjams create partial obstructions, but at 40-90 feet the river is generally wide enough to allow free passage. From CR-414 to the mouth of the river, at the town of Ford River, we found no obstructions that required portaging, although it is likely that the long, remote, and less-often-floated section above 414 will have some.

CR-537, 2.5 miles downstream from CR-414, has fair access and roadside parking. Another 2.5 miles downstream is the CR-533 Bridge with no access.

From here to US-2, expect more or less continuous light rapids and riffles over gravel and bedrock. Stretches flow between flat ledge formations similar to those found on the Escanaba River. Homes and cottages are scattered along the entire length of the river, though not in large numbers.

At US-2 access and parking are good upstream and left of the bridge at the carpool parking lot, ❷.

US-2 BRIDGE to M-35 ACCESS SITE
7 ¼ MILES / 3 – 4 HOURS

This is the fastest section of the Ford and should not be attempted by beginning paddlers during high water conditions. There are long stretches of nearly continuous light rapids and riffles, and even the intervals of slower water are over rock and gravel bottom. Many of the riffles are shallow but runnable well into June, most years. The rapids are generally straightforward and easily negotiated by paddlers with average whitewater skills.

The exception is a short drop of intense water encountered about halfway through the section. These unnamed rapids are formed by a pair of ledge-drops at a point where the river narrows between other ledges. It is easily recognized, coming after the river divides around a large island, converges, then bends to the right at the rapids. At least one source lists these rapids as Class II-III because of the high waves that develop. Even in relatively low water, the waves are substantial and—since they do not look large from above—come as a surprise. Scouting is recommended. Portage either right or left.

After these rapids, light rapids continue for a mile or more, with descent gradually increasing until it is fairly extreme and creates long Class I-II rapids during high-water periods. During low water, expect to have to pick your way through channels between rocks, scraping and bumping along the way. Ledges and low cliffs are, again, similar to those found on the Escanaba.

The lower end of this section slows and deepens, with stretches of riffles getting shorter and more widely spaced. Houses become more frequent.

Access and parking are good at the public site and boat launch ❸ just below M-35 near the town of Ford River.

FOX RIVER

COUNTY: Schoolcraft
START/END: Wagner Dam Access to M-77 Bridge in Germfask
MILES: 32
GRADIENT: 5 ft/mile
PORTAGES: Numerous fallen trees, logjams
RAPIDS/FALLS: None
CAMPGROUNDS: Several
CANOE LIVERIES: One (see Appendix D)
SKILL REQUIRED: I
TOPO. MAPS: Sunken Lake, Seney NW, Seney, Hardwood Island (7.5 min.)

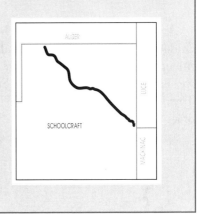

This slow- to moderate-flowing cold-water river has long been known for its outstanding trout fishing. It has also earned fame for being the river Ernest Hemingway had in mind when he wrote his famous short story, "Big Two-Hearted River." Mounted 18- to 20-inch brook trout on the walls of stores and taverns in Seney and Germfask lend credence to the theory that Hemingway wanted to disguise the identity of this great trout stream. The Fox and the Two Hearted are at present the only Michigan Natural Rivers in the Upper Peninsula.

Paddlers will find the Fox to be an interesting and mild-tempered river. Numerous access sites, campgrounds and adjacent roads in the section above Seney tend to diminish the sense of isolation and remoteness that pervades this portion of the Upper Peninsula. Below Seney, however, a total lack of streamside development preserves the more expected atmosphere.

Fallen trees create occasional problems along the entire river. It is best to allow plenty of time and be prepared for frequent short portages and lift-overs. Numerous sunken logs and the remnants of water-control dams are evidence of heavy early twentieth-century logging activities. The surrounding plains in the Seney area are dotted with the aged stumps of pines and hemlocks that once covered the entire region.

Of the several tributaries to the Fox, only the East Branch is navigable, but only in the five-mile section between the mouth of Cold Creek and M-28. It is closed to watercraft above Cold Creek to protect habitat used by brook trout for spawning. Below M-28, fallen trees and other obstructions clog the East Branch and make watercraft impractical.

Water levels in the Fox River system do not fluctuate greatly, and low water is seldom a problem, even in dry summers. Most of the region is within the Grand Sable and Manistique River state forests. Streamside camping possibilities are quite good in spite of large areas of lowlands and mosquito breeding grounds. High, pine-crested knolls open to the wind are recommended, as are liberal supplies of insect repellent.

The entire mainstream and all tributaries of the Fox are designated "Wild-Scenic" by the Michigan Natural Rivers Program.

The Fox River Natural River Plan discourages watercraft use upstream of the Seney Township Campground near M-28, because of the fragile nature of the river there. Although we have included a brief description of this section, we do not recommend paddling it.

WAGNER DAM PUBLIC ACCESS to SENEY TOWNSHIP CAMPGROUND
16 MILES / 11 – 14 HOURS

Expect many fallen trees and logjams in this small, ecologically fragile section.

Access ❶ at Wagner Dam Public Access is good with good parking. The river here is 25 – 35 feet wide and 1 – 4 feet deep with moderate current over sand bottom. Terrain is lowland forests with mixed hardwoods and conifers and very thick undergrowth of tag alders. Deadfalls begin almost immediately, and will need to be skirted or towed over. Dragging a canoe through the undergrowth can be unforgettable during mosquito season. Occasional high banks and clearings lead to stump-dotted plains, but campsites are rare.

The Little Fox River joins the mainstream about 2.5 miles above Fox River State Forest Campground. ❷ Access at the campground is fair, down a steep stairway. Facilities are primitive.

Below the campground, the river remains similar to above, with frequent windfalls blocking the way. Moderate current and sand bottom are consistent throughout. Deep water at the bends makes wading difficult for fishermen.

Three-quarters of a mile above Seney is the Seney Township Campground, ❸ with good access and parking as well as drinking water and vault toilets.

SENEY TOWNSHIP CAMPGROUND to M-77 BRIDGE IN GERMFASK (MANISTIQUE RIVER) 16 MILES / 8 – 10 HOURS

Access is fair at best at the M-28 Bridge and at the bridge on Railroad Street immediately downstream, so we recommend putting in at Seney Township Campground, three-quarters of a mile above M-28.

This is the most remote and least visited section of the Fox. Although we once completed it in 4½ hours of hard paddling, we recommend a much slower pace. Most paddlers find it takes about 10 hours.

The river from here is 40 – 60 feet wide and 2 – 6 feet deep. Bottom is almost entirely sand. Most of the terrain is lowland forests, with large silver maples predominating. Tag alders frequently border the water. Fallen trees are common, though many have been partially cleared.

About 1 mile below Seney is a "spreads" similar to one on the East Branch of the Fox. The river divides and re-divides into channels through a large marshland of grasses and cattails. The prominent channels tend to lead toward the left. Most channels are deep and fairly quick, even when only 3 to 4 feet wide, and there is not much chance of getting stranded or lost.

The remainder of the trip is through lowland forests. A few adequate campsites are found on knolls, where large hemlocks and pines protrude. The sites are not frequent, so it is better to stop at the first or second site after the spreads than risk spending the night on low ground.

The East Branch joins the mainstream just before the junction with the Manistique. It enters on the left and is dark and very slow. The Manistique, which also joins from the left, is clouded and has moderate current.

From here to the town of Germfask, the Manistique River is 60 – 80 feet wide, darkly colored, and flows generally at a moderate rate. Fishing is for pike, bass, walleyes and occasional trout. Deadfalls and jams are piled at the bends and occasionally obstruct passage. There are one or two short stretches of quicker water over rocks.

Near Germfask a few houses appear. There is private access at Northland Outfitters (canoe livery, store, cabins, and private campground) shortly before Ten Curves Road Bridge (CR-498). Access at the bridge is poor.

Good access and parking are found at the roadside park ❹ on the left upstream side of the M-77 Bridge.

Small water on the Upper Fox

INDIAN RIVER

COUNTIES: Alger, Schoolcraft
START/END: Widewaters Campground to Indian Lake
MILES: 36
GRADIENT: 2.4 ft/mile
PORTAGES: Occasional fallen trees
RAPIDS/FALLS: None
CAMPGROUNDS: Several
CANOE LIVERIES: None
SKILL REQUIRED: I-II

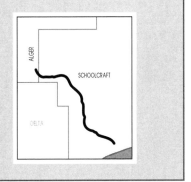

The Indian River is a National Scenic River from its origin at Hovey Lake in Alger County to Indian Lake. Because it is small and plagued by fallen trees, it would probably not be navigable except for the efforts of the U.S. Forest Service. Trees that fall due to bank erosion are regularly cleared by forest-service crews. The river lies almost entirely within the Hiawatha National Forest, and numerous access sites and excellent campgrounds are conveniently located for paddlers.

Generally, the river maintains a steady, moderately strong current, has a bottom of mixed sand and gravel, and flows through upland forests of jack pines and hardwoods. Water quality appears good and, though slightly tea-colored, the water is much clearer than many Upper Peninsula rivers. Water flow is relatively stable, making the river an excellent midsummer choice for canoeists.

Fishing is for brown and brook trout and was once considered outstanding. Erosion, however, has caused sand to choke many of the gravel stretches essential for spawning, and as a result, trout populations have suffered. Efforts have been made to halt this erosion, and it is particularly important that canoeists and fishermen avoid walking on the sand banks found at almost every bend in this river.

WIDEWATERS CAMPGROUND to THUNDER LAKE ROAD BRIDGE
12 MILES / 5 – 7 HOURS

This might be the most beautiful headwaters you can paddle on any Michigan river—a series of ponds and small lakes strung like a necklace beneath stands of mature pines. Put in either at the public access site at beautiful Widewaters USFS Campground ❶ or one-half mile upstream at Fish Lake Public Access. Between Fish Lake and the campground, the river progresses through small lakes connected by narrow channels with little current. Below the campground the river narrows and current increases to flow steadily over sand bottom, with some stretches of light riffles over gravel and stone. Some fairly fast riffles are found just above FH-13, where there is fair access and roadside parking. The terrain along this section, as along much of the river, is upland forest of low hills and hardwoods with scattered birch, poplar, and pines. Some tag alders and cedars line the banks. The river is small—15- to 30-feet wide—with depths of 1 to 3 feet.

One to two hours below Widewaters is Tommy Page Bridge ❷ on FS-2258, where there is good access but limited roadside parking. From here, and at scattered intervals, are twelve "dispersed" USFS campsites along the river. The USFS asks that campers stay only in these designated sites, on a first-come-first-serve basis. No fee or permit is required.

By Tommy Page Bridge the river has gained volume from lake outlets and tributary streams and has increased to 30 – 50 feet wide, with depths of 1 – 3 feet. Shortly before the bridge a channel allows access to Straights Lake, which in turn leads to several other lakes. Most of the property around the lakes, however, is privately owned, and several cabins line the shores. There are also a few houses and cabins beside the river in this area; otherwise, it remains within the national forest. Deadfalls and sweepers are frequent, but most have at least a narrow passage cleared. Basic maneuvering abilities will get most paddlers through with little trouble. McCormack Canoe Access is located about two-thirds of the way through this section, off Little Indian Road. A short stairway leads to the river, and there is good parking, vault toilets, and an unofficial campsite.

Access ❸ at Thunder Lake Road (CR-437) is good, with adequate parking beside the river on the left, before the bridge.

THUNDER LAKE ROAD BRIDGE to EIGHT MILE BRIDGE
16 MILES / 7 – 9 HOURS

The river remains similar in size and character from Thunder Lake Road to below the town of Steuben. Although

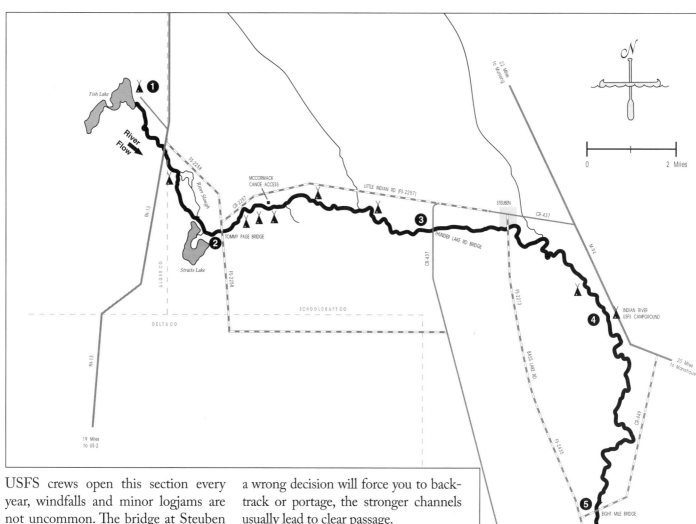

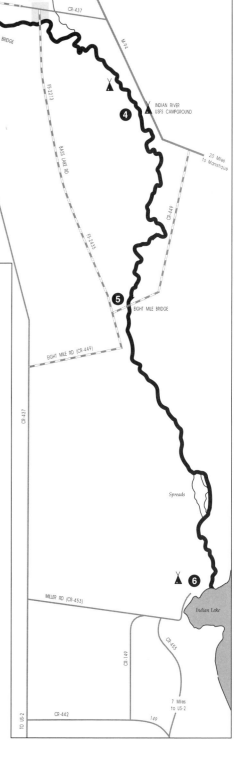

USFS crews open this section every year, windfalls and minor logjams are not uncommon. The bridge at Steuben has poor access and poor parking.

Set beneath stately pines, Indian River USFS Campground ❹ has fair access down wooden stairs at the back of campsite #5. It can be difficult to see from the river. Look for wooden bank stabilizers and the wooden stairs.

Below the picnic area and campground, expect a 2- to 3-hour float to Eight Mile Bridge. 5 The river continues to flow through pine and hardwood forest, though the banks become steeper and the river slightly faster and more narrow. Very tight bends and frequent, partially cleared deadfalls call for fairly complex maneuvering. Beginners may have difficulty, although it should be no problem for those with intermediate or higher skills. The wooded hills give way gradually to marshlands and the current slows. Just before Eight Mile Bridge and beyond to Indian Lake, the river divides into spreads with narrow channels winding through the marsh grasses. Although

a wrong decision will force you to back-track or portage, the stronger channels usually lead to clear passage.

At Eight Mile Bridge, take out on the pine-wooded point just upstream on the left, where access is good and parking is adequate for three or four vehicles.

EIGHT MILE BRIDGE to INDIAN LAKE
8 MILES / 4 – 6 HOURS

Marshes continue through this entire section to Indian Lake. It contains a second area of spreads that is more extensive and complex than the one above and can be confusing.

At Indian Lake, hug the right (west) shoreline 2 miles to the public access site at Palms Book State Park, ❻ where there are camping and picnicking facilities. Use caution on the open lake where large waves can occur.

The river below Indian Lake is wide, slow, and joins the Manistique River a few miles downstream near the city of Manistique.

MANISTIQUE RIVER

COUNTIES: Luce, Schoolcraft
START/END: Ten Curves Road Access to City of Manistique
MILES: 67
GRADIENT: 1.5 ft/mile
PORTAGES: One dam, easy
RAPIDS/FALLS: None
CAMPGROUNDS: Several
CANOE LIVERIES: One (see Appendix D)
SKILL REQUIRED: I

Emerging from the west end of Manistique Lake, the Manistique River flows southwest to the city of Manistique, at Lake Michigan. Through most of its length after the junction with the Fox River, the Manistique has slow to moderate current and sand bottom, making it well suited for combined camping and fishing trips by paddlers of all abilities. Veterans of Fox River trips will be glad to know that fallen trees and logjams do not obstruct the Manistique.

Fishing is primarily for pike, bass, and walleyes, with some trout in the upper reaches. Camping possibilities are good to excellent except in the 10 miles of Seney Wildlife Refuge below M-77, where it is prohibited, and in the lower river, where lowland and swamps limit dry access.

TEN CURVES ROAD (CR-498) ACCESS to MEAD CREEK CAMPGROUND
16 MILES / 5 – 7 HOURS

Put in at the public access site ❶ on Ten Curves Road 2.5 miles east of Germfask. This is the Lake Branch of the Manistique and although it may be possible to start a few miles upstream at Manistique Lake, it is not a large river and may be obstructed by fallen trees above, and for a short distance below, the access site.

A few bends below the bridge on Ten Curves Road is a low-head dam that can be portaged on the right. Just below the dam is the junction with the Fox River. From here, the Manistique is always large enough for unobstructed passage.

Average width is 60 – 80 feet with depths of 2 – 8 feet. In the Lake Branch, water tends to be discolored—stained dark from the Fox—and clouded, with almost a milky hue. Bottom is primarily sand, except for a few short stretches of gravel and rock above Germfask.

In Germfask, the second bridge at Ten Curves Road has poor access and parking. Access at the M-77 Bridge ❷ is good at Manistique River Roadside Park, where there is drinking water, a picnic area, toilets, and good parking. Access is via a trail that passes behind the restrooms and down a short bank on the upstream left side of the river.

From M-77 to just above Mead Creek Forest Campground, the Manistique passes through the Seney National Wildlife Refuge. Camping is prohibited in the refuge, as is access to the banks. Wildlife is abundant, especially waterfowl. Terrain is low hills of upland forests with hardwoods, birch, spruce, and pine. Cedars predominate in low areas near the river. Some streamside banks are steep and eroding. Fallen trees and logjams are frequent, but the width of the river ensures clear passage. The bottom is almost entirely sand. Current varies from slow to moderate.

Mead Creek State Forest Campground ❸ marks the end of the Seney Wildlife Refuge and the beginning of the Manistique River State Forest. The campground is on the left bank and is obvious from the river. There is a developed access site with good parking, and the campground has primitive facilities with toilets and water.

MEAD CREEK CAMPGROUND to MERWIN CREEK CAMPGROUND
29 MILES / 8 – 12 HOURS

The river remains virtually unchanged through this section. Topography alters slightly to include abandoned farmlands and lowland forests. Riverside Truck Trail (CR-436) and CR-433 parallel the river but do not detract from the sense of isolation and quiet. Surrounding lands are almost entirely within the Manistique River State Forest.

Access and parking are good at Cookson Bridge. ❹ The current here is gentle, bottom is sand, and width is 90 – 120 feet—characteristics that remain basically the same through the remainder of the river.

There is good access at the boat ramp at Merwin Creek State Forest Campground ❺ where campsites are open and airy and located on a low bank above the river. Facilities are primitive with toilets, water, and picnic tables. We ended our trip here, choosing not to continue through the remaining 22 miles of slow water.

MERWIN CREEK CAMPGROUND to CITY OF MANISTIQUE
22 MILES / 7 – 10 HOURS (est.) (Not on Map)

Although our information is incomplete for this section, we were told that the river is wide and slow and passes primarily through lowland forests. The most striking feature of this section is the large number of backwaters or sloughs it contains. Many are large enough to warrant names: Klegstad's Slough, Clear Slough, Catfish Slough, Bear Town Slough, Sturgeon Hole Slough, and Island Slough. This area offers interesting possibilities for exploring and fishing. Most of the region is within the state forest, but campsites are limited because of low ground. Be aware that mosquitoes, black flies, and deer flies can be an annoyance in season.

In Manistique, dams and viaducts make passage difficult. We recommend taking out on the north side of the city at the North Cedar Street Access Site, where parking and access are good. It is preceded by a series of major backwaters and sloughs that include Jamestown Slough and the junction with the Indian River.

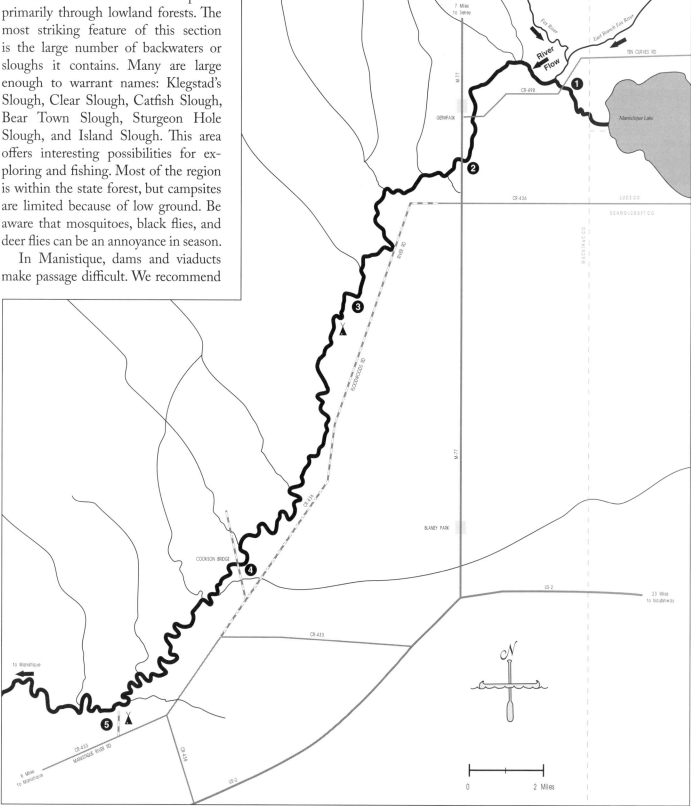

MICHIGAMME RIVER

COUNTIES: Marquette, Dickinson, Iron
START/END: Republic Dam to M-69 Bridge
MILES: 40.5
GRADIENT: Republic Dam to Michigamme Reservoir—8.6 ft/mile
      Hemlock Falls Dam to M-69—4.4 ft/mile
PORTAGES: Two dams, moderately difficult
RAPIDS/FALLS: Witbeck Rapids, above M-95 Bridge—Class I-II
CAMPGROUNDS: None
CANOE LIVERIES: Two (see Appendix D)
SKILL REQUIRED: I-II

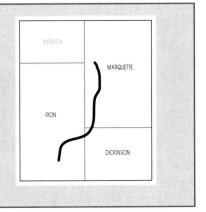

This major tributary of the Menominee River system begins in Lake Michigamme, in western Marquette County. Dams at Lake Michigamme, Republic, Michigamme Reservoir (Way Dam), Hemlock Falls, Peavy Falls and Lower Michigamme Falls interrupt what would otherwise be a fine river for extended expeditions. As it is, paddlers can plan on a several-day trip with almost half the distance through backwaters. Without meaning to discourage such a trip, we must advise that crossings of Michigamme Lake, Michigamme Reservoir and Peavy Reservoir are formidable. Each of these impoundments is a significant wilderness area, with numerous islands, bays and channels that make navigation difficult. The sections of river between the dams are not as isolated and inaccessible as the reservoirs themselves but are interesting and well worth investigating.

It is important to note that the large drainage area of the Michigamme system and the influence of the many dams causes extreme water-level fluctuations. High-water marks are 8 to 10 feet above normal summer levels and indicate that this otherwise hospitable river might not be kind to beginners in the spring. Several light rapids and a slightly more difficult stretch at Witbeck Rapids should not be difficult at normal water levels for paddlers with average ability.

Fishing in the river and impoundments is outstanding for walleye, pike, smallmouth bass and muskie, with occasional trout reported in the river below Hemlock Falls Dam.

REPUBLIC DAM to MICHIGAMME RESERVOIR
25 MILES / 8 – 12 HOURS

The river above Republic is navigable as far upstream as Lake Michigamme, but access is so difficult we chose not to include that section in this description. An ambitious alternative is to put in to Lake Michigamme at the state park off US-41 west of Marquette, make the long, difficult crossing of the reservoir, portage the dam, and continue downstream on the river.

Access in and near Republic is complicated by iron-mining operations with barricaded access roads and a series of backwaters in the shadows of slag heaps from Republic Mine. One alternative is to put in at Munson Park ❶ near the tiny downtown district, and paddle south through the narrows of Michigamme Basin and across a mile

and a half of backwaters to Republic Dam. To bypass the backwaters, put in at the bridge on Willow Drive, a short distance below the dam, where access is fair and parking limited to a small lot.

Below Republic Dam the river is 60 – 75 feet wide, shallow, and rocky with slow to steady current. Water is clear. Terrain alternates open meadows with thickets and woodlots of hardwoods. From Republic to Witbeck Rapids, shallow riffles alternate with long, deep pools, some as large as small lakes. Banks are lightly developed, with only a few houses and farms visible from the river.

Halfway to Witbeck Rapids is a state roadside park ❷ with access, parking, water, toilets, and picnic area. The river here spreads wide, is very shallow, and may need to be walked through during low-water periods. It is followed by long stretches of still water to Witbeck.

Witbeck Rapids Public Access ❸ has

good access and parking with vault toilets just upstream of the rapids. The rapids consist of a series of dense rock gardens with table-size to automobile-size boulders stacked to form natural reefs. Passage is through channels and short, quick chutes in and among the rocks. At least one short portage is required during low water. Most of the stretch can be tricky—if not treacherous—during high water because of tight corridors, sharp drops and the need for precise maneuvering. Current is only moderately fast during normal water levels but increases dramatically as the levels go up. Rapids extend for over a mile, then the river slows and deepens before the M-95 Bridge south of Witch Lake.

M-95 Bridge has poor access and parking along the highway and is not recommended. Newberg Road Bridge has poor access and very limited parking.

Below M-95, generally slow to

moderate current gives way to still water as the river widens and deepens entering Michigamme Reservoir. At the upper end of the reservoir, off Race Landing Road, is good access and parking, with vault toilets, at Wisconsin Electric (WE) Public Recreation Area 29 ❹. Take out here or continue the eight miles across Michigamme Reservoir to Way Dam. If you continue across the reservoir (we didn't), plan on adding 3 or 4 hours to your trip. Four WE campgrounds are scattered along the south shore of the reservoir. Another is located beside the river immediately below Way Dam.

WAY DAM to M-69 BRIDGE
7.5 MILES / 2 ½ – 3 ½ HOURS

Below Way Dam are 3 miles of slow river and backwaters before Hemlock Falls Dam. ❺ Portage this dam on the right and follow the gravel road downhill and to the left. There is good access and parking at the end of Stream Road. The river here is 80 – 125 feet wide, 1 – 2 feet deep in the riffles, and 3 – 6 feet deep in the slow pools. From the dam to the bridge at M-69 is an easy float through

alternating riffles and pools, with light Class I rapids shortly below the dam and near Old 69 Bridge. Basic paddling skills are sufficient. Bottom is generally gravel and stone. Terrain is hills, some large, of hardwoods. Occasional houses and cabins are visible from the river. There is reported to be excellent fishing for pike, smallmouth bass, muskie, and occasional rainbow and brown trout.

Access and parking are fair at Old M-69 Bridge. Two miles farther, at M-69 Bridge, ❻ is Michi-Aho Resort, with a canoe livery, lodging, and tackle shop, where access and parking are available with permission.

Below M-69, the backwaters of Peavy Pond begin almost immediately and extend for 9 miles to Peavy Falls Dam. Many older county and topographical maps will have "Glidden Rapids" marked just below M-69, but these rapids are now submerged under the backwaters.

Below Peavy Falls Dam is another three miles of backwaters before Michigamme Falls Dam. Immediately below this final dam, the Michigamme River joins with the Brule River to become the Menominee.

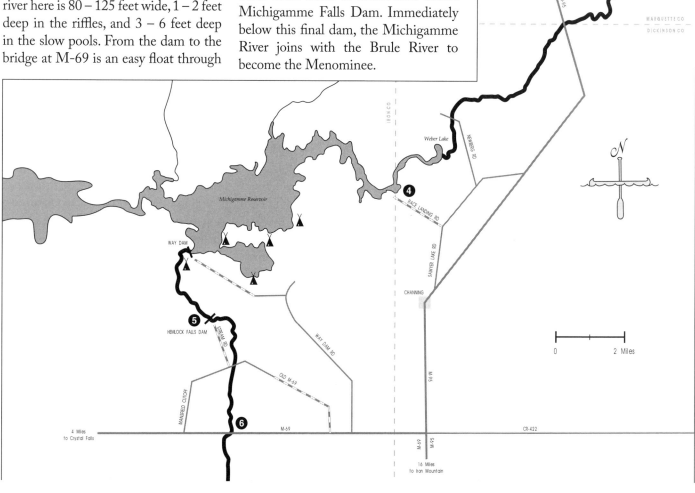

MONTREAL RIVER

COUNTY: Gogebic
START/END: US-2 Bridge (West Branch) to Lake Superior Road Bridge
MILES: 16.5
GRADIENT: US-2 to Saxon Falls Power Dam—10.8 ft/mile
　　　　　　　Saxon Falls Dam to Lake Superior Road—40 ft/mile
PORTAGES: Saxon Dam and Falls, difficult
CAMPGROUNDS: None
CANOE LIVERIES: None
SKILL REQUIRED: II-III
TOPO. MAPS: Ironwood, Little Girls Point (15 min.)

L ike the Menominee and Brule rivers, the Montreal forms a boundary between Michigan and Wisconsin and is claimed by paddlers from both states. This westernmost Michigan river is also one of the state's most spectacular. The final 3.5-mile section above Lake Superior is an unforgettable, nearly continuous run of Class I-III rapids through a deep gorge in remote, seldom-visited country.

Upstream, the Montreal has many Class I rapids and riffles and passes through equally remote, though less spectacular, country. In the cities of Ironwood, Michigan, and Hurley, Wisconsin, the Montreal has been the site of kayak and canoe whitewater competition but is only runnable in this area for short periods each year. We were there in September and again at the beginning of June, and water levels were too low for practical navigating both months.

Generally, only consider the river below the junction with the West Branch to be consistently runnable, with only the lower section below Saxon Falls runnable during very dry seasons. Whitewater fanatics would do well to contact the Ironwood Chamber of Commerce, local DNR, and USFS field offices for up-to-the-minute reports on the upper sections that include Ironwood and, below it, Interstate Falls. (See Appendix C: Further Information.)

Fishing is for brook and brown trout. Camping facilities are limited, but the river passes through public land where there are abundant riverside campsites. The municipal campground in Ironwood is conveniently located but plagued by traffic noise. A much better atmosphere is found at Little Girls Point—five miles northeast of the mouth of the river on Lake Superior Road (CR-505)—where camping and picnicking are on a bluff overlooking Lake Superior.

US-2 (WEST BRANCH) to SAXON FALLS POWER DAM
13 MILES / 3 ½ – 5 ½ HOURS

There is no easy access to this remote, seldom-paddled section. During high water, advanced paddlers can get there by putting in on the mainstream in Ironwood. Otherwise, the best approach is to put in on the little West Branch a mile inside the Wisconsin border and paddle down to the junction with the mainstream. Access is fair with road-side parking beside the bridge along busy US-2. ❶ Note that the river is unmarked on the highway, but a sign for River Road is immediately west of the river crossing. The river is 20 – 30 feet wide, shallow, and very rocky. Water is

Montreal River in the gorge below Saxon Falls

clear and current is fast. During spring or when water is being released from Giles Flowage Dam upstream, this can be a challenging little river. During low water expect to bump and scrape. Tight bends and occasional obstructions require fairly advanced maneuvering skills. Terrain is low hills of hardwoods and mixed conifers with willows common at the banks. The junction with the mainstream is about 1 mile downstream.

During the summer it is not unusual for the mainstream above the junction to be smaller than the West Branch. It also tends to be discolored from red clay and mud. From the junction of the rivers, there are several miles of continuous Class I rapids and rock gardens, some of which are quite shallow during low-water periods. Rocks vary from grapefruit-size to wheelbarrow-size and are jagged. The river is 30 – 40 feet wide and generally clear, although the potential for obstruction from fallen trees exists. High-water marks indicate levels 5 to 6 feet above early summer levels.

Closer to Saxon Flowage the current slows, and sections of light riffles alternate with slow water over sand bottom. Some high banks of eroding clay contribute to the river's discoloration. Rock stretches give way entirely to a narrow backwater before Saxon Flowage, where numerous bays and channels can be confusing, especially during heavy fogs that are not unusual off Lake Superior.

Take out at the boat ramp left of Saxon Falls Dam ❷ where access and parking are good.

Whitewater paddlers wanting to access the Montreal below Saxon Falls will find it among the most difficult-to-reach rivers in Michigan. To put in here follow Saxon Falls Road to the end, turn right and follow the signage to the dam, sub-station, boat landing, and Saxon Falls. (The powerhouse straight ahead, where we recommended access in earlier editions, is now a restricted area with prominent no-trespassing signs.) To reach the river below Saxon Falls Dam requires portaging 350 yards along

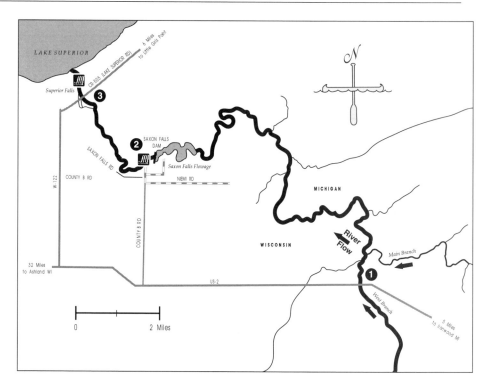

a catwalk on top of a 6-foot-diameter flume that runs from the dam to the power station below the falls. At the end of the flume climb down a 10-foot ladder and take the long and extremely steep steel stairs to the river. This rather arduous route is recommended only for the physically fit.

SAXON FALLS DAM to LAKE SUPERIOR ROAD (CR-505) BRIDGE
3.5 MILES / 2 – 3 HOURS

The Montreal River Gorge is one of the most beautiful places in Michigan and contains one of the state's finest sections of whitewater. Saxon Falls are immediately upstream from the grassy landing at the bottom of the stairs and make an unforgettable sight.

The river from the falls downstream consists of nearly continuous Class I-III rapids for at least three miles, with difficulty dependent upon the amount of water coming over Saxon Falls. According to paddlers who have made the trip many times, when there are three "fingers" of water coming over Saxon Falls, expect a wild trip with much Class III and perhaps, Class IV water. We made the trip twice, both

times when one finger came over the falls, and found it to be a wonderful, fairly challenging run through much Class II-III water. At that level, there were only a few rock gardens and riffles shallow enough to be bottom-draggers and one or two stretches that required short walk-throughs. Even at low levels, however, this is not a section recommended for beginning paddlers or even intermediate paddlers without whitewater experience.

At any water level, numerous chutes with high standing waves and backrollers have the potential to swamp open canoes, and the remoteness of the region and total lack of intermediate access means that, in the event of mishap, a long and difficult hike is necessary to find assistance. Some drops and chutes require scouting at all water levels, and all require care and attention.

The river within the gorge is 50 – 100 feet wide. Water is discolored. Terrain is spectacular with high, sheer cliffs of conglomerate rock rising 100 – 200 feet above the river in many places. Forests of pines and hemlocks dominate the low hills that line the river between bluffs. Through the gorge, high rock walls on one side of the river are usually opposed

One "finger" at Saxon Falls, Montreal River

by lower ground on the other side, so that access to shore is possible in most places. Good potential campsites can be found, but many of the lower banks are covered with thick underbrush.

The river slows and widens shortly before the bridge at Lake Superior Road (CR-505). ❸ Take out upstream, left of the bridge, but note that parking is limited to one or two cars on the roadside. Further progress to Lake Superior is impeded shortly beyond the bridge by a power dam and Superior Falls.

Unnamed Rapids, Montreal River

ONTONAGON RIVER EAST BRANCH

COUNTY: Ontonagon
START/END: FS-208 to US-45 Bridge
MILES: 7.5
GRADIENT: 24 ft/mile
PORTAGES: Occasional fallen trees
RAPIDS/FALLS: Numerous unnamed rapids—Class I-III
CAMPGROUNDS: None
CANOE LIVERIES: None
SKILL REQUIRED: II-III
TOPO. MAPS: Rockland (15 min.)

This small river is noted for having one of the finest and longest stretches of Class II-III rapids in Michigan. Although access is possible as far upstream as the M-28 Bridge in Kenton, extensive logjams and frequent fallen trees make passage difficult and discouraging. The East Branch is a National Wild and Scenic River from its origin in northwest Iron County to the Ottawa National Forest boundary—far upstream of the short section described in this book.

We chose to include only the final 7.5 miles above the junction with the Middle Branch. This remote section of nearly continuous rapids is best run in spring, when the rapids rate Class II-III. Some of the kayakers who paddle the river regularly make a point of paddling it as soon as the ice goes out to take advantage of high water. In summer and fall the rating drops to Class I-II, with passage during very low water difficult and tedious through shallow rock gardens. Only experienced whitewater paddlers should attempt this section during high water.

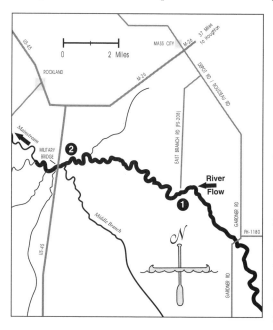

FS-208 ROAD (EAST BRANCH ROAD) to US-45 BRIDGE (MILITARY BRIDGE)
7.5 MILES / 2 ½ – 4 HOURS

The put-in best suited for paddling the 7.5 miles of whitewater is at the site of the washed-out FS-208 Bridge, ❶ reached via a two-track that begins at the end of FS-208 and leads across a gated cow pasture to the river. This is private property, and permission must be obtained from the owner, who lives in the farmhouse on the right, at the end of the paved road.

Should permission be denied or the owner unavailable an alternative is to put in at the bridge on Gardner Road/FH-1180, where access is fair and parking is on the roadside. This will require an additional 7 miles of paddling on slow to moderate current, with fallen trees and other obstructions not uncommon.

The river throughout is 40 – 80 feet wide and the color of coffee with cream. Current is moderate near the FS-208 access but increases quickly downstream. Terrain is mostly low hills of hardwoods with many eroding clay bluffs. Occasional fallen trees partially obstruct the river.

Most of the riverbed is strewn with bushel-basket-size boulders and smaller, many of them quite jagged. The low visibility of the water makes it difficult to detect rocks, especially during low water, and collisions are inevitable. Passage through the rapids is relatively straightforward. Rock gardens and chutes require some precise maneuvering, but the runs are primarily down steep descent through standing waves. The action is fast and relentless for several miles and demands good whitewater skills. Because of the river's nearly due-west course, late-afternoon sun and glare proved a hindrance to us in reading the water. A morning or early afternoon trip would be better.

Take out at the roadside park ❷on the right, before Military Bridge. Access is fair up a steep bank, parking is good, and there are water and toilet facilities as well as a picnic area.

ONTONAGON RIVER MAINSTREAM

COUNTY: Ontonagon

START/END: US-45 Bridge to Ontonagon

MILES: 24

GRADIENT: 2.5 ft/mile

PORTAGES: None

RAPIDS/FALLS: Irish Rapids, 4.5 miles below Victoria Road—Class I-II

Grand Rapids, 7.5 miles below Victoria Road—Class I-II

CAMPGROUNDS: None

CANOE LIVERIES: None

SKILL REQUIRED: I-II

TOPO. MAPS: Rockland, Ontonagon (15 min.)

The mainstream of the Ontonagon and its major tributaries—the East Branch, the Middle Branch and the South Branch—make up one of the most interesting and varied river systems in the Upper Peninsula. The entire system drains an area of 1,340 square miles, bigger than Rhode Island. Remote country, excellent fishing, and many stretches of Class I-III rapids are characteristic of the entire system. Although several dams and waterfalls make extended expeditions difficult, trips of one to several days are possible on each of the branches.

The mainstream begins after the confluence of the East Branch and the Middle Branch at Military Bridge on US-45. This large, generally slow river is the tamest of the major branches, but two sets of rapids may require caution, especially during high water.

Camping possibilities are good on abundant public land along the river. Fishing is excellent for walleye and other warm-water species and for lake-run trout and salmon in April/May and September/October. Angling pressure can be heavy in the vicinity of Military Bridge, but diminishes downstream.

Flatwater paddling on Sunday Lake, in Upper Peninsula whitewater country (photo by Gail Dennis)

US-45 BRIDGE (MILITARY BRIDGE) to CITY OF ONTONAGON
24 MILES / 8 – 10 HOURS

There is a developed roadside park ❶ —with good parking, a picnic area, toilets and water—on the right, upstream side of the river at Military Bridge. Access is only fair down a steep bank. The mouths of the East Branch and Middle Branch are visible just upstream. The river here is 125 to 200 feet wide and flows over light riffles. Visibility is less than 1 foot through red-brown water.

One mile below the put-in, the West Branch (already joined by the South Branch) enters on the left and increases water volume noticeably. Levels on the mainstream are usually sufficient for good floating even during dry summers, although some shallow riffles and sand bars may avoid detection in the discolored water and cause bottom-dragging.

Three and a half miles below US-45 is fair access and good parking on the left upstream side of the Victoria Road Bridge. ❷ This is the last access before Ontonagon and also an alternative put-in for paddlers wishing to reach Ontonagon in one day without hurrying. We made the trip from here in 5½ hours of steady paddling. Current in the final half of the section is nearly nonexistent and will not aid progress. It is also worth noting that prevailing northwest winds can hinder progress significantly; we fought winds strong enough to blow whitecaps on the river.

A few scattered cabins can be seen from the river, but most of the way is through a deep, wooded valley with few signs of habitation or other development. Banks up to 150 feet high or more are wooded with hardwoods and pines; low valleys and banks have hardwoods, birch, pine, and hemlock. Much of the bordering land is in the Ottawa National Forest and the Baraga State Forest. Not far to the west is Porcupine Mountains State Park. Good campsites are abundant on low, wooded banks and frequent large sandbars. The river alternates long stretches of slow water with short, light riffles.

Irish Rapids are 8 miles below US-45. During low water, take the right channel around the island at midriver, where most of the water volume is forced—the shallow riffles to the left will probably not float a canoe. Standing waves in the channel may create difficulties for beginners even during low water. During high water they have the capacity to swamp open canoes and should be scouted from the right bank. The length of the rapids is only a few hundred feet, and portaging would not be difficult.

Grand Rapids are 3 miles below Irish Rapids and are preceded by long stretches of slow water. These several-hundred-yard-long rapids are formed by a series of low rock shelves. The river is wide over them, creating very shallow water in summer with no obvious channels or chutes. During high water, standing waves develop that could be difficult. Light riffles continue downstream, with several islands immediately below the rapids.

The remainder of the river is generally deep and wide (from 300 to 500 feet), with slow to barely noticeable current. Terrain becomes gradually lower with many eroding clay banks. Large sandbars at nearly every bend create ideal campsites at most water levels. Power boats frequently come upriver the final few miles from Ontonagon.

In Ontonagon, there is public access and parking ❸ at the community park and marina on the left past the big highway bridge and railroad trestle.

LAKE SUPERIOR

LAKESHORE RD

❸ ONTONAGON

US-45

Grand Rapids

N

0   2 Miles

Irish Rapids

US-45

ROCKLAND

M-26

River Flow

US-45

❷

VICTORIA RD

MILITARY BRIDGE

❶ East Branch

Middle Branch

Flume

Victoria Basin

VICTORIA DAM

ONTONAGON RIVER MIDDLE BRANCH

COUNTIES: Gogebic, Ontonagon
START/END: Watersmeet to Bond Falls Dam
MILES: 20.25
GRADIENT: Watersmeet to Burned Dam Campground—2.2 ft/mile
  Burned Dam to Bond Falls Flowage—7.3 ft/mile
PORTAGES: 2-3 small falls, fairly easy; occasional fallen trees
RAPIDS/FALLS: Several unnamed rapids below Burned Dam Campground—Class I-II
  Little Falls, just before Bond Falls Flowage—Class II
  Mex-i-min-e Falls, at Burned Dam Campground
CAMPGROUNDS: One
CANOE LIVERIES: One (see Appendix D)
SKILL REQUIRED: II
TOPO. MAPS: Watersmeet (15 min.)

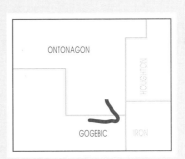

This small, clear trout stream begins at Crooked Lake, in the Sylvania Tract Recreation Area, but is not large enough to be navigable until 10 miles downstream near the town of Watersmeet. From Watersmeet, there are about 50 miles of river until the junction with the East Branch near Military Bridge, but only the section to Bond Falls Flowage is consistently navigable at this time. At Bond Falls Flowage, at least half the water in the Middle Branch has for years been diverted via a flume to the South Branch, leaving the Middle Branch downstream depleted.

Water levels above Bond Falls are consistently high enough for good paddling, even in midsummer. Several short rapids and occasional tight bends require basic paddling skills, especially below Burned Dam Campground. The ledge-drops at Little Falls, before Bond Falls Flowage, should be portaged by all but experienced whitewater paddlers. Good streamside campsites are available on public land in the Ottawa National Forest and at Burned Dam Campground. Fishing is excellent for brook trout, with browns and rainbows also present.

The entire Middle Branch from its origin to the northern boundary of the Ottawa National Forest—including the entire portion described in this book—is designated a National Wild and Scenic River.

WATERSMEET to BURNED DAM USFS CAMPGROUND
9.25 MILES / 4 – 5 HOURS

Good access and parking are found at the public site at the US-45 Bridge ❶ in Watersmeet. Here the river is 15 – 25 feet wide and 2 – 4 feet deep over sand and gravel bottom. Water is clear, though slightly tea colored. Current is slow to moderate, with several short chutes and drops of fast water that will not be difficult for moderately experienced paddlers. Terrain is generally low hills of hardwoods away from the river, with tag alders and cedars predominant near the water.

At Buck Lake Road Bridge access is poor with no parking. Below here are several miles of slow, wide river through marshlands. The river is paralleled by Old US-2 (CR-208), and occasional houses and cabins are visible from the river. After a low railroad trestle the river narrows, and current increases over mild riffles.

Burned Dam USFS Campground ❷ is at Mex-i-min-e Falls. The falls are a short, furious drop that could be run by advanced paddlers in covered boats but should be portaged by all others. The portage trail is on the right and is about 100 yards long. Camping facilities are primitive, with outhouses and no water.

BURNED DAM USFS CAMPGROUND to BOND FALLS DAM
11 MILES / 4 – 5 HOURS

This section is highlighted by several moderately difficult Class I-II rapids.

Tight bends, minor logjams, and occasional fallen trees combine with the rapids to make this the most difficult portion of the river and one that is not recommended for beginners. The longest set of rapids are 1½ hours below Mex-i-min-e Falls and are a 300- to 400-foot-long run of steep descent with standing waves and exposed rocks. Not much maneuvering is required—stay to the center but watch for a large rock midstream at the bottom of the run. Other short rapids follow in succession, alternating with stretches of slow water.

Those who wish to avoid the rapids before Bond Falls Flowage and the long crossing of the reservoir should take out at Interior Road Bridge ❸ (FH-5250), where there is good access and a small parking area above the bridge on the right. Fairly fast water below the bridge gives way to slower water through low-lands of silver maple, where fallen trees are not uncommon. Several trees and minor jams may require short portages.

About an hour below Interior Bridge, just before the river enters Bond Falls Flowage, are several sets of rapids at Little Falls. During high water, only one drop is visible; during low water three drops will need to be negotiated. To scout or portage, take out on the left, through heavy underbrush. (At the top of the ridge, the two-track FH-5255 makes a convenient portage trail; this road will require four-wheel drive in wet seasons.) At the first drop, a zig-zag course through the only clear chute requires precise maneuvering. The second and third drops follow almost immediately. The final 3-foot drop and jagged, exposed rocks make portaging advisable, although the stretch may be runnable by advanced paddlers when high water covers most rocks.

It's possible to take out on the left, just as the river opens into Bond Falls Flowage. Or cross the flowage 2.5 miles to the northeast, heading toward the white dam-house. We recommend taking out at the UPPCO boat ramp ❹ , where there is good parking and vault toilets half a mile south of the dam. As an alternative, Bond Falls Park, with a campground and picnic area, offers good access and parking on the right (east) side of the dam. Bond Falls are immediately below the dam.

Should U.P. Power Company agree to increase minimum flow from the dam to an average of 85 cfs or more (this has been discussed as a possibility for years), the river from here should become navigable, at least in spring and fall. Keep in mind that Agate Falls, at M-28, requires a long and difficult portage. From there to the junction of the East Branch is an estimated 10-hour float—including some fast water—through remote country. Below Agate Falls, clay banks and tributaries change the clear water of the Middle Branch to the red-brown more characteristic of the Ontonagon system.

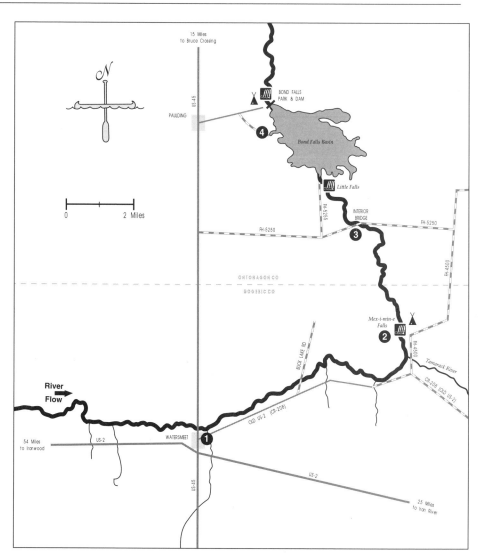

ONTONAGON RIVER SOUTH BRANCH

COUNTY: Ontonagon
START/END: Ewen to Victoria Dam
MILES: 26.5
GRADIENT: 7.5 ft/mile
PORTAGES: At least one section of rapids may require portaging
RAPIDS/FALLS: Flannigan Rapids, 12 miles below Ewen—Class I-II
　　　　　　　 Unnamed rapids 25 miles below Ewen—Class II-III
CAMPGROUNDS: One
CANOE LIVERIES: One (see Appendix D)
SKILL REQUIRED: II
TOPO. MAPS: Matchwood, Rockland (15 min.)

The South Branch may be the least-known and least-often paddled of the major branches of the Ontonagon, yet we found it to be the most attractive and challenging. Although in this description we have included only the final section from Ewen to Victoria Dam, the upper river, from its origin at Cisco Lake Dam to its confluence with Ten-Mile Creek south of Ewen, is a National Wild and Scenic River and deserves mention. It begins as the Cisco Branch of the Ontonagon, a small but navigable stream in southwestern Gogebic County, better known for trout fishing than canoeing. About 8 miles south of Ewen, in the area of 18 Mile Rapids, it is joined by Sucker Creek which is the final channel for water diverted from the Middle Branch into the flume at Bond Falls Basin. The addition of this water increases the size and volume of the Cisco Branch significantly, and from there it becomes known as the South Branch. Water levels for the remainder of the river are dependent on flow from the flume and from Sucker Creek, which in turn depends on power-generating needs of the hydroelectric plant at Victoria Dam.

Fishing in the Cisco Branch and South Branch is excellent for brook trout. Most of the surrounding lands downstream from Ewen are in the Ottawa National Forest, and suitable riverside campsites are abundant. With the exception of the rapids in the final 1.5 to 2 miles before Victoria Dam Basin, paddlers with average ability should not have difficulty on the South Branch. Those final rapids, however, are very heavy and very difficult during medium to high water and should be attempted only by advanced whitewater paddlers.

EWEN to VICTORIA DAM
26.5 MILES / 8 – 10 HOURS

Because there are no intermediate access points in this section, paddlers planning to complete the trip in one day are advised to start early. Put in at the public access site at M-28 Bridge ➊ in Ewen. Here, the river is 40 – 60 feet wide, slow, and muddy. Water is the color of coffee with cream, and current is slow to moderate. Plan on about an hour and a half of steady paddling before the current increases to anything more than moderate. At first, terrain is low hills of hardwoods with lowlands of maples and dead elms near the river. Farther downstream, high, wooded hills predominate with hardwoods, pines,

and hemlocks most common.

Flannigan Rapids are the only rapids marked on most county and topographical maps we have seen, and they are shown to be about half a mile long through several tight bends. It is difficult to determine just which are Flannigan Rapids, since rapids of varying length occur for at least 10 miles beginning about 12 miles below Ewen. Most are either riffles or Class I-II rapids with standing waves and bushel-basket-size boulders to avoid. Channels are clear and easily detected, although during low water shallow riffles and rock gardens will need picking through. The discolored water makes detecting rocks sometimes difficult, especially in slower water. Rapids alternate with stretches of slow water through much of the section.

Two runs of virtually constant Class I-II rapids are several miles long each. After the junction with the West Branch, the river slows and widens to 80 to 120 feet. From here the South Branch is technically known as the West Branch, though the West Branch is the smaller river. The West Branch itself is considered navigable from the M-28 Bridge—just below its outlet from Gogebic Lake at Bergland Dam—but only during high water in spring, when it is said to be a fast, challenging trip. It is a National Wild and Scenic River from its confluence with Cascade Falls to Victoria Basin.

After the junction of the West Branch and South Branch, a long stretch of slow water leads to a final 1-hour run of rapids that culminates in major rapids about 1.5 miles above Victoria Basin. After a gradual right bend, the river drops out of sight. You will hear the rapids before you see them. Take out on the left and scout carefully. In high water, these rapids are runnable only by advanced paddlers and probably only in covered boats. We ran it during medium-high water with the banks close to overflowing. The initial drop is about 4 to 5 feet, with the most intense water and a very large backroller near the left shore. A chute just right of center squeezes between intimidating standing waves and backrollers—easily large enough to swamp an open canoe—and huge partially submerged rocks immediately downstream need to be avoided. We made it through, but barely. Someone who came before us wasn't so fortunate; we found an aluminum canoe wrapped around rocks just below the steepest pitch.

Portaging around these unnamed rapids is difficult over uneven ground and thick underbrush. But it is not nearly as difficult as the walk out—the nearest road, at Victoria Dam, is 3 miles as the crow flies. About a thousand yards of relatively easy Class I-II rapids follow the first difficult drop, followed by one-quarter mile of still water through a steep, wooded canyon. Around a bend to the left is another set of rapids down a steep descent. Although shorter and less intense than the water upstream, these are solid Class II rapids with quite high standing waves and should be negotiated with care. They empty directly into Victoria Basin.

Follow the left shore of the reservoir and make the long crossing to the dam. ❷ Portage on the left at the landing, where access and parking are good. Avoid the right side of the dam and the spillway leading to spectacular Victoria Falls. A small, primitive campground is located on the left (north) side of the dam, a short walk up the old gravel road.

No good access is available below Victoria Dam, and the river there is considered unnavigable. Much of the flow is diverted down a flume that

follows a gravel service road about 1.5 miles to a generating station. The portage is so long—and the remainder of river before the mainstream of the Ontonagon so short—we recommend taking out at Victoria Dam and shuttling to either the Victoria Falls Road Bridge or Military Bridge on US-45 to continue on the mainstream.

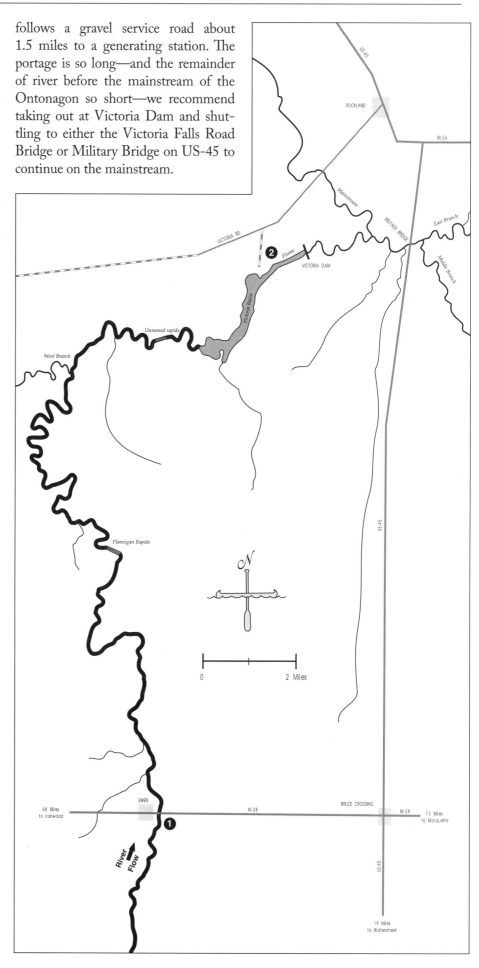

PAINT RIVER

COUNTY: Iron
START/END: Gibbs City to Little Bull Dam
MILES: 38
GRADIENT: 4.2 ft/mile
PORTAGES: Possibly two at rapids, fairly difficult
          One dam, difficult
RAPIDS/FALLS: Unnamed rapids below the junction with the Net River—Class I-II
          Hemlock Rapids, Upper and Lower, 13 miles below Gibbs City—Class II-III
          Unnamed rapids immediately below Crystal Falls Dam—Class I-II
          Horserace Rapids, below Little Bull Dam—not runnable
CAMPGROUNDS: Several
CANOE LIVERIES: One (see Appendix D)
SKILL REQUIRED: Rapids—III; all other sections—I
TOPO. MAPS: Gibbs City, Sunset Lake, Amasa, Kelso Junction, Crystal Falls (7.5 min.)

The Paint is part of the large river system—including the Brule and Michigamme rivers—that comes together in the southeast corner of Iron County to form the Menominee River. Except for Hemlock Rapids (about halfway between the Forks and Crystal Falls) and the gorge with rapids and falls at Horserace Rapids (near the end of the river), it is a generally quiet, moderately paced river well-suited to beginning paddlers and families. Because of its length and the relatively undeveloped country it flows through, it makes one of the finest expeditions in the U.P.

Camping potential is good, with several USFS campgrounds as well as abundant streamside sites in the long stretches that run through state and national forest land. The upper reaches support brook, brown, and rainbow trout, and the lower reaches hold smallmouth bass and northern pike. Other wildlife is abundant, especially deer and bald eagles, which we saw in numbers greater than anywhere else in Michigan.

The entire lengths of the North and South Branches and the mainstream from the Forks to the Ottawa National Forest boundary (just below Blockhouse USFS Campground) are National Wild and Scenic Rivers.

PAINT RIVER FORKS CAMPGROUND to BATES-AMASA ROAD BRIDGE (CR-643)
17 MILES / 6½ – 9½ HOURS

This long section has much slow water but also several sets of rapids, two of which—the Upper and Lower Hemlock—may require portaging. The wide range of paddling time indicated above is to allow for the portages at Hemlock. We completed the trip in 6½ hours, running all rapids, after spending 30 to 45 minutes scouting Hemlock Rapids, a delay that is absolutely necessary. Allow at least 2 hours more for portaging, if necessary, or plan to make it a two-day trip. Several well-used campsites are found in the area of the rapids.

Paint River Forks USFS Campground ❶ is located just above the non-existent town of Gibbs City. The campground has only four campsites, an outhouse, and no water facilities. No fee is required. Good access and parking are available at the campground.

The river at the Forks is low by late summer, when some riffles will be too shallow to float through. During periods of higher water, trips can begin on either the North or South Branch well above their junction at Gibbs City.

The Paint mainstream near Gibbs City is 40 – 75 feet wide and rocky and flows through high country of mixed forests, with thickets of tag alders frequent. From the beginning there are sections of very slow water that give way to quick, shallow riffles—a riffle-and-pool pattern that is repeated all the way to Crystal Falls. Occasional cabins—or "camps" as they're known in the Upper

Peninsula—line the river much of the trip, but they affect wildlife very little and do not detract from the sense of remoteness and wildness that lingers over the Paint. We saw two eagles fly from perches apparently in the front yard of one cabin; deer were bedding down at another.

Blockhouse USFS Campground ❷ is located 5 miles below the Forks. It has only four sites and no water or other services and is a free-use camp. Access and parking are from the campsites.

The Net River joins the Paint about 2 miles below Blockhouse Campground. The Net is often mentioned as a canoeable river, but when we saw it, after a week of heavy rains in September, it was still much too shallow to run. Reports are that it is a beautiful river through remote country and well worth

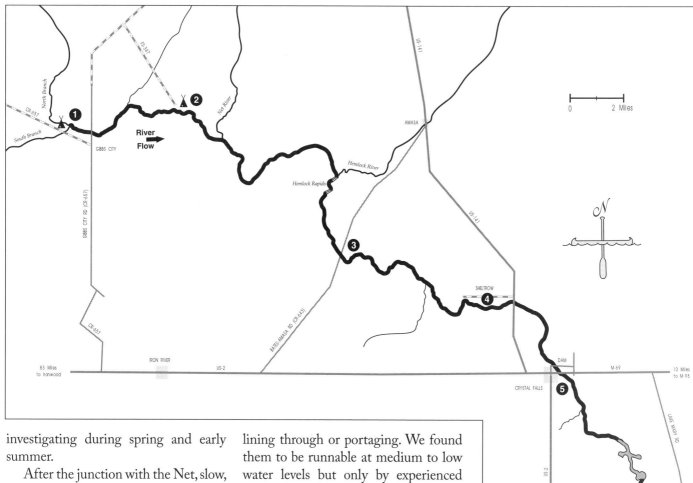

investigating during spring and early summer.

After the junction with the Net, slow, deep water becomes more predominant, culminating finally in several miles of still water. Current is nearly imperceptible. Silver maples and cedars are reminiscent of some southern-Michigan rivers. One or two hours of this ends at a sudden, fast chute of whitewater. This 100-foot-long run of standing waves can be taken down the center, but use caution. A similar, though shorter and less intense drop is found about a mile below the first; it should not be difficult for most paddlers.

Upper Hemlock Rapids can be heard not long after the Hemlock River—visible as a cascading stream in a small bay on the left—enters the Paint. The rapids are approximately 13 miles, or 4 to 6 hours paddling time, from Gibbs City. The first drop is fairly straightforward. Run it down the center and take out on the left in the quiet pool below to scout the remainder of the rapids.

Most references we've seen consider both Upper and Lower Hemlock Rapids unrunnable and strongly recommend

lining through or portaging. We found them to be runnable at medium to low water levels but only by experienced whitewater paddlers. Fairly complex maneuvering is required through chutes and standing waves capable of swamping an open canoe. During high water in spring, these rapids are, as a local resident told us, "awesome" and are perhaps unrunnable in open boats.

The trickiest spot on Upper Hemlock is a 90-degree turn to the left near the beginning of the rapids. Scout carefully and seek out the strongest chute, or V, to run. Backrollers could be a problem in higher water, and standing waves are always present. Total length of the rapids is about 1,400 feet. There is a good trail on the left, so portage if in doubt.

A quarter-mile stretch of still water follows Upper Hemlock. Lower Hemlock, like the upper rapids, is audible well in advance. Take out on the left and scout carefully. These are more difficult than the upper rapids and require serious consideration. One Class III drop of approximately 4 feet is followed by a potentially dangerous backroller. Total length of the rapids is about 2,000

Fishing for smallmouth bass on the Paint River

feet, with much of it difficult, extremely fast water over bushel-basket- to picnic-table-size boulders. Chutes are narrow and require precise maneuvering. The one-half-mile portage is more difficult than the one on the upper rapids, but don't let it be a deterrent to portaging. These rapids are not suited for canoeists inexperienced in whitewater. Much of the land bordering the rapids is within state forest, and there are several good and often-used campsites near the river.

Three miles below Lower Hemlock Rapids, access and parking are good at the Bates-Amasa Road Bridge. **3**

BATES-AMASA ROAD BRIDGE (CR-643) to CRYSTAL FALLS POWER DAM
13 MILES / 4 – 6 HOURS

From Bates-Amasa Road to Crystal Falls, the river is wide (75 to 125 feet) and alternates shallow riffles with slow, deeper water, most of it over rock and gravel bottom. We found good small-mouth bass fishing in the slower, deeper water.

Erickson Landing is a state-maintained access site **4** with good access

and parking.

US-141 Bridge has no public access or parking. From here the river slows and widens into the backwaters of Crystal Falls Power Dam. The backwaters are little more than a mile long, but the portage at the dam is fairly difficult. Take out on the left side at the grassy access site about 200 feet before the power station and carry to the steep bank across the road. Follow the portage signs. The bank down to the river is heavily overgrown, but there is a narrow trail leading to the rocks below the dam. Below the dam is a short, fairly difficult stretch of Class I-II rapids followed by milder riffles that extend beyond the access site and bridge at M-69.

M-69 BRIDGE to LITTLE BULL DAM
8 MILES / 2 ½ – 4 HOURS

Access and parking are good at the public site on the right upstream side of the M-69 Bridge **5** in Crystal Falls. From here, riffles diminish quickly, and the river widens and slows considerably. This is some of the most isolated country on the river. We saw only one cabin

and much wildlife, especially waterfowl, eagles and deer.

Little Bull Dam might as well be considered the end of the Paint River. Downstream was once several miles of extremely challenging and beautiful water climaxing at Horserace Rapids. However, Wisconsin Electric's Little Bull Diversion Canal now runs much, if not most, of the Paint River's water over to Peavy Pond and the Michigamme River for power production, leaving the Paint below the dam too depleted for good paddling. Horserace Rapids are virtually unrunnable, except perhaps in spring and then only by the most experienced whitewater experts. The diversion canal is navigable, but somewhat uninspiring, and makes possible a long expedition to Peavy Pond, down the Michigamme and into the Menominee river.

Access and parking are good at Wisconsin Electric Recreation Area 22 at Little Bull Dam, where there are vault toilets. **6** The dam is identified at the site as "Lower Paint Dam." Camping is permitted, although space is limited, and it is very much like camping in a parking lot.

PRESQUE ISLE RIVER

COUNTIES: Gogebic, Ontonagon
START/END: M-28 Bridge to South Boundary Road Bridge
MILES: 17.5
GRADIENT: M-28 to Steiger's Bridge—17.5 ft/mile
Steiger's Bridge to South Boundary Road—46.5 ft/mile
PORTAGES: Several falls and rapids, moderately difficult to very difficult
RAPIDS/FALLS: Many unnamed rapids—Class I-IV
Minnewawa, Nimikon, Nakomis, Lepisto, and Iagoo Falls
CAMPGROUNDS: One
CANOE LIVERIES: None
SKILL REQUIRED: III-IV
TOPO. MAPS: Thomaston (15 min.)

The Presque Isle below M-28 is the most challenging whitewater river in Michigan, if not the entire Midwest. Canoe Magazine once listed it as one of the ten North American rivers "that define the outer edge of contemporary whitewater paddling," and it has a reputation among experienced whitewater paddlers for being a difficult, unpredictable river that tests their abilities. Local DNR, USFS, and law-enforcement agencies report having to frequently transport stranded and injured paddlers out of the Presque Isle. The country is wild, access is extremely limited, and it cannot be stressed too strongly that only experienced, well-equipped and safety-minded kayakers and canoeists should attempt this trip.

Although navigable water is found as far upstream as the West Branch of the Presque Isle—above Presque Isle Flowage in south-central Gogebic County—we decided to include only the 17.5 miles of whitewater from US-28 to the series of falls shortly before Lake Superior. The section above M-28 contains primarily slow water through lowland forests and tag alders, with light rapids below Presque Isle Flowage and below Yondota Falls, north of Marenisco. Fishing is said to be good in the upper reaches, and paddling is suitable for those with intermediate ability. Expect occasional logjams and downed trees as well as a quarter-mile portage around Yondota Falls.

To paddle the 17.5 miles of Class II-IV rapids below M-28, it would be ideal to divide the trip in half. We have heard of advanced kayakers who know the river well making the entire trip in one long day, but the usual time required is at least two days. Figure an average paddling time of a little more than 1 mile per hour, which takes into account numerous stops to scout rapids and negotiate several short portages as well as one long one. The river divides conveniently at a bridge known as both Connorsville Bridge and Steiger's Bridge. Unfortunately, liability issues have caused the property owners to close the access road to this bridge, leaving paddlers with no option but to camp on the river or attempt the entire stretch in one day.

Water levels fluctuate greatly on the Presque Isle. In the past, water gages were located at the M-28 bridge and at South Boundary Road Bridge. Both are currently gone, though local paddlers are lobbying for replacement. Readings of 7 to 7.8 feet were considered optimum, with higher levels too dangerous, and lower levels creating the need for many more portages. Ideal levels are usually found in May to early June. April levels tend to be high, and cold water makes neoprene suits advisable. USGS water-gauge data indicates a flow-rate range from 1,500 cubic feet per second in April to as low as 40 cfs in August. It is worth noting that the Presque Isle does not lose navigable water levels as quickly as the nearby Black River, nor does it rise as readily after heavy rains.

The Presque Isle is a National Wild and Scenic River from the confluence of the East and West Branches south of Marenisco to Minnewawa Falls.

Minnewawa Falls

M-28 BRIDGE to STEIGER'S BRIDGE
8.5 MILES / 7 – 9 HOURS

Access ❶ and parking are good at M-28, where the river is 60 – 80 feet wide and 3 – 6 feet deep, with slow current. Water is tea colored. Terrain is lowland forests with thickets of tag alders and underbrush near the river. Slow water extends for about 2 miles, to the site of the washed-out bridge on FS-481 (Underwood Tower Road) one mile west of the M-28 Bridge. (Access to the washed-out bridge is blocked and requires a lengthy hike to the river.)

From here to Steiger's Bridge, rapids increase steadily in intensity and duration. Initially, light rapids over small to medium-size rocks alternate with wide, lake-like pools of still water. Many of the pools have narrow outlets over natural rock reefs. Some of these outlets are short, fierce chutes of whitewater over 2- to 4-foot drops. Gradually the pattern alters to include stretches of rapids between pools.

Typical rapids consist of stretches of broken water—over small to medium-size jumbled rocks—punctuated by ledge-drops. The ledges generally occur in a series of steps, some as high as 4 to 5 feet, and they often stretch across the entire 80- to 100-foot width of the river. Usually one or two chutes will funnel water over the ledges and create a tongue that allows clear passage. At the bottom of these chutes, watch for standing waves, side-curlers and backrollers—many can easily swamp an open canoe, even at lower water levels.

Minnewawa Falls are a difficult but runnable series of ledgedrops and chutes forced between car- and house-size boulders. Two major Class III drops require precise maneuvering through narrow and not always obvious channels and should be scouted. The second, especially, demands careful consideration, although it is somewhat forgiving in that a large pond-size pool at the bottom makes rescue comparatively easy. There are several cabins on the shore of the pool, with two-track roads available in emergencies.

Class I-II rapids continue downstream less than a mile to Nimikon Falls. This is a 12- to 15-foot drop that should be portaged, although kayakers have been known to run it on the left side during high water. Portage on the right. From here to Steiger's Bridge are about 3.5 miles of Class III rapids, with occasional drops that might require scouting.

The dirt road to Steiger's Bridge ❷ (labeled "Old Camp Four Grade" on some maps, but unmarked at the road) is located about 5 miles north of M-28, off CR-519. As mentioned above, it is gated and closed to public use.

STEIGER'S BRIDGE to SOUTH BOUNDARY ROAD BRIDGE
9 MILES / 7 ½ – 10 HOURS

The section of river below Steiger's Bridge is considerably more challenging than the one above. Beginning just below the bridge are about 8 miles of continuous Class II-IV rapids with an average descent of 46.5 feet per mile. Access to the banks is difficult through much of this section, with small eddies often the only places to rest and scout.

Rapids increase in intensity, with drops becoming more frequent and larger as you progress through the first mile of river.

After about 1 mile, Triple Drop, a trio of small falls and chutes, marks the beginning of the infamous gorge of the Presque Isle—a mile-long pitch of intense Class III-IV rapids (Class V in high water) in which the river descends 140 feet. The gorge is through a steep valley with densely wooded banks 120 to 150 feet high. Access to the banks from within the canyon is possible but extremely difficult due to fast water near shore, steep banks, and heavy growth of underbrush and trees. Portage is recommended for all but the most advanced paddlers.

Triple Drop can be scouted and run, but the proximity of the gorge directly downstream makes mishaps so hazardous that we recommend portaging the entire stretch. Take out on the left before Triple Drop, where the banks are about 75 feet high, and fight through underbrush to the top of the ridge. The portage is long and exhausting but highly recommended over entering the gorge. The river makes a wide swing to the left (west), and by hiking northwest you can intercept the river below the gorge. There is no portage trail, but one-quarter mile inland is a series of logging trails that makes passage considerably easier than trailblazing through the woods. Hike at least a mile until the trail descends to the river. Nakomis Falls marks the end of the gorge and is visible just upstream from the point where the trail comes closest to the river. Access is down a 15-foot bank. From here to Lepisto Falls, rapids continue without let-up. Drops rate Class III, possibly IV, and the rapids between them are a solid Class II. Lepisto Falls is a Class IV drop that should be portaged on the left, although it can be run by experts in covered boats.

Below Lepisto Falls, rapids continue, with several major drops that require scouting and perhaps portaging, but intensity gradually lowers. The final 2

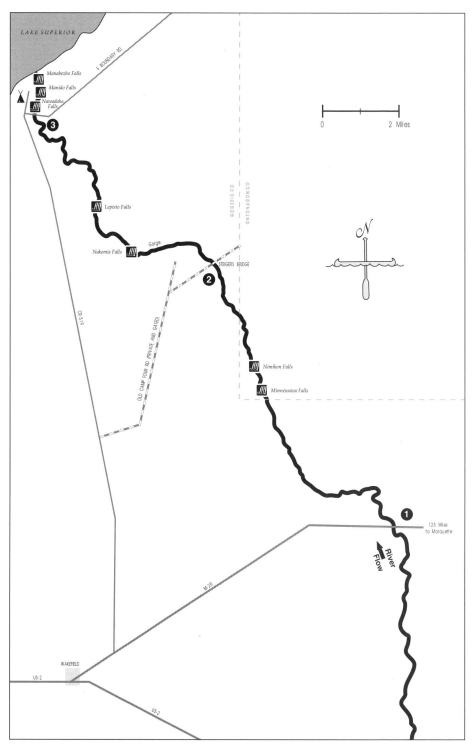

miles are through Class I-II rapids with some stretches of light riffles and slower water. These final miles are within the Porcupine Mountains State Park and are dominated by enormous virgin pines and hemlocks. Wildlife, including bald eagles, is abundant.

Access is fair at South Boundary Road Bridge ❸ with fair roadside parking. Take out on the left upstream side of the bridge. Nawadaha, Manido and Manabezho falls are directly downstream and make continuing the final mile to Lake Superior dangerous and inadvisable. Advanced kayakers sometimes run these falls at optimum water flow, but all others should stay on shore. Full camping facilities are available at Presque Isle Campground near the mouth.

STURGEON RIVER

COUNTY: Delta
START/END: CR-442 to Flowing Well Campground
MILES: 13
GRADIENT: 7 ft/mile
PORTAGES: Occasional fallen trees
RAPIDS/FALLS: 10 Mile Rapids, below Hwy 13 Bridge—Class I-II
CAMPGROUNDS: One
CANOE LIVERIES: None
SKILL REQUIRED: I-II

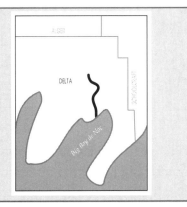

Located almost entirely within the Hiawatha National Forest, the Sturgeon is a medium paced, easily accessible river that passes through remote and unspoiled country. Like the nearby Whitefish, it is seasonal, with May and June offering ideal water levels, although a wet autumn will bring enough water for enjoyable trips.

Fishing is primarily for brook trout in the upper reaches, with warm-water species such as pike and smallmouth bass predominating in the lower reaches.

Our description does not include the final 7 to 8 miles below Flowing Well Campground and the US-2 Bridge. The river there is slow, meandering, and passes through lowlands of drowned hardwoods and cedars where fallen trees and logjams make passage nearly impossible. Likewise, we have not included the 19 miles of river upstream of CR-442. USFS information indicates that this stretch can be paddled starting at CR-440, 3 miles west of FH-13 on the Delta-Alger county line, but we found that upper water too narrow, shallow, and choked with logjams and fallen trees for enjoyable canoeing.

Nearly 45 miles of the Sturgeon, including the entire section described in this book, is protected as a National Wild and Scenic River.

CR-442 to FLOWING WELL CAMPGROUND
13 MILES / 5 – 7 HOURS

Although we paddled the entire length of this section in one easy day, the river divides conveniently for a two-day trip at 14 Mile Bridge on FH-13. The upper half of the trip passes through the remotest country on the river and offers the best camping possibilities other than the USFS campground at Flowing Well.

Put in at CR-442, where access ❶ is fairly good but parking is limited to a small pull-off. The river here is 30 to 40 feet wide and shallow. Bottom is rock and gravel, current is quick, and the water is stained dark. Downstream, the current slows and the river meanders through lowlands and tag-alder thickets most of the way to FH-13. Expect a few minor logjams and occasional fallen trees. About midway through the section, the country opens up into beautiful and expansive meadows with great camping possibilities. Shortly beyond the meadows, the current increases over bedrock riffles that continue until the bridge at FH-13.

Access is fair at 14 Mile Bridge ❷ on FH-13, with parking limited to the roadside. Riffles here give way quickly to slow water and meanders through lowlands and hardwoods. Fallen trees most of the way to the public access site just above 10 Mile Rapids force many short but tedious portages.

At a spot a half mile above the FH-2231 Bridge is a pull-off from FH-13 that provides access down a short bank. Ten Mile Rapids are immediately downstream. The rapids are composed of a 50-yard-long series of low ledge-drops, with easy passage between minor obstacles. Although not challenging to experienced whitewater paddlers, others should use caution, especially during high water, when large standing waves may be created. Downstream, there are similar, less notable drops and generally quick current. Access and parking are poor at the bridge on USFS-2231 (28th Road), where there is a USGS water gauge.

Flowing Well Campground ❸ is about a mile below F-2231 Bridge, where access is fair and parking is limited to one vehicle. The campground is not marked from the river; look for trails to the banks and a clearing at the top of a low ridge on the right, where picnic tables may be visible. The best access is at the picnic area by the flowing well, at the downstream end of the campground. Access is up a short bank; be cautious on the slippery rocks.

US-2 is 5 miles below Flowing Well Campground. Expect slow water and increasing numbers of fallen trees to there. Access at US-2 is only fair, with parking limited to the shoulders of the highway. Passage below US-2 is not recommended due to blockage by fallen trees and logjams.

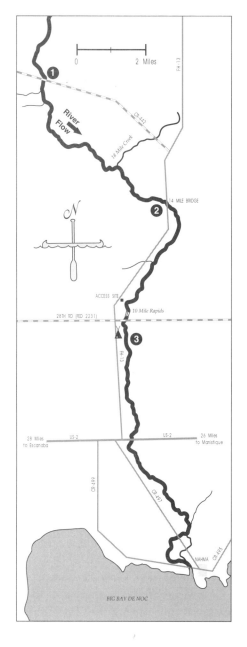

TWO HEARTED RIVER

COUNTY: Luce

START/END: High Bridge on CR-407 to rivermouth

MILES: 20.5

GRADIENT: High Bridge to Reed and Green Bridge—4.2 ft/mile
Reed and Green Bridge to mouth—3.6 ft/mile

PORTAGES: Occasional fallen trees

RAPIDS/FALLS: None

CAMPGROUNDS: Several

CANOE LIVERIES: One (see Appendix D)

SKILL REQUIRED: I

TOPO. MAPS: Muskallonge Lake SE, Muskallonge Lake East, Betsy Lake NW (7.5 min.)

I f only on the strength of its unforgettable name, the Two Hearted is certainly the best-known river in the Upper Peninsula. Ernest Hemingway contributed greatly to its fame when he used it for the title of his short story about the Fox River, "Big Two-Hearted River." For Hemingway the appeal, as he once wrote, was simply that "it's poetry." But many anglers and canoeists have long considered the river to have other appeals as well.

Fishing is excellent for steelhead during spring and fall runs, and for brook trout in the upper reaches and tributaries.

Canoeing opportunities are somewhat limited on the Two Hearted. While it is possible to navigate a canoe on both the South Branch and East Branch, these tributaries are very small and frequently obstructed and are therefore not recommended.

Much of the river passes through Lake Superior State Forest, and several state-forest campgrounds are located along it. Basic paddling skills are sufficient to handle any of the Two Hearted's light riffles, except in early spring when extremely high water creates hazards. Early and midsummer plagues of black flies are legendary and should be prepared for.

The Two Hearted is one of only two Upper Peninsula rivers designated as Michigan Natural Rivers (the Fox is the other). It is the only river in the Natural Rivers Program to be classified as "Wilderness."

HIGH BRIDGE (CR-407) to
REED AND GREEN BRIDGE (CR-410)
9.5 MILES / 5 – 8 HOURS

Float time will vary on this section depending on the number of obstructions. Expect at least a dozen fallen trees to require lift-over or portaging. The river near High Bridge is small (30 to 40 feet wide) and quite fast over rocks and gravel. In summer expect to bump rocks in shallow riffles. From here downstream, the current alternates quick over light riffles with sections of slower, deeper water. Depths are 1 to 3 feet with some deep holes at the bends. Water is tea colored. Terrain is hills of hardwoods near the bridge with lowlands of tag alders and marshes downstream.

High Bridge offers poor access down a steep bank, with roadside parking. Better access and limited parking are found at the washed-out bridge just below High Bridge. **❶** To reach it, take the road to the right immediately after pulling into High Bridge State Forest Campground. The campground has water, outhouses, and spacious, widely spaced campsites under the pines.

Most of the fallen trees are encountered in the upper three-quarters of the section. A state forest canoe campground known as Lone Pine is closed now and no longer has water or toilets, but can still serve as a campsite.

Access and parking are good at Reed and Green Bridge **❷** (CR-410). The small state forest campground just downstream has rustic facilities, water, and fair access to the river.

REED AND GREEN BRIDGE (CR-410) to RIVERMOUTH
11 MILES / 4 – 6 HOURS

This is the most frequently paddled section of the Two Hearted, but it will seldom be crowded, except, perhaps, in spring and fall when steelhead and salmon are running.

The river is 35 – 45 feet wide, and depth is 2 – 4 feet over a bottom of gravel and scattered large rocks or sand. Low hills of oaks, birch, pines, and spruce rise away from the river's occasionally short, steep banks; tag alders are common near the water. Moderate current and fairly deep water alternate with short, light riffles over gravel bars. Occasional fallen trees hinder progress—most can be bypassed, although one or two may need portaging.

Dunes line the river near the end of this section. The Lake Superior surf can be heard long before the river reaches it. Although the pine forest continues, scattered houses and cabins are visible along this section. Numerous sandbars make convenient resting and picnic stops.

Access and parking are good beyond the foot bridge just before the mouth of the river at Two Hearted River State Forest Campground **❸**.

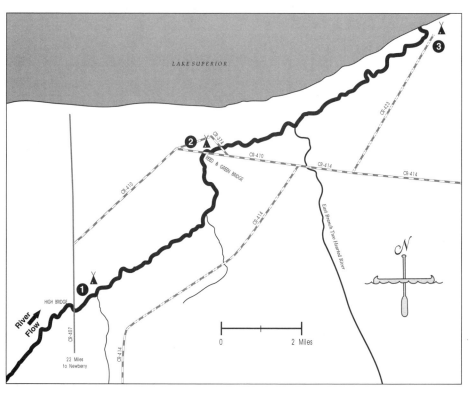

WHITEFISH RIVER

COUNTY: Delta
START/END: CR-448 Bridge to US-2 Bridge
MILES: 18
GRADIENT: 6.9 ft/mile
PORTAGES: Occasional fallen trees
RAPIDS/FALLS: None
CAMPGROUNDS: None
CANOE LIVERIES: None
SKILL REQUIRED: I

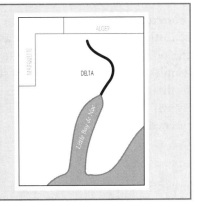

This short river flows through remote country and makes a good choice for a one-day float or fishing trip. Water quality is excellent, and current varies from slow to quick. There are many riffles and light rapids, especially in the upper reaches, but they should create trouble for beginning paddlers only during the high water of early spring. A more likely difficulty exists for paddlers making trips during low water in mid and late summer, when many stretches will simply be unfloatable. Most years, the best months for ideal water levels are May and June.

Camping potential is only fair due to private property and thick underbrush in many places. Fishing is for brook trout in the upper reaches and smallmouth bass from near the junctions of the East and West Branches downstream.

The lower ends of the East and Big West branches, and the mainstream from the confluence of the branches to Lake Michigan, are designated as National Wild and Scenic Rivers.

CR-448 ON EAST BRANCH to LITTLE BAY DE NOC PUBLIC ACCESS
18 MILES / 6 – 9 HOURS

According to the U.S. Forest Service, access to the East Branch of the Whitefish is possible as far upstream as its headwaters in Trout Lake in western Alger County. We found that section too small and congested with fallen trees to be enjoyable, although it would be a challenging trip through remote country for anyone with the energy to take it. Interestingly, a short portage north of Trout Lake will take you to the Au Train River Basin, which flows north into Lake Superior. European explorers noted that Native Americans often used the Whitefish/Au Train rivers as a shortcut between lakes Michigan and Superior.

Access at CR-448 Bridge ❶ is fair with limited roadside parking. The river from here is 30 to 50 feet wide, quick, shallow, and rocky, over a substrate of gravel and bedrock. Water is shallow except during spring runoff and periods of heavy rain. Mixed hardwoods, conifers, cedars, and tag alders line the banks. From here until the junction with the Big West Branch, shallow riffles alternate with slow, deep, boulder-paved pools. Some suitable campsites can be found on state land between stretches of private property. A few houses and cottages are scattered through the section.

After the junction with the Big West Branch, water volume nearly doubles and is probably sufficient for floats during dry summers. However, because there are no access sites below the junction of the two branches, the shallow upper water is a necessary inconvenience.

The Big West Branch is said to be canoeable in early spring, at least from CR-444 down to the bridge on CR-448 (a few miles west of the bridge over the East Branch on the same road). Farther upstream are several falls that make passage difficult, and we have heard that in the section below CR-444 are rapids that can be run successfully in April and May. Low water makes the Big West Branch extremely shallow, however, and when we were there near the beginning of June, water levels were already too low for sensible paddling. USFS information indicates a float time of 1 to 1½ hours from CR-444 to CR-448, with no information available for the stretch from CR-448 to the junction with the East Branch.

The remainder of the mainstream has long riffles, some of which are wide and shallow, but for the most part, expect easy passage to US-2. The final 2 to 3 miles of river slows—with long, pool like stretches lined with dead trees and drowned logs—before the marshes that characterize the rivermouth region of the Whitefish. The final few miles can be tedious in a strong headwind; otherwise, they are a pleasant, quiet trip through meadows and marshes with waterfowl abundant.

Access at US-2 is fair below the bridge, on the left. Parking, however, is limited to the shoulder of the highway. This access is best used only if strong south winds make Little Bay de Noc unsafe.

If the wind allows, a better alternative is to continue past the bridge into the protected, near-shore waters at the head of Little Bay de Noc. Bear right around the point and small bay approximately 2 miles to the municipal access site ❷ in the town of Rapid River. This facility, with excellent access and parking, is reached via Main Street.

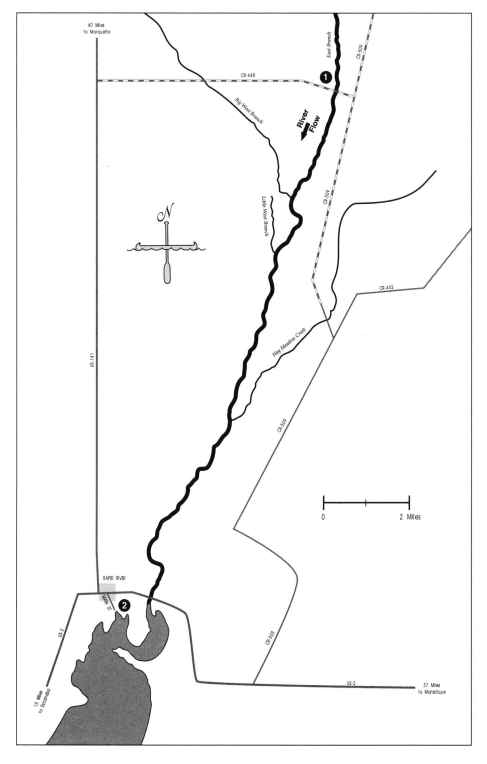

APPENDIX A: THE INTERNATIONAL SCALE OF RIVER DIFFICULTY

CLASS I   Fast moving water with riffles and small waves. Few obstructions, all obvious and easily missed with little training. Risk to swimmers is slight; self-rescue is easy.

CLASS II: NOVICE Straightforward rapids with wide, clear channels which are evident without scouting. Occasional maneuvering may be required, but rocks and medium-sized waves are easily missed by trained paddlers. Swimmers are seldom injured and group assistance, while helpful, is seldom needed.

CLASS III: INTERMEDIATE Rapids with moderate, irregular waves which may be difficult to avoid and which can swamp an open canoe. Complex maneuvers in fast current and good boat control in tight passages or around ledges are often required; large waves or strainers may be present but are easily avoided. Strong eddies and powerful current effects can be found, particularly on large-volume rivers. Scouting is advisable for inexperienced parties. Injuries while swimming are rare; self-rescue is usually easy but group assistance may be required to avoid long swims.

CLASS IV: ADVANCED Intense, powerful but predictable rapids requiring precise boat handling in turbulent water. Depending on the character of the river, it may feature large, unavoidable waves and holes or constricted passages demanding fast maneuvers under pressure. A fast, reliable eddy turn may be needed to initiate maneuvers, scout rapids, or rest. Rapids may require "must" moves above dangerous hazards. Scouting may be necessary the first time down. Risk of injury to swimmers is moderate to high, and water conditions may make self-rescue difficult. Group assistance for rescue is often essential but requires practiced skills. A strong Eskimo roll is highly recommended.

CLASS V: EXPERT Extremely long, obstructed, or very violent rapids which expose a paddler to added risk. Drops may contain large, unavoidable waves and holes or steep, congested chutes with complex, demanding routes. Rapids may continue for long distances between pools, demanding a high level of fitness. What eddies exist may be small, turbulent, or difficult to reach. Scouting is recommended but may be difficult. Swims are dangerous, and rescue is often difficult even for experts. A very reliable Eskimo roll, proper equipment, extensive experience, and practiced rescue skills are essential.

CLASS VI: EXTREME RAPIDS These runs have almost never been attempted and often exemplify the extremes of difficulty, unpredictability and danger. The consequences of errors are very severe and rescue may be impossible. For teams of experts only, at favorable water levels, after close personal inspection and taking all precautions.

(Thanks to American Whitewater. For more information or to join the organization, go to www.americanwhitewater.org.)

Appendix B: Rapids

LOWER PENINSULA

RIVER	NAME OF RAPIDS	LOCATION	DIFFICULTY	PAGE
Black	Crocket Rapids	above South Black River Road Bridge	I	12
Boardman	Beitner Rapids	below Beitner Road Bridge	I-II	15
Chippewa	Unnamed rapids	above Deerfield County Park	I	20
	Unnamed rapids	below Chippewa Road Bridge	I-II	21
Flat	Unnamed rapids	at old dam site before Ingall's Bridge	I	25
Huron	Unnamed rapids	at Territorial Road Bridge	I	28
	Delhi Rapids	above Delhi Road Bridge	I-II	29
Little Manistee	Several unnamed rapids	below Nine Mile Bridge	I-II	37
Little Muskegon	Several unnamed rapids	below West County Line Road Bridge	I	39
Muskegon	Big Rapids	below Baldwin Street Bridge in Big Rapids	I-II	47
Ocqueoc	Numerous unnamed rapids	below County Road 638 Bridge	I-II	50
Pere Marquette	Rainbow Rapids	below Rainbow Rapids Landing	I	53
Pigeon	Numerous unnamed rapids	below Pigeon River Road Bridge	I	56
	Numerous unnamed rapids	below M-68 Bridge	I-II	56
Pine	Numerous unnamed rapids	above and below M-37 Bridge	I-II	58
Rifle	Overhead Pipeline Rapids	below M-55 Bridge	I-II	61
	Unnamed rapids	below Greenwood Road Bridge	I	62
Sturgeon	Numerous unnamed rapids	below Wolverine Park	I-II	67
Thornapple	Unnamed rapids	at Ruehs Park in Alaska	I	69
Thunder Bay	Speehley Rapids	below M-65 Bridge	I	71

UPPER PENINSULA

RIVER	NAME OF RAPIDS	LOCATION	DIFFICULTY	PAGE
BLACK	Granite Rapids	below County Road 513 Bridge	II	76
	Numerous unnamed rapids	above and below Ramsay	I-II	77
	Numerous unnamed rapids	below US-2 Bridge	II-III	77
	Numerous unnamed rapids	below Narrows Park	II-III	78
BRULE	Several unnamed rapids	below M-189 Bridge	I-II	80
	Unnamed rapids	below Pentoga	II	81
	La Chapelle Rapids	below US-2 Bridge	I-II	81
ESCANABA	Unnamed rapids	below Gwinn	I-II	82
	Unnamed rapids	before junction with West Branch Escanaba	I-II	82
	Unnamed rapids	before Boney Falls Basin	I-II	83
	Unnamed rapids	below Boney Falls Dam	II-IV	83
FORD	Several unnamed rapids	below US-2 Bridge	I-III	86
MENOMINEE*	Big Bull Rapids	below Brule River Dam	III	81
	Piers Gorge	below Little Quinnesec Falls Dam	III-IV	81
MICHIGAMME	Witbeck Rapids	above M-95 Bridge	I-II	93
MONTREAL	Numerous unnamed rapids	below US-2 Bridge	I-II	96
	Numerous unnamed rapids	below Saxon Falls Dam	II-III	96
ONTONAGON, EAST BRANCH	Numerous unnamed rapids	below FS-208 Road	II-III	98
ONTONAGON, MAINSTREAM	Irish Rapids	4.5 miles below US-45 Bridge	I-II	100
	Grand Rapids	7.5 miles below US-45 Bridge	I-II	100
ONTONAGON, MIDDLE BRANCH	Several unnamed rapids	below Burned Dam	I-II	
	Little Falls Rapids	before Bond Falls Flowage	II-III	
ONTONAGON, SOUTH BRANCH	Flannigan Rapids	below M-28 Bridge	I-II	103
	Unnamed rapids	before Victoria Falls Basin	II-III	104
PAINT	Unnamed rapids	below junction with Net River	I-II	106
	Hemlock Rapids	Upper and Lower below Gibbs City	II-III	105,106
	Unnamed rapids	below Crystal Falls Dam	I-II	107
	Horserace Rapids	below Little Bull Dam	Not Runnable	107
PRESQUE ISLE	Numerous unnamed rapids	below M-28 Bridge	I-III	109
	Continuous rapids	from Steiger's Bridge to Lake Superior	I-IV	109
STURGEON	10 Mile Rapids	below Highway 13	I-II	111

*Although we have not included the Menominee River in this book, we have given a brief description of these two notable rapids at the end of the Brule River section.

Appendix C: Further Information

LOWER PENINSULA

AU SABLE, Mainstream
Huron-Manistee National Forest
Mio Ranger District
107 McKinley Road
Mio, MI 48647
(989) 826-3252

Huron-Manistee National Forest
Huron Shores Ranger Station
5761 North Skeel Road
Oscoda, MI 48750
(989) 739-0728

Grayling Regional C of C
213 N. James St
Grayling, MI 49738
(989) 348-2921

AU SABLE, South Branch
DNR—Roscommon OSC
1-75 and M-18 South
8717 North Roscommon Road
Roscommon, MI 48653
(989) 275-5151

BOARDMAN
Traverse City C of C
202 East Grandview Parkway
Traverse City, MI 49684
(231) 947-5075

HURON
Huron-Clinton Metropolitan
Authority
13000 High Ridge Drive
Brighton, MI 48114
(800) 477-2757

Proud Lake Recreation Area
3500 Wixom Rd.
Milford, MI 48382
(248) 685-2433

Island Lake Recreation Area
12950 East Grand River Ave.
Brighton, MI 48116
(810) 229-7067

JORDAN
DNR—Gaylord Field Office
1732 W M-32
Gaylord, MI 49735
(989) 732-3541

KALAMAZOO
DNR—Plainwell
621 North 10th Street
Plainwell, MI 49080
(269) 685-6851

MANISTEE
Manistee Ranger Station
412 Red Apple Road
Manistee, MI 49660
(231) 723-2211

Grayling Regional C of C
213 N James St
Grayling MI 49738
(989) 348-2921

Manistee Area C of C
11 Cypress Street
Manistee, MI 49660
(231) 723-2575

PERE MARQUETTE
Manistee National Forest Baldwin/
White Cloud Ranger Station
650 North Michigan Avenue
Baldwin, MI 49304
(231) 745-4631

Baldwin C of C
PO Box 804
Baldwin, MI 49304
(516)223-8080

Ludington Area Chamber of
Commerce
5300 US-10
Ludington, MI 49431
(231) 845-0324

PIGEON
DNR—Pigeon River Country
Headquarters
9966 Twin Lakes Road
Vanderbilt MI 49795
(989) 983-4101

PINE
Huron-Manistee National Forest
Supervisor's Office
1755 S. Mitchell Street
Cadillac, MI 49601
(800) 821-6263

DNR – Cadillac
8015 Mackinaw Trail
Cadillac, MI 49601
(231) 775-9727

Baldwin/White Cloud
Ranger Station
650 North Michigan Avenue
Baldwin, MI 49304
(231) 745-4631

PLATTE
Sleeping Bear Dunes
National Lakeshore
9922 Front Street
Highway M-72
Empire, MI 49630
(231) 326-5134
www.nps.gov/slbe

RIFLE
Tawas Area C of C
402 E Lake Street
Tawas City, MI 48763
(989) 362-8643

THUNDER BAY
Alpena Area C of C
235 West Chisholm Street
Alpena MI 49707
(989) 354-4181

UPPER PENINSULA

BLACK
Western U.P. Convention & Visitor Bureau
648 W Cloverland Drive
Ironwood, MI 49938
(906) 932-4850

Ottawa National Forest
E6248 US-2
Ironwood, MI 49938
(906) 932-1330

BRULE
DNR—Crystal Falls Field Office
1420 US-2 West
Crystal Falls MI 49920
(906) 875-6622

USFS—Iron River Ranger District
990 Lalley Road
Iron River MI 49935
(906) 265-5139

ESCANABA
Delta County Area C of C
230 Ludington Street
Escanaba MI 49829
(906) 786-2192

USFS—Hiawatha National Forest
820 Rains Dr
Gladstone, MI 49837
(906) 786-4062

FORD
See Escanaba River

FOX
DNR—Newberry OSC
5100 M-123
Newberry, MI 49868
(906) 293-5131

Newberry Area C of C
4947 Twin Lakes Road
Newberry, MI 49868
(906) 293-5562

INDIAN
Schoolcraft County C of C
1000 W Lakeshore Dr
Manistique MI 49854
(906) 341-5010

USFS—Hiawatha National Forest
820 Rains Dr
Gladstone, MI 49837
(906) 786-4062

MANISTIQUE
See Indian River

MICHIGAMME
DNR—Marquette
1990 US-41 South
Marquette, MI 49855
(906) 228-6561

Marquette Area C of C
501 South Front Street
Marquette MI 49855
(906) 226-9658

Dickinson County Area C of C
600 South Stephenson Avenue
Iron Mountain, MI 49801
(906) 774-2002

MONTREAL
See Black River

ONTONAGON
USFS—Bergland Ranger District
M-28
Bergland MI 49910
(906) 575-3441

USFS—Kenton Ranger District
Kenton MI 49943
(906) 852-3500

USFS—Ontonagon Ranger District
1209 Rockland Road
Ontonagon MI 49953
(906) 884-2411

USFS—Watersmeet Ranger District
Old US-2
PO Box 276
Watersmeet MI 49969
(906) 358-4551

PAINT
See Brule River

PRESQUE ISLE
See Black River

STURGEON
See Indian River

TWO HEARTED
See Fox River

WHITEFISH
See Indian River

APPENDIX D: CANOE LIVERIES

LOWER PENINSULA

AU SABLE RIVER

ALCONA CANOE RENTAL
(canoes/kayaks/campground/
cabins/ store/shuttles)
6351 Bamfield Road
Glennie, MI 48737
(989) 735-2973
(800) 526-7080
www.alconacanoes.com

BORCHER'S AU SABLE CANOE/KAYAK
(canoes/kayaks/store/shuttles/
bed-and-breakfast)
101 Maple Street
Grayling, MI 49738
(989) 348-4921
(800) 762-8756
chunter@borchers.com
www.canoeborchers.com

CARLISLE CANOES
(canoes/kayaks/campground/
cabins/ store/shuttles)
110 State Street
Grayling, MI 49738
(989) 348-2301
info@carlislecanoes.com
www.carlislecanoes.com

GOTTS' LANDING CANOES AND
KAYAKS
(canoes/kayaks)
701 Morenci Ave
Mio, MI 48647
(989) 826-3411
(888) 226-8748
Canoe@GottsLanding.com
www.gottslanding.com

HINCHMAN ACRES CANOE RENTAL
(canoes/kayaks/cabins)
702 North M-33
P.O. Box 220
Mio, MI 48647
(989) 826-3267
(800) 438-0203
info@hinchman.com
www.hinchman.com

HUTT'S CAMPING AND CANOEING
(canoes/campground/store/
shuttles)
3989 M-72 East
Grayling, MI 49738
(989) 348-8405

JIM'S CANOE LIVERY
(canoes/cottages/guide service)
1706 S Wakeley Bridge Road
Grayling, MI 49738
(989) 348-3203
www.jimscanoe.com

OSCODA CANOE RENTAL
(canoes/kayaks)
678 River Road
Oscoda, MI 48750
(989) 739-9040
www.oscodacanoe.com

PENROD'S PADDLESPORTS CENTER
(canoes/kayaks/cabins/store)
100 Maple Street
P.O. Box 432
Grayling, MI 49738
(989) 348-2910
(888) 467-4837
penrods@grayling-mi.com
www.penrodscanoe.com

RAINBOW RESORT
(canoes/kayaks/cabins)
731 Camp Ten Road
Mio, MI 48647
(989) 826-3423
(800) 737-4133
info@rainbowresortmio.com
www.rainbowresortmio.com

RAY'S AU SABLE CANOEING
(canoes/kayaks/store/shuttles)
1-75 Business Loop
Grayling, MI 49738
(989) 348-5844

WYANDOTTE CANOE AND
OUTFITTERS
(canoes/campground)
1320 McMasters Bridge Road
Grayling, MI 49738
(989) 348-8354
WyandotteLodge@aol.com

ROLLWAY CANOE RENTAL
(canoes/kayaks/cabins)
6160 Rollways Road
Hale, MI 48739
(989) 728-3322
www.rollwayresort.com

AU SABLE RIVER, SOUTH BRANCH

CAMPBELL'S CANOE LIVERY
(canoes/kayaks)
1112 Lake Street (M-18)
Roscommon, MI 48653
(989) 275-5810
(800) 722-6633
www.canoeatcampbells.com

HIAWATHA CANOE LIVERY
(canoes/kayaks/lodge)
1113 Lake Street
Roscommon, MI 48653
(989) 275-5213
www.canoehiawatha.com

PADDLE BRAVE CANOE LIVERY AND
CAMPGROUND
(canoes/kayaks/campground/
cabins)
10610 Steckert Bridge Road
Roscommon, MI 48653
(989) 275-5273
(800) 681-7092
www.paddlebrave.com

Watters Edge Kayak And Canoe Livery
(canoes/kayaks/shuttles)
10799 Dana Dr
Roscommon, MI 48653
(989) 275-5568
bobstair@gmail.com
www.wecl.8k.com

Wyandotte Canoe And Outfitters
(canoes/campground)
1320 McMasters Bridge Road
Grayling, MI 49738
(989) 348-8354
WyandotteLodge@aol.com

BETSIE RIVER

Alvina's Canoe And Boat Rental
6470 S Betsie River Road
Interlochen, MI 49643
(231) 276-9514

Betsie River Canoes And Campground
(canoes/kayaks/campground/store)
13598 Lindy Road
Thompsonville, MI 49683
(231) 378-2386
www.brcanoesandcampground.com

Hanmer's Riverside Resort And Livery
(canoes/kayaks/cabins)
2252 Benzie Hwy
Benzonia, MI 49616
(231) 882-7783
(800) 252-4286
www.hanmers.com

BOARDMAN RIVER

Ranch Rudolf
(canoes/kayaks/lodging)
6841 Brown Bridge Road
Traverse City, MI 49684
(231) 947-9529
info@ranchrudolf.com
www.ranchrudolf.com

Traverse City Kayak Rental
Clinch Park
Traverse City, MI 49684
231-883-7890
www.therivertraversecity.com/
kayak-rental

CHIPPEWA RIVER

Buckley's Mountainside Canoes
(canoes/kayaks/store/shuttles)
4700 West Remus Road
Mt. Pleasant, MI 48858
(989) 772-5437
buckleydonna@hotmail.com
www.buckleyscanoe.com

Chippewa River Outfitters
(canoes/kayaks/store/shuttles)
3763 S. Lincoln Road
Mount Pleasant, MI 48858
(989) 772-5474
(888) 775-6077
info@chipoutfitters.com
www.chipoutfitters.com

Tuck's Paddlesports
830 Whitetail Dr
Midland, MI 48640

DOWAGIAC RIVER

Niles Canoe And Outfitting
(canoes/kayaks/shuttles)
1520 North Business US-31
Niles, MI 49120
(269) 683-5110

Doe-Wah-Jack's Canoe Rentals
(canoes/kayaks)
P.O. Box 9063
Benton Harbor, MI 49023
(269) 782-7410
(888) 782-7410
info@paddledcri.com
www.paddledcri.com

HURON RIVER

Argo Canoe Livery
(canoes/kayaks/rafts)
1055 Longshore Dr
Ann Arbor, MI 48105
(734) 794-6241

Gallup Canoe Livery
(canoes/kayaks)
3000 Fuller Road
Ann Arbor, MI 48105
(734) 662-9319

Heavner Canoe Rental
(canoes/kayaks)
2775 Garden Rd
Milford, MI 48381
(248) 685-2379
alheavner@hotmail.com
www.heavnercanoe.com

Michigan Paddlesports
(canoes/kayaks/store)
9260 McGregor Road
Pinckney, MI 48169
(734) 426-1651

Skip's Huron River Canoe Livery
(canoes/kayaks)
3780 Delhi Court
Ann Arbor, MI 48103
(734) 769-8686
www.skipshuronrivercanoeliveryllc.com/

Village Canoe Livery
(canoes/kayaks)
1216 Garden Road
Milford, MI 48381
(248) 685-9207

JORDAN RIVER

Jordan Valley Outfitters
(canoes/kayaks/rafts/store/shuttles)
311 North Lake Street (M-66)
East Jordan, MI 49727
(231) 536-0006
info@jvoutfitters.com
www.jvoutfitters.com

Swiss Hideaway Canoe Rental
(canoes/kayaks)
1953 Graves Crossing Road
Mancelona, MI 49659
(231) 536-2341
swisshideaway@gmail.com
www.jordanriverfun.com/

KALAMAZOO RIVER

HIGHLAND RIVER ADVENTURES
(kayaks)
227 Central St
Battle Creek, MI 49017
(269) 339-0771
www.highlandriveradventures.com

TWIN PINES CAMPGROUND AND
CANOE LIVERY
(canoes/campground/store/
shuttles)
9800 Wheeler Road
Hanover, MI 49241
(517) 524-6298

OLD ALLEGAN CANOE RENTAL
(canoes/kayaks/shuttles)
2722 Old Allegan Road
Fennville, MI 49408
(269) 561-5481
canoe@i2k.com
www.oldallegancanoe.com

RUNNING RIVERS PADDLE BOARD
AND KAYAK RENTALS
(Lower Kalamazoo and Kalamazoo
Lake)
Center Street
Wade's Bayou Memorial Park
Douglas, MI 49406
(616) 218-5021
www.running--rivers.info

LITTLE MANISTEE

ENCHANTED ACRES CANOE AND
CAMPGROUND
(canoes/kayaks/cabins/camping)
9581 N Brooks Rd
Irons, MI 49644
(231) 266-5102
www.enchantedacrescamp.com

INSTALAUNCH CAMPGROUND AND
MARINA
(canoes/kayaks/cabins/RV
campground)
22 Park Ave
Manistee, MI 49660
(231) 723-3901
(888) 452-8642
jim@instalaunch.com
www.instalaunch.com

PINE CREEK LODGE
(canoes/kayaks/campground/
cabins/ motel)
13544 Caberfae Highway
Wellston, MI 49689
(231) 848-4431
pcl@kaltelnet.net
www.pinecreeklodge.com

LITTLE MUSKEGON RIVER

TALL PINES CAMPGROUND
(campground/shuttles/
no canoes at this time)
550 South Talcott
Morley, MI 49336
(231) 856-4556

MANISTEE RIVER

ENCHANTED ACRES CANOE AND
CAMPGROUND
(canoes/kayaks/cabins/camping)
9581 N Brooks Rd
Irons, MI 49644
(231) 266-5102
www.enchantedacrescamp.com

CHIPPEWA LANDING
(canoes/kayaks/rafts/campground)
10420 Chippewa Landing Road
Manton, MI 49663
(231) 313-0832
contact@chippewalanding.com
http://www.chippewalanding.com/

PINE CREEK LODGE
(canoes/kayaks/campground/
cabins/ motel)
13544 Caberfae Highway
Wellston, MI 49689
(231) 848-4431
pcl@kaltelnet.net
www.pinecreeklodge.com

PINE RIVER PADDLESPORTS CENTER
(canoes/kayaks/rafts/campground/
cabins/store)
9590 South M-37
Wellston, MI 49689
(231) 862-3471
(800) 717-4837
prpc@thepineriver.com
www.thepineriver.com/

RAY'S AU SABLE CANOEING
(canoes/kayaks/store/shuttles)
1-75 Business Loop
Grayling, MI 49738
(989) 348-5844

SHEL-HAVEN
(canoes/kayaks/store)
11852 W M-72
Grayling, MI 49738
(989) 348-2158
www.shel-haven.com

SMITHVILLE LANDING
(canoes/kayaks/rafts/campground)
M-66 on the Manistee River
13177 Old M-66 SE
Fife Lake, MI 49663
(231) 839-4579
www.smithvillelanding.com

WILDERNESS CANOE TRIPS
(canoes/kayaks/store/shuttles)
6052 Riverview Rd
Mesick, MI 49668
(231) 885-1485
(800) 873-6379
www.wildernesscanoetripsonline.
com

MUSKEGON RIVER

CROTON DAM FLOAT TRIPS
(canoes/kayaks)
5355 Croton Road
Newaygo, MI 49337
(231) 652-6037
wwofn@yahoo.com

CHINOOK CAMPGROUND AND
CANOES
(canoes/kayaks/raftrs/campground/
store/restaurant)
5471 W 112th Street
Grant, MI 49327
(231) 652-6915
www.chinookcamping.com

DUGGAN'S CANOE LIVERY AND
CAMPGROUND
(canoes/kayaks/campground/store)
12 Miles West of Harrison, M-61
P.O. Box 29
Harrison, MI 48625
(989) 539-7149
info@dugganscanoes.com
www.dugganscanoes.com

J&J's River Run
(canoes/kayaks/rafts)
11426 Benzing Road
Evart, MI 49631
(231) 287-0008
Riverrun6001@gmail.com
www.jjriverrun.com

Old Log Resort
(canoes/kayaks/campground/
cabins)
12062 M-115
Marion, MI 49665
(231) 743-2775
www.oldlogresort.com

White Birch Canoe Trips And
Campground
(canoes/kayaks/campground)
5569 S Paradise Road
Falmouth, MI 49632
(231) 328-4547
www.whitebirchcanoe.com

Vic's Canoes At Salmon Run
Campground
(canoes/kayaks/rafts/campground)
8845 Felch Avenue
Grant, MI 49327
(231) 834-5494
info@salmonrunmi.com
www.salmonrunmi.com

Sawmill Canoe Livery
(canoes/kayaks)
226 Baldwin St
Big Rapids, MI 49307
(231) 796-6408
www.sawmillmi.com

Areawide Canoe Rental By
Wisner
(canoes/kayaks/rafts)
25 Water St
Newaygo, MI 49337
(231) 652-6743
info@wisnercanoes.com
www.wisnercanoes.com

Muskegon River Camp And
Canoe
(canoes/kayaks/campground/store)
6281 River Road
Evart, MI 49631
(231) 734-3808
info@campandcanoe.com
www.campandcanoe.com

River Rat Canoe Rental
(canoes/kayaks)
8702 River Dr
Grant, MI 49327
(231) 834-9411
www.riverratcanoerental.com

PERE MARQUETTE RIVER

Baldwin Canoe Rental
(canoes/kayaks/rafts/campground/
motel)
P.O. Box 269
Baldwin, MI 49304
(231) 745-4669
(800) 272-3642
bcr@baldwincanoe.com
www.baldwincanoe.com

Henry's Landing Campground
And Canoe Rental
(canoes/kayaks/campground)
701 S Scottville Rd
Scottville, MI 49454
(231) 757-0101
henryslanding@yahoo.com
www.henryslanding.com

Ivan's Canoe Rental And
Campground
(canoes/kayaks/campground/
cabins/ shuttles)
7332 Michigan 37
Baldwin, MI 49304
(231) 745-3361
ivanscampground@sbcglobal.net
www.ivanscanoe.com

River Run Canoe Livery
(canoes/kayaks)
600 S Main St
Scottville, MI 49454
(231) 757-2266
www.riverruncanoerental.com

PINE RIVER

Bosman's Pine River Canoe
Rental
(canoes/kayaks)
8027 Grandview Hwy
Wellston, MI 49689
(231) 862-3661
(877) 6canoes
bosmancanoe@hotmail.com
www.bosmancanoe.com

Horina Canoe Rental
(canoes/kayaks)
9889 M-37
Wellston, MI 49689
(231) 862-3470
Horinacanoes@yahoo.com
www.horinacanoe.com

Pine River Paddlesports Center
(canoes/kayaks/rafts/campground/
cabins/store)
9590 South M-37
Wellston, MI 49689
(231) 862-3471
(800) 717-4837
prpc@thepineriver.com
www.thepineriver.com

Shomler Canoes And Kayaks
(canoes/kayaks)
11390 M-37
Irons, MI 49644
(231) 862-3475
cliff@shomlercanoes.com
www.shomlercanoes.com

Sportsman's Port
(canoes/kayaks/store/campground)
10487 West M-55
Wellston, MI 49689
(231) 862-3571
(888) CANOE-01
www.sportsmansport.com

PLATTE RIVER

Honor Canoe Rental
(canoes/kayaks/lodging)
2212 Valley Rd/US-31 North
Honor, MI 49640
(231) 325-0112
info@HonorCanoeRentals.com
www.honorcanoerentals.com

Honor Trading Post Canoe
Rental
(canoes/kayaks/store)
8294 Deadstream Rd
Honor MI 49640
(231) 325-2202
info@canoeplatteriver.com
www.sportsmansport.com

RIVERSIDE CANOES
(canoes/kayaks/store)
M-22 and Platte River
5042 N Scenic Highway
Honor, MI 49640
(231) 325-5622
www.canoemichigan.com

RIFLE RIVER

WHITE'S CANOE LIVERY
(canoes/kayaks/campground/
cabins/store)
400 S Melita Rd
Sterling, MI 48659
(989) 654-2654
www.whitescanoe.com

RIVERBEND CAMPGROUND AND
CANOE RENTAL
(canoes/kayaks/campground/store)
1165 North Main Street
Omer, MI 48749
(989) 653-2576
www.riverbendomer.com

RUSSELL'S CANOES AND
CAMPGROUNDS
(canoes/kayaks/campground)
146 Carrington St
Omer, MI 48749
(989) 653-2644
(800) 552-4928
www.russellcanoe.com

CEDAR SPRINGS CAMPGROUND AND
CANOE RENTAL
334 Melita Road
Sterling, MI 48659
(989) 654-3195

RIVER VIEW CAMPGROUND AND
CANOE LIVERY
5755 Townline Road
Sterling, MI 48659
(989) 654-2447
www.riverviewcampground.com

TROLL LANDING CAMPGROUND AND
CANOE RENTAL 2660 RIFLE RIVER
TRAIL
West Branch, MI 48661
(989) 345-7260
office@trolllanding.com
www.trolllanding.com

RIFLE RIVER CANOEING
AND CAMPING
(canoes/kayaks/campground/store)
5825 Townline Road
Sterling, MI 48659
(989) 654-2556
www.riflerivercampground.com

WHISPERING PINES CAMPGROUND
AND CANOE LIVERY
538 South Hale Rd (M-65)
Twining, MI 48766
(866) 871-3092
(989) 653-3321
www.whisperpines.com

SHIAWASSEE RIVER

CHEFF'S CANOE RENTAL AND
WALNUT HILLS CAMPGROUND
(canoes/kayaks)
7685 Lehring Road
Durand, MI 48429
(989) 288-7067
(989) 494-9955
www.cheffscanoerental.com

STURGEON RIVER

ARTS & ADVENTURE PADDLESPORTS
(kayaks/standing paddleboards)
6240 Mack Avenue
Indian River, MI 49749
(231) 238-4843
info@artsandadventure.com
www.artsandadventure.com

BIG BEAR ADVENTURES
(canoes/kayaks/rafts/store/
shuttles/lodging)
4271 South Straits Highway
Indian River, MI 49749
(231) 238-8181
(888) 75-NORTH
bigbear@freeway.net
www.bigbearadventures.com

HENLEY'S CANOE & KAYAK RENTALS
13062 Railroad St
Wolverine, MI 49799
(231) 525-9994
info@henleysrentals.com

THORNAPPLE RIVER

INDIAN VALLEY CAMPGROUND AND
CANOES
(canoes/kayaks/campground)
8200 108th Street SE
Middleville, MI 49333
(616) 891-8579

U-RENT-EM CANOE LIVERY
(canoes/kayaks)
805 W Apple St
Hastings, MI 49058
(269) 945-3191
www.urentemcanoe.com

THUNDER BAY RIVER

CAMPERS COVE CAMPGROUND AND
CANOE
(canoes/kayaks/campground/store)
5005 Long Rapids Road
Alpena, MI 49707
(989) 356-3708
www.camperscovecampground.
com

BACKWOODS CANOE LIVERY
12520 Airport Road
Atlanta, MI 49709
(989) 785-4081

WHITE RIVER

KELLOGG'S CANOES AND KAYAKS
(canoes/solo canoes/kayaks/
shuttles)
250 West Michigan Ave
Hesperia, MI 49421
lkellogg@verizon.net
(231) 854-1415

HAPPY MOHAWK CANOE LIVERY
(canoes/kayaks/campground/
cabins)
735 Fruitvale Road
Montague, MI 49437
(231) 894-4209
happy@aol.com
www.happymohawk.com

UPPER PENINSULA

BRULE RIVER

MICHI-AHO RESORT AND MARINE
(canoes/lodging/store/shuttles)
2181 M-69
Crystal Falls, MI 49920
(906) 875-3514
pjhingos@yahoo.com

NORTHWOODS WILDERNESS
OUTFITTERS
(canoes/kayaks/store/cabins/
shuttles by reservation)
4088 Pine Mountain Road
Iron Mountain, MI 49801
(906) 774-9009
(800) 530-8859
www.northwoodsoutfitters.com

ESCANABA RIVER

UNCLE DUCKY OUTFITTERS
(canoes/kayaks)
434 East Prospect
Marquette, MI 49855
(877) 228-5447
www.paddlingmichigan.com

FOX RIVER

NORTHLAND OUTFITTERS
(canoes/kayaks/campground/
cabins/store/shuttles)
8174 Hwy M-77
Germfask, MI 49836
(906) 586-9801
(800) 808-3FUN
northlan@up.net
www.northoutfitters.com

BIG CEDAR CAMPGROUND AND
CANOE LIVERY
(canoes/kayaks/campground)
7936 Hwy M-77
Germfask, MI 49836
(906) 586-6684
bigcedar_up@yahoo.com
www.bigcedarcampground.com
Uncle Ducky Outfitters (canoes/
kayaks)
434 East Prospect
Marquette, MI 49855
(877) 228-5447
www.paddlingmichigan.com

MANISTIQUE RIVER

NORTHLAND OUTFITTERS
(canoes/kayaks/campground/
cabins/store/shuttles)
8174 Hwy M-77
Germfask, MI 49836
(906) 586-9801
(800) 808-3FUN
northlan@up.net
www.northoutfitters.com

BIG CEDAR CAMPGROUND AND
CANOE LIVERY
(canoes/kayaks/campground)
7936 Hwy M-77
Germfask, MI 49836
(906) 586-6684
bigcedar_up@yahoo.com
www.bigcedarcampground.com

UNCLE DUCKY OUTFITTERS
(canoes/kayaks)
434 East Prospect
Marquette, MI 49855
(877) 228-5447
www.paddlingmichigan.com

MICHIGAMME RIVER

MICHI-AHO RESORT AND MARINE
(canoes/lodging/store/shuttles)
2181 M-69
Crystal Falls, MI 49920
(906) 875-3514
pjhingos@yahoo.com

NORTHWOODS WILDERNESS
OUTFITTERS
(canoes/kayaks/store/cabins/
shuttles by reservation)
4088 Pine Mountain Road
Iron Mountain, MI 49801
(906) 774-9009
(800) 530-8859
www.northwoodsoutfitters.com
Uncle Ducky Outfitters (canoes/
kayaks)
434 East Prospect
Marquette, MI 49855
(877) 228-5447
www.paddlingmichigan.com

ONTONAGON RIVER, Middle and South Branches

SYLVANIA OUTFITTERS
(canoes/kayaks/store/shuttles)
E23423 US-2
Watersmeet, MI 49969
(906) 358-4766
www.sylvaniaoutfitters.com

PAINT RIVER

MICHI-AHO RESORT AND MARINE
(canoes/lodging/store/shuttles)
2181 M-69
Crystal Falls, MI 49920
(906) 875-3514
pjhingos@yahoo.com

TWO HEARTED RIVER

TWO HEARTED CANOE TRIPS AT
RAINBOW LODGE
[Note: Rainbow Lodge was
destroyed in a forest fire in 2012.
As of this writing, the owners were
uncertain whether they would
rebuild]
32752 County Rd 423
Newberry, MI 49868
(906) 658-3357
rbl2hrt@up.net
www.exploringthenorth.com/
twoheart/rainbow.html

UNCLE DUCKY OUTFITTERS
(canoes/kayaks)
434 East Prospect
Marquette, MI 49855
(877) 228-5447
www.paddlingmichigan.com

WHITEFISH

UNCLE DUCKY OUTFITTERS
(canoes/kayaks)
434 East Prospect
Marquette, MI 49855
(877) 228-5447
www.paddlingmichigan.com

THE AUTHORS

Jerry Dennis grew up exploring the rivers and lakes of his native Michigan and has earned his living since 1986 writing about nature and the outdoors. His essays and articles have appeared in The New York Times, Smithsonian, Audubon, Canoe and Kayak, Field and Stream, Orion, and many other publications, and his books have been translated into half a dozen languages and have received numerous awards, including the Sigurd Olson Nature Writing Award and the Great Lakes Culture Award. He lives near Traverse City, Michigan, with his wife, Gail. Visit his website at www.jerrydennis.net.

Craig Date currently resides with his wife, Dora, in Sanford, Michigan and is employed as a Clinic Manager in Midland, Michigan. He enjoys travel, photography, wood-working, and playing bluegrass guitar. Visit his website at www.michiganfolk.net.

For updates and further information go to the official website of Canoeing Michigan Rivers:
www.canoeingmichiganrivers.net